Recipes from

ACROSS INDIANA

THE BEST OF HEARTLAND COOKING

GUILD PRESS OF INDIANA, INC.

Copyright © 1998 by WFYI-MIPB

The title "Across Indiana," the Across Indiana logo, and the WFYI TelePlex logo
are the exclusive property of WFYI-MIPB

WFYI
TELEPLEX

GUILD PRESS OF INDIANA, INC.
435 GRADLE DRIVE
CARMEL, IN 46032
TEL.: 317-848-6421 • FAX: 317-848-6810

ISBN 1-57860-060-X

Library of Congress
Catalog Card Number 98-73932

Cover photograph by Matthew Musgrave
Cover design by Steven D. Armour
Text design by Sheila G. Samson

Thanks to the following underwriters for helping make this book possible:

THE RED GERANIUM ENTERPRISES, NEW HARMONY

THE INDIANA HISTORICAL SOCIETY

Contents

Foreword

It is certainly my pleasure to have the chance to welcome you to *Recipes from Across Indiana*. Truly, the recipes you will find here are from all across Indiana, and reflect the diversity, rich heritage, and *flavor* of our state.

In thinking about what a book like this represents, memories of family meals, both large and small, in happy times and sad, came to mind. Additionally, I recalled new residents to our small town of Corydon, who brought with them recipes for ethnic foods that had been passed down for generations, then placed on the table at a community pitch-in. I also smiled as I recalled that in the O'Bannon family we always seem to end up gathered around the old chopping block in our kitchen—munching food, talking, laughing, and sharing. In my life, as I am sure is true in yours, food always seems to be present when we gather together with family, friends, and neighbors.

Food expresses our family traditions. In many families, certain foods are always served for Sunday meals or on picnics. These recipes tell us much about the way of life our ancestors experienced, about hard times and prosperity, about convenience and the things of which they were most proud.

More than just the biological needs, food brings with it nourishment of character, community, and confidence. Most often it is with food that we offer an arm of support, a hug of reassurance, a pat on the back, and a laugh over time well spent. With food often comes symbols of our role and place in the world around us.

In the pages that follow, I hope that you will find new recipes to share with family and friends and create some new traditions of your own. At least I am sure that is the hope of all who have been committed to sharing these recipes with you.

Enjoy this taste of our Hoosier heritage.

Judy O'Bannon
First Lady of Indiana
August 1998

Acknowledgments

From the first glimmer of a concept through its completion, this cookbook is the result of a collaborative effort at its finest.

Heading the committee were Judy O'Bannon, honorary chairperson; Diana Davis and Sally Lugar, co-chairpersons; and Barbara Wynne, advisor. Thanks to Mary Rinck, recipe selection chairperson, and Marcella Taylor, proofing chairperson. Also, committee members Gloria Barron, Cecelia Dodson, Janet Gibson, Miriam Lazo, Barbara Lewis, Kathy Mulvaney, Sally Ouweneel, and Angie Wylde. Their sharp eyes and creative input were invaluable.

Special contributions were greatly appreciated: Barbara's Bouquets, for the beautiful floral arrangements that appear in the color photos and on the cover; Gloria Barron, whose delightful sketches grace many of the pages; J. Robert Cook, WFYI writer/producer, for his outstanding black and white photographs; and Hugh Gibson, for his painstaking computer work in entering the recipes. Thanks also to Liz Appel Rinck, who wrote the *Across Indiana* stories that appear throughout the book and the vignettes that open each section; and Sheryl D. Vanderstel, historical writer.

Thanks to Nancy Niblack Baxter, president of Guild Press of Indiana, for her creativity and acumen in the conceptualization process; and to Sheila Samson, editor and designer, for her tireless efforts in producing such a polished and beautiful book.

A very special thanks to WFYI volunteers for the distribution of this cookbook.

And of course, we especially appreciate the hundreds of Hoosier cooks who shared family recipes with the stories of their heritage. Although we do not claim that all of these are original recipes, we hope your family will enjoy this collection of what we think is indeed "the best of heartland cooking."

Special thanks to Matthew Musgrave for the beautiful color food photography in this book; Lilly Harris, food design consultant, for the food arrangements; Barbara Lewis of Barbara's Bouquets for the floral designs; and the following master chefs whose wonderful dishes appear in the photographs:

Steven Oakley, Executive Chef
  Something Different and Snax, Indianapolis

Rolf Meisterhans, Owner and Executive Chef
  Chef Rolf's Café, Carmel

Joseph Heidenreich, Executive Chef
  California Café, Circle Centre, Indianapolis

Sue Kobets, Owner
  Illinois Street Food Emporium, Indianapolis

Introduction

After Indiana attained statehood in 1816, thousands of people migrated into the area over the next several decades, looking for opportunities in these new western lands. In the beginning, most settlers were farmers, coming primarily from the Upland South—Kentucky, Tennessee, Virginia, and the Carolinas. They brought with them a foodways tradition of pork and corn, two agricultural products that were well-suited to the Hoosier soil and climate. Early travelers through Indiana sometimes complained of the monotonous and unimaginative cooking found in the homes of these simple, hard working farmers. But as prosperity broadened, so did the dietary habits of Indiana's residents. Soon, shopkeepers were offering regionally grown produce along with imported spices, coffee, tea, preserved fishes, and meats. Seville oranges, lemons, and other exotic fruits regularly appeared in advertisements for local stores.

English immigrant Seira Hine, writing in an 1836 letter, discussed the foods of her new western homeland. She admitted that most Hoosiers "subsist a good deal on Indian corn" but noted that it could be cooked a variety of ways. She described the lovely cakes, puddings, custards, and preserves that she had eaten at parties, as well as chicken, ham, and tongue as fine as that found in England.

As more people of diverse social and economic backgrounds called Indiana home, a greater variety of foods found their way into Hoosier households. In 1851, the only cookbook published in Indiana prior to the Civil War was printed in New Albany. Mrs. Angelina Collins, author of *Table Receipts Adapted to Western Housewifery*, still noted that no Hoosier table would be complete without hominy at every meal. But she also provided recipes for Blanc Mange, Charlotte Russe, Lamb the Russian Way, and Soup à la Jardiniere.

Foreign immigration also introduced new food traditions to Indiana. The Germans and Irish arrived beginning in the 1830s. Scandinavian, Eastern European, Greek, and Italian immigrants were joined by African Americans in the state's urban areas during the late nineteenth and twentieth centuries. Finally, Hispanic, Asian, and Middle Eastern peoples of the most recent immigration waves have helped to create a global culinary culture. Today, no cuisine is too distant or too exotic to be found on some table in the Hoosier state.

Sheryl D. Vanderstel
Food Historian

In gratitude to Ardath Y. Burkhart

The roots of public broadcasting run deep. There are incredible stories that describe the community-based origins and hometown initiatives that created public television in cities all across America. Nowhere is there a more inspiring tale of heroic proportions than the founding of Indianapolis based public TV station WFYI and the leadership that made it a reality.

In 1970, Ardath Y. Burkhart led some three thousand volunteers in a door-to-door fund-raising "battle" to bring public television to Indianapolis. At the time, Indianapolis was the largest city in the country without a public TV station. Comprised primarily of mothers of young children, "Ardath's Army," as the group affectionately became known, raised the money needed to put WFYI on the air and to operate that first year. The community-wide effort was one of *The Indianapolis Star*'s "Top Ten News Stories" of 1970, and prompted the city's mayor, Richard G. Lugar, to proclaim "the accomplishment makes a mere male feel humble."

Over the years, Ardath Burkhart led numerous fund-raising projects, and from 1972 to 1983 she served as chair of the WFYI board of directors. All these years later, seldom does a day at WFYI go by that Mrs. Burkhart's name is not mentioned in reference to her commitment and dedication to public broadcasting.

In 1995, the station's silver anniversary, the WFYI Foundation was established and an endowment fund created to assure that future generations would benefit from the services of WFYI. As part of this foundation, the Ardath Y. Burkhart Memorial Fund was put in place to pay tribute to the many contributions made to WFYI by this remarkable community leader.

You'll see several references to Mrs. Burkhart throughout this book. WFYI is pleased that proceeds from the sale of *Recipes from Across Indiana* will be directed to the Ardath Y. Burkhart Memorial Fund. It's one small way to honor the memory of someone who played a vital role in the creation of public broadcasting across Indiana. And it's good knowing that Ardath Burkhart's name will forever be linked to WFYI and that, once again, she is associated with a project that will support the mission of public broadcasting.

Lloyd Wright, President and General Manager
WFYI TelePlex
August 1998

Remembering Ardath . . .

Throughout this book are several of Ardath Burkhart's special recipes, called "Ardath's Favorites" and highlighted by the above symbol. Ardath was a consummate cook and entertainer. Her daughter, Gay, remembers her mother's gracious style:

> *Mother always loved entertaining. She very rarely had anything catered. Although she might hire help for serving and cleaning up, as a general rule she felt she could not accept compliments on food if she had not fixed it herself.*

Ardath's Army

Photo by Casalini

"Commander-in-Chief" Ardath Y. Burkhart

Ardath loved to give parties—big ones. The biggest and longest-lasting was the extraordinary gatherings that brought public television to the state. At one such gathering, the possibility for public TV was studied. Ardath was the only woman in attendance. The men voted it down, but Ardath said, in effect, "Nonsense! Women will do it!"

She called together a few capable women—in her home, of course—and that started it. I covered the meeting for *The Indianapolis Star.* That small group, fired by Ardath's enthusiasm and leadership, recruited hundreds of women who knocked on practically every door in the area, seeking support for our own PBS station. In my reporting for *The Star*, I named the corps "Ardath's Army." We never did know how many recruits there were, but we estimated somewhere between twenty-five hundred and three thousand. And that's how WFYI came into being.

Robbie DuBois

Ardath Burkhart had a battalion of women who battled for public television in Indianapolis in the late 1960s. Called the "Pantyhose Platoon," it was made up of young moms who in turn recruited hundreds of other volunteers for the cause. Among other tasks, they taught how to make bow-tie antennae from twisted wire coat hangers and hook them up to TVs to make them UHF compatible in those pre-cable days. These ingenious homemade gizmos enabled us to get Channel 20 so our children could watch *Sesame Street*, and we adults could enjoy the symphony and the opera.

Ardath made volunteering fun. She invited her Pantyhose Platoon to her home on West Kessler Boulevard where we all tried to be her "think tank." There was no generation gap between Ardath and her volunteers. She served in the front lines with us, never looking on with binoculars.

Like all good hostesses, she always served wonderful refreshments. The canapés, finger sandwiches, cookies, and cakes were her recipes, and she always made some or all of the goodies herself. She loved food, and its presentation was one of her trademarks. There was always a bouquet of fresh flowers on her dining room table and food was served on beautiful trays and platters. Even though there was always a relaxed atmosphere when working with Ardath, the surroundings were elegant. She always made us feel welcome, a valued part of her organization, and with an essential role in the outcome of the event. We left her meetings knowing we *would* accomplish our mission.

I remember a large oil painting in the Burkhart home of a teacher sharing her love of learning with her pupils. Ardath was an educator, and I believe she taught her Pantyhose Platoon and the entire brigade how to love serving the community.

Barbara Wynne
August 1998

Scenes from across Indiana . . .

Even in something as functional as a barn, Hoosier ingenuity can be found, as in the distinctive air vent in the shape of an old-style cross on this abandoned Martin County barn.

Farm folk in Hendricks County know that no matter how hard you try, no one can impress a cow.

PHOTOS BY J. ROBERT COOK

Scenes from across Indiana . . .

Some enterprising resident of Brown County, a place renowned for being a hotbed of creativity, has taken the term "flower bed" literally.

The old Bailey Farm in Porter County is within walking distance of the Indiana Dunes. Visitors to this historic landmark can see a working farm as it was in settlers' days.

PHOTOS BY J. ROBERT COOK

Great Beginnings

APPETIZERS AND BEVERAGES

Special occasions call for special food! Whether it's a patio party celebrating the Indy 500, a costumed get-together for Halloween, or a family gathering for the holidays, festive hors d'oeuvres and beverages help set the tone for a celebration.

Dallas Cowboys' Play-Off Guacamole

½	medium onion, finely chopped
1	fresh jalapeño pepper, finely chopped
1	medium tomato, diced
1	garlic clove, minced
4	teaspoons chopped cilantro
4	medium avocados, coarsely mashed
½	teaspoon salt
	Juice from ½ a medium lime

In a medium bowl, combine the onion, jalapeño, tomato, garlic, and cilantro. Add the avocado, salt, and lime juice. Cover with plastic wrap and let stand about 30 minutes or so for the flavors to blend. Serve with tortilla chips. To store guacamole, cover with plastic wrap and refrigerate. Makes about 3 cups.

Linda Lugar
Carmel

Swiss and Bacon Canapés

Easy but good!

1	8-ounce package refrigerator crescent rolls
10	slices bacon, fried and crumbled
12	ounces shredded Swiss cheese
1	tablespoon minced onion
3	eggs, beaten
¾	cup milk
½	teaspoon salt

Preheat oven to 375°F. Unroll the crescent rolls and press into a 9 x13-inch baking dish. Combine the rest of the ingredients and pour over the rolls. Bake for about 30 minutes. Remove from oven and let set for 5 minutes. Cut into small squares and serve warm.

Friend of WFYI
Bloomington

Jeré's Chicken Tidbits

1	cup Parmesan cheese
1	cup fine bread crumbs
1	stick butter or margarine
4	boneless skinless chicken breasts

Preheat oven to 350°F. Mix bread crumbs and cheese in one bowl. Melt butter in another bowl. Cut chicken into pieces. Dip chicken pieces in butter, then roll in the crumb mixture. Place in 9 x13-inch baking dish. Bake for 15–20 minutes.

(Note: I cut chicken into larger portions if I'm serving as an entrée.)

Jeré Sturges
Greensburg

Sun Dried Tomato Cheese Spread

This recipe has been in the Harris family for over $\frac{1}{300}$ of a century. I threw it together for a party over the holidays, and—as luck would have it—it worked. Even my kids liked it! I guess this means I can cook, but don't look for a restaurant with my name on it anytime soon.

1	8-ounce package cream cheese
3	ounces sharp cheddar, grated
3	ounces Edam cheese, grated (Gouda optional)
½	teaspoon onion powder
1	small clove garlic, finely chopped
2	teaspoons Worcestershire sauce
¼	cup finely chopped sun dried tomatoes

Put all ingredients in a microwave-safe bowl. Heat in microwave on high for 3–5 minutes; stop halfway to stir, and stir when finished. Work until smooth. Add cayenne pepper if you like it spicy. Serve hot or cold with crackers, bread or tortilla chips. Serves 6–8.

George Harris and Jo DuMontelle
Pendleton

Mexican Chicken Won-Ton Snacks

Also tastes great using ground beef in place of chicken breasts.

4–5 boneless chicken breasts, boiled and chopped
1 cup sour cream
1 package taco seasoning (hot or mild)
1 package won ton wrappers
1 package Mexican cheese, shredded

Preheat oven to 350°F. Boil chicken breasts and finely chop or shred when cool. Mix chicken with sour cream and taco seasoning. Place won ton wrappers in greased cupcake pans. Place in oven for about 1–2 minutes or until the tips are crisp. Remove from oven, spoon in chicken mixture and top with shredded cheese. Return to oven for about 5 minutes or until cheese begins to bubble. Serve hot as a snack.

Kelcy Santuro
Indianapolis

Mushroom Puffs

1 loaf thin bread rounds
1 8-ounce package cream cheese, softened
2 egg yolks
⅛ teaspoon Worcestershire sauce
1 teaspoon onion flakes
1 can mushroom caps, drained

Toast bread rounds. Beat together cream cheese, egg yolks, Worcestershire sauce, and onion flakes until fluffy.

Preheat oven to 400°F. Place a mushroom cap, round side up, on each toasted bread round. Cover with the cream cheese mixture. Bake for 10 minutes or until bubbly.

(Note: To always have these on hand, freeze on cookie sheet and then store in freezer bags. When ready to use, thaw and bake as above.)

Friend of WFYI
Crown Point

Braunschweiger Ball

¾   pound braunschweiger
1   8-ounce package cream cheese
1   package onion soup
½   teaspoon garlic powder
1   cup walnuts, chopped

Soften braunschweiger and cream cheese. Mix with garlic powder and onion soup. Add ½ cup nuts. Form into ball and roll in remaining nuts. Refrigerate 2 or 3 days before serving. Serve with crackers.

Linda Arnot
Indianapolis

Deviled Ham Chip Dip

6   tablespoons salad dressing or mayonnaise
16   ounces cream cheese
4   ounces pimentos, chopped
2   teaspoons onion juice or onions, finely chopped
1   teaspoon Worcestershire sauce
4 ¼   ounces deviled ham spread

Combine all ingredients well. (This is best when made at least a day ahead so flavors blend well.) Serve with chips or crackers.

Jane Carlson
Indianapolis

Hot Crab Spread

6 ½   ounces crabmeat
2   tablespoons onion, chopped
3   tablespoons milk
1   teaspoon horseradish, creamy style
1   dash salt
1   8-ounce package cream cheese, softened
    Sliced almonds

Preheat oven to 350°F. Be sure all cartilege and shell pieces are removed from the crabmeat. Combine with all ingredients except the almonds, and blend well. Spread the mixture in a 9-inch pie pan. Sprinkle with the sliced almonds and bake for 15 minutes. Serve with crackers. Serves 8. (Note: This recipe works as well with mock crabmeat.)

Sally Ouweneel
Indianapolis

Hawaiian Meatballs with Sweet-Sour Sauce

Mother used to make these by the hundreds. She would put them on baking sheets, put them in the freezer, and when frozen, she would transfer them to plastic freezer bags to store. When she was ready to use them, she would bake them, add the Sweet-Sour Sauce and serve them in a chafing dish with toothpicks.

SAUCE

1	13 ½ ounce can pineapple chunks
	water
2	tablespoons cornstarch
½	cup brown sugar
2	tablespoons soy sauce
½	cup vinegar
2	tablespoons lemon juice
1	cup green pepper, chopped
1	tablespoon pimento, chopped

MEATBALLS

1 ½	pounds ground beef
⅔	cup cracker crumbs
½	cup onion, chopped
⅔	cup evaporated milk
1	teaspoon seasoned salt

FOR THE SAUCE: Drain the pineapple, reserving the juice. Add enough water to the pineapple juice to make one cup of liquid. Add cornstarch and blend until smooth. Stir in the remaining ingredients and pineapple. Simmer over low heat for 15 minutes or until thickened.

FOR THE MEATBALLS: Combine all ingredients, mixing lightly. (This is best done with your hands, not stirring.) Shape into 1-inch balls.

Preheat oven to 350°F. Arrange the meatballs on a baking sheet. Bake for 30 minutes. Drain and transfer to serving dish. Pour the Sweet-Sour Sauce over the meatballs and serve. Makes about 30 meatballs.

(Note: To fry, roll the meatballs in a little flour. In a skillet, heat about 3 tablespoons of oil over medium-high heat and add the meatballs. Cook until brown, drain, and return to the skillet. Reduce heat to low and add the Sweet-Sour Sauce. Simmer covered for 15 minutes.)

Gay Burkhart
Zionsville

Shrimp Dip

This will go quickly at a family gathering!

2	3-ounce packages cream cheese, softened
⅓	cup mayonnaise
3	tablespoons chili sauce
2	teaspoons lemon juice
2	teaspoons onion, grated
¼	teaspoon Worcestershire sauce
½	pound medium shrimp, cooked and finely chopped
¼	cup chopped celery
¼	cup grated carrots

Combine all ingredients, mixing well. Chill. Serve with assorted crackers or vegetables.

Helen Davis
Martinsville

Chicken Surprise Cheese Ball

State Senator Sandra Dempsey treated us with this recipe during some long working evenings when the State Legislature was in session.

1	8-ounce package cream cheese, softened
½	cup chopped cooked chicken
1	small can chopped green chilies, drained well
2	tablespoons finely chopped onion
¾	teaspoon garlic powder
½	teaspoon chicken bouillon granules
¾	cup chopped pecans

Mix the first 6 ingredients well. Shape the mixture into a ball and roll in the chopped pecans. Wrap with plastic and chill overnight. Serve with your favorite snack crackers.

Angie Wylde
Indianapolis

Sweet and Sour Chicken Wings

This is always a popular dish to take to a pitch-in. I think they are even better when cooled a little. They warm up great, too, if you're lucky enough to have any left.

2	cups sugar
1	cup white vinegar
6	tablespoons soy sauce
6	tablespoons water
1	teaspoon salt
5	pounds chicken wings
2	eggs, beaten
1½	cups flour
½	cup shortening or vegetable oil

In a saucepan, combine the sugar, vinegar, soy sauce, water, and salt. Simmer over medium-low heat for about 2 minutes, stirring constantly. Remove from heat and set aside.

Preheat oven to 375°F. Dip the chicken wings in beaten eggs. Dredge in flour to just coat lightly, using more if needed. Over medium-high heat, heat the shortening or oil; cook the chicken wings in batches until lightly browned, adding more shortening or oil as needed. Drain the wings and arrange on a baking sheet. Pour the sugar and vinegar mixture over the wings, making sure they are thoroughly coated. Bake uncovered for about 40 minutes and serve.

Alta Virginia "Casey" Hayes
Attica

Tortilla Roll-ups

1	package large tortillas
1	16-ounce sour cream
1	8-ounce cream cheese
4–5	green onions, chopped
1	can sliced black olives
	taco cheese
	salsa

Mix sour cream, cream cheese, green onions and olives all together. Spread mixture evenly over tortillas. Sprinkle each with taco cheese. Roll up each tortilla. Refrigerate several hours (overnight is best). Then slice into bite-size pieces. Secure with a toothpick and serve with a good salsa for dipping.

Tish Balentine
South Bend

Southwest Dip

1	8-ounce package cream cheese, softened
1	large avocado, peeled, seeded, and cut into pieces
½	cup sour cream
1	tablespoon lemon juice
2	tablespoons mayonnaise
	Salt and pepper to taste
1	bunch green onions, chopped
½	head lettuce, shredded
2	medium tomatoes, chopped
1	cup shredded cheddar cheese
	Chili powder to taste
½	cup chopped green olives

In a blender container or food processor bowl, combine cream cheese, avocado, sour cream, lemon juice, mayonnaise, and salt and pepper. Process until the mixture is almost smooth. Spread on large plate. (This part can be done several hours ahead. If so, cover with clear plastic wrap and refrigerate.)

In layers over the cream cheese mixture add the onion, shredded lettuce, tomatoes, and cheddar cheese. Sprinkle lightly with chili powder and chopped green olives. Serve with tortilla chips.

Cheryl Carlson
Indianapolis

Pecan Cheese Dip

3	whole eggs, beaten
2	tablespoons sugar
3	tablespoons vinegar
1	8-ounce package cream cheese, softened
½	green pepper, finely chopped
1	small onion, grated
½	cup pecans, chopped

In a saucepan, combine the eggs, sugar, and vinegar. Cook over medium-low heat, stirring, about 5 minutes or until mixture thickens. Remove from heat and cool slightly.

Add the cream cheese to the cooled egg mixture and beat until well blended. Add the green pepper, onion, and pecans. Serve with raw vegetables. Serves 12.

Ann C.
Indianapolis

Crab Mousse

This is a good party hors d'oeuvre as it makes a beautiful presentation and serves a crowd.

2	envelopes unflavored gelatin
½	cup cold water
1	cup mayonnaise
2	7-ounce cans crabmeat
½	cup diced celery
¼	cup green stuffed olives, sliced
1	tablespoon chopped onion
2	tablespoons lemon juice
1 ½	teaspoons horseradish
1	cup sour cream

Soften gelatin in cold water in top of double boiler. Heat water in bottom of double boiler and combine top and bottom, stirring in gelatin until it dissolves or becomes clear. Remove from heat and stir in mayonnaise. Add crabmeat and all other ingredients except sour cream. Blend well. Gently fold in sour cream. Pour into well-oiled fish mold. Chill. To serve, unmold on leaf lettuce or endive. Use olive halves for "eyes" and garnish top with chopped parsley. Serve with your favoite snack crackers.

Susie McFall
Indianapolis

Spinach Squares

5	tablespoons butter
3	eggs
1	cup flour
1	cup milk
1	teaspoon salt
1	teaspoon baking powder
1	pound Monterey jack cheese, grated
3	cups chopped fresh spinach (well rinsed and drained)

Preheat oven to 350°F. Melt butter in 9 x 13-inch pan. Beat together eggs, flour, milk, salt, and baking powder. Mix in cheese.

Spread spinach over the top of the butter and pour the egg mixture over this. Bake for about 40 minutes, or until edges are slightly brown. Cool and cut in squares.

Note: Spinach squares can be frozen. To reheat, place the frozen squares on a cookie sheet and bake at 350°F for about 15 minutes.

In memory of Sarah Schnaiter Byram
Martinsville

Reuben Paté

1 tablespoon vegetable oil
1 cup minced onion
¾ pound corned beef, minced
1 cup sauerkraut, drained
¾ cup mayonnaise
4 ounces cream cheese
1 cup shredded Swiss cheese
½ cup fresh parsley, minced
2 tablespoons Dijon mustard
4 tablespoons minced fresh dill
1 tablespoon ketchup
  Coarsely ground pepper to taste
1 teaspoon caraway seed (optional)

Heat oil in a medium-size sauté pan and brown the onions until golden brown; cool slightly.

Combine the onions, corned beef, sauerkraut, mayonnaise, cream cheese, Swiss cheese, parsley, mustard, dill, ketchup, and pepper in a food processor. Process until fairly smooth. Remove the processor blade and stir in caraway seeds. Place in a serving container and refrigerate 6 hours or overnight. It may also be frozen. Makes about 5 cups.

To serve, transfer to a decorative bowl, surround with crackers, and serve.

Marcia Adams
Fort Wayne

Taco Cheese Dip

1 pound ground beef
1 pound sausage
1 medium onion, chopped
1 can cream of mushroom soup
8 ounces sour cream
1 pound processed American cheese
¼ cup jalapeño relish or chopped jalapeño peppers

Brown meat and onion; drain off fat. Cut cheese in ½-inch cubes. Combine all ingredients in a crock pot and turn to high. Stir occasionally until cheese is melted. Continue to heat on low until thoroughly heated. Serve with corn chips or tortilla chips.

Sherri Rapp
Indianapolis

Tuna Ball

1   8-ounce package cream
     cheese
1   teaspoon onion, minced
1   teaspoon hot pepper sauce
2   tablespoons chili sauce
1   9-ounce can water packed
     tuna, drained
     Parsley

Blend all ingredients except tuna and parsley in food processor or blender. Stir in tuna. Shape into a ball and sprinkle with parsley. Chill at least 3 hours. Excellent served on small crackers or party rye.

Cathy Peden
New Albany

The Rathskeller Restaurant is located in the historic, turn-of-the-century Athenaeum Building in downtown Indianapolis. The Athenaeum, originally known as Das Deutsche Haus, *was designed in the German Renaissance Revival style by the architectural firm of Vonnegut and Bohn, headed by Bernard Vonnegut, grandfather of author Kurt Vonnegut. The Rathskeller is reminiscent of both a quaint Bavarian inn and a lively Munich beer hall, and offers an award-winning menu featuring authentic German cuisine as well as steaks, seafood, chicken, pork, and vegetarian entrées. The bar offers a wide variety of both domestic and imported beers. (See recipe next page.)*

Brat & Sauerkraut Balls

SPICY BREADING

2   cups cornflake crumbs
1   cup bread crumbs
1 ½   cups flour
1   tablespoon seasoned salt
¾   tablespoon granulated garlic
¾   tablespoon granulated
      onion
1 ½   teaspoon celery salt
1 ½   teaspoon black pepper

BEER SAUCE

2   cups (1 pint) sour cream
1 ½   teaspoons granulated onion
1 ¼   teaspoons garlic, freshly
      chopped
2   teaspoons horseradish
1 ½   tablespoons pork drippings
1   chicken bouillon cube,
      crushed
¾   cup beer

BRAT & SAUERKRAUT BALLS

1   pound ground pork sausage
1   pound lean ground beef
1   pound bratwurst, ground *
2   pounds sauerkraut, chopped
1   8-ounce package cream
      cheese
1 ½   cup brat mustard (or use
      yellow mustard with 4
      tablespoons horseradish
      added)
1   cup onion, minced
1   cup celery, minced

2   tablespoons black pepper
2   tablespoons salt
6   eggs
1   cup milk

FOR SPICY BREADING:

Combine all ingredients and mix until thoroughly blended.

FOR BEER SAUCE:

Combine all sauce ingredients in mixing bowl and blend well.

FOR BRAT & SAUERKRAUT BALLS:

Preheat oven to 350°F. Combine the first 10 ingredients in large mixing bowl. Roll into 1-inch balls and place on ungreased baking sheet. Bake for 30 minutes or until fully cooked. Transfer to paper toweling to drain and let cool. (While the meatballs bake, prepare the Spicy Breading and Beer Sauce.)

Heat vegetable oil in a deep fryer or deep pan. Whisk together eggs and milk. Dust cooled meatballs lightly in flour, dip in egg mixture, and roll in the Spicy Breading. Fry meatballs in hot oil until golden brown. Serve with Beer Sauce.

* Have meat cutter grind the bratwurst for you, or grind yourself with meat grinder. Another option is to remove casings and work until of ground consistency.

Rathskeller Restaurant
Indianapolis

13

Asparagus and Prosciutto Appetizer

Refreshing and pretty—a good luncheon entree, too!

30   asparagus spears
Salt and pepper to taste

5   tablespoons olive oil

6   slices (2-ounces each)
prosciutto, thinly sliced

6   slices Swiss cheese, thinly
sliced

3   medium onions, julienned
Salt and pepper to taste

¾   cup Mango Coulis (recipe
follows)

1 ½ cups Melon Berry Salsa
(recipe follows)

1   mango, peeled, pitted,
thinly sliced

Snap the tough ends off asparagus and toss with salt and pepper and 2 tablespoons olive oil. Grill over hot fire until asparagus is tender and has grill marks, but still a bright green. Chill .

To serve, top a slice of prosciutto with a slice of Swiss cheese. Lay 5 pieces of asparagus at the narrow end and tightly roll prosciutto and cheese around the asparagus so that the tips and ends are exposed. (Can be made ahead to this stage; chill until ready to serve.)

Over a high heat bring remaining olive oil to just below the smoking point. Add onions and reduce to a medium heat. Sauté onions, stirring frequently, until they have reached a soft brown color. Season with salt and pepper.

Preheat oven to 350°F. Place asparagus rolls on baking sheet and bake just until cheese is just melted. Ladle 2 tablespoons of Mango Coulis onto a plate. Place 2 heaping tablespoons of the sautéed onion in the center of the coulis. Place an asparagus roll on top of the onion. Surround with Melon Berry Salsa. Garnish with two mango slices crossed over the asparagus roll. Serves 6.

Joseph Heidenreich, Executive Chef
California Café, Indianapolis

Mango Coulis

15   tablespoons frozen mango purée *

2 ¼ teaspoons honey

½   tablespoon balsamic vinegar

Blend ingredients and chill until ready to serve.

* Found in the freezer section of grocery.

Melon Berry Salsa

½   cantaloupe, diced

½   mango, diced

1   cup strawberries, diced

2   tablespoons julienned fresh basil

1   tablespoon chopped chives

¾   teaspoon balsamic vinegar
Salt and pepper to taste

Combine all ingredients and chill.

Pierogies

1 ½ cups mashed potatoes
½ teaspoon salt
2 eggs
¼ cup farina
1 ½ cup flour
1 pound dry cottage cheese
1 egg
½ teaspoon salt
1 small onion, grated

Mix first 5 ingredients well to form dough. Roll out on floured surface in rectangle, about ⅛ inch thick. Cut into squares or circles about 3 inches in diameter.

Combine cottage cheese, egg, salt, and onion; mix well. Place a spoonful of cottage cheese filling mixture on one side of dough circles or squares; dampen edges of dough and fold, press together firmly to seal. Drop into boiling soup or salted water and boil 15 minutes. (Note: Sauerkraut or finely minced beef can also be used to fill pierogies.) Serves 4–8.

Helen Cybulski
South Bend

Lumpia Shanghai

1 pound lean pork, ground
½ pound shrimp, finely chopped
2 large carrots, finely chopped
1 bunch spring onions, finely chopped
1 egg
3 tablespoons soy sauce
salt and pepper to taste
1 package of lumpia wrappers, cut in half *

Combine the first 4 ingredients in bowl. Add egg and soy sauce and mix thoroughly. Season with salt and pepper. Spoon about 1 teaspoonful of pork mixture in one corner of a lumpia wrapper. Fold the corner over toward the center; fold the side corners over. Brush opposite corner of the wrapper lightly with water to seal, and fold over.

Heat oil in deep fryer or deep pan and fry lumpias until golden brown. Serve with ketchup or hot sauce. Makes 50 lumpias.

* Lumpia wrappers can be purchased in Oriental groceries.

Eddie Barrientos
Indianapolis

Jerry's Eggnog

My brother, Jerry Eubank, originated this recipe. For a number of years he was the head chef at the former Jefferson House Smorgasbord in Lafayette, Indiana. Later, before his retirement and death, he was the beloved chef at Wabash College's Beta Theta Pi Fraternity in Crawfordsville, Indiana.

6	egg yolks, well-beaten
1 ½	cups sugar
½	cup golden rum
1	quart dairy eggnog
3	cups coffee cream or half-and-half
1	pint bourbon
3	cups whipping cream, whipped
6	egg whites
½	cup sugar
	Nutmeg to taste

Beat egg yolks. Add sugar, rum, eggnog, and cream or half-and-half, beating well each time after each ingredient is added. Add bourbon and beat another 15 minutes. Fold in whipped cream.

Beat egg whites until frothy; gradually add sugar and beat until stiff peaks form. Fold egg whites into eggnog mixture. Add nutmeg to taste. Keep refrigerated. Stir well before serving, and top each serving with a sprinkle of nutmeg if desired. Makes a half gallon. (This recipe doubles well.)

In memory of Jerry Eubank
Indianapolis

Strawberry Milkshake

My husband and I raised goats for their milk. One of our grandchildren's favorite ways of drinking it was in this milkshake recipe I developed. We also grew our own strawberries.

1	cup unsweetened frozen strawberries
1	cup goat's milk or regular milk
2–3	tablespoons sugar
1	teaspoon vanilla, optional

Combine all ingredients in a blender container and process until smooth. Makes 1 large shake.

Ann Axton
New Harmony

Wassail, a Christmas Drink

Perfect for holiday parties.

4	cups pineapple juice
1 ½	cups apricot nectar
4	cups apple cider
2	sticks of cinnamon
2	teaspoons whole cloves
1	teaspoon nutmeg

Combine all ingredients in a large pan and simmer until hot. Strain out the spices and serve warm.

Marti Hood
Wabash

Cider Warm-Up

The simmering aroma will greet your guests at the door. A great "after the game" warm-up drink.

1	gallon apple cider
1	quart cranberry juice
1	quart orange juice
2	quarts tea
2–3	cinnamon sticks
5–6	cloves

Mix all the ingredients together in a large kettle. Simmer for 20 minutes. Remove the cloves and discard. Serve the cider warm with a fresh half stick of cinnamon in each mug or cup. Makes 2 gallons—enough for a crowd!

Friend of WFYI
West Lafayette

Coffee with Punch

Stand back and watch everyone have a good time!

½	gallon chocolate ice cream
1	quart half-and-half
24	cups (6 quarts) brewed coffee
1	cup coffee liqueur (Tia Maria or Kahlua)

Chop up the ice cream in a punch bowl. Pour the half-and-half over it, then add the cooled coffee. Stir and mix well with a large spoon. Add the coffee liqueur and serve.

Geneva Parker
Indianapolis

A Cut Above

"We're not business people," explains Linda Kirkendall. "We're artists. We graduated from Indiana State with art degrees, and for us to be able to keep a little glimmer of that means everything. Every piece is hand done; every piece is individual. That's just kind of where our integrity is."

Linda and Randy Kirkendall of Warsaw, Indiana, aren't your run-of-the-mill entrepreneurs. Where other members of their generation have invented new businesses by going all-out with high tech, Linda and Randy's business takes glasscutting back to its roots and the way things were in their grandparents' day.

Linda relates the history of the Warsaw Cut Glass Factory. "This factory was built in 1911, and when they started out they had forty-five glasscutters. Two were master glasscutters who had come down from Chicago, and the rest were locally trained gentlemen from this area.

"The factory was busy till World War I broke out. All the blanks [plain, uncut crystal pieces] were made in Germany, and the Germans stopped making lead crystal and started making lead bullets. This almost ruined the cut-crystal business in the United States.

"But one of the master glasscutters at the time did not want to see this factory close down. He developed a type of cutting called gray, or fine cutting. It could be used on the American-made blanks, which were mouth-blown and much thinner. That's generally what we do today.

"The glasscutter sits behind a revolving stone wheel and presses each individual piece against it to grind the patterns into the glass. We can cut anything you desire. We can match great-grandmother's cut glass patterns."

Linda and Randy acquired the glass factory in 1980. They have maintained its operation in traditional manner, even using some of the original equipment. At other companies, glass is cut by computer; here, Randy or his apprentice guide the glass shapes across the cutting wheel to create patterns and forms.

"The rhythm and the magic would be gone if we went to automated machinery," says Randy. "And I really don't think that the modern equipment can do what the old stone wheels can."

Using traditional methods, however, presents challenges. "Lightening up my touch was an immense challenge for me," Randy recalls. "Plus, think about how hard it would be to draw if the pencil were stationary and paper moved around it. That's what I have to imagine when I carve. I have to visualize a two-dimensional drawing onto a three-dimensional piece of glass. That is very challenging."

Although the Warsaw Cut Glass Factory produces dozens of works and a variety of styles and designs, they don't offer a catalogue. With a catalogue, sales would increase. That would mean more demand for their glass, and that would mean changing the way they do things now. And where would be the fun in that?

Orange Julius

Pretty as a picture—and so refreshing. Your guests will love this!

1	6-ounce can frozen orange juice concentrate
1	cup ice water
1	cup milk
½	cup sugar
12	ice cubes
6	strawberries

Combine all ingredients in a blender and process until smooth and well-blended. Pour into plastic container and place in the freezer for about 30 minutes. When ready to serve, remove from freezer and stir. It should be a slushy consistency. (If frozen solid, take out of freezer 1 hour before serving.)

Serve in long-stemmed glass and garnish with additional strawberries.

Peggy Rapp
Indianapolis

Hot Bloody Mary

This is a great warm-up for tailgate parties!

4	cups V-8 juice
4	tablespoons oil
4	bouillon cubes
2	tablespoons vinegar
1	teaspoon salt
½	teaspoon basil
¼	teaspoon paprika
1	teaspoon celery salt
1	medium cucumber
1	large green pepper

Combine juice, oil, bouillon, vinegar, salt, and spices. Heat but do not boil. Peel and seed cucumber. Remove seeds and membrane from pepper. Finely chop cucumber and pepper. Add to the hot juice mixture. Vodka may be added. Serves 8–12.

Friend of WFYI
South Bend

Banana Punch

2	cups sugar
3	cups water
1	12-ounce can orange juice concentrate, thawed
3	cups pineapple juice
3	bananas, pureed
3	quarts ginger ale

Dissolve sugar in water. Add orange juice, pineapple juice and bananas; stir well. Freeze in large plastic containers. To serve, thaw and mix with ginger ale in punch bowl. (Rum may be added if desired.) Makes 5 quarts. Serves 25–30.

Friend of WFYI
New Albany

Williamsburg Favorite

Pretty, easy, and delicious any time of the year.

½	gallon coffee
½	gallon chocolate milk
1	quart vanilla ice cream
½	pint heavy cream, whipped
	Ground nutmeg
	Chocolate curls

Combine the coffee, chocolate milk and ice cream. Pour into individual cups or mugs, top with whipped cream, sprinkle with nutmeg, and top with chocolate curls.

Friend of WFYI
Seymour

Sunshine Punch

1	6-ounce can frozen orange juice concentrate
1	6-ounce can frozen lemonade concentrate
1	6-ounce can frozen limeade concentrate
4	cups cold water
1	quart 7-Up, chilled
10	fresh cherries

Combine all ingredients except cherries and chill. Serve in large punch bowl with ice ring. (The ice ring may be decorated by adding cherries before the ring is fully frozen.)

Sally Lugar
Indianapolis

Summer Party Punch

This recipe can be easily doubled or tripled for a large party. Pretty served at a bridal luncheon with fresh flowers around the punch bowl.

1	quart iced tea
1	6-ounce can frozen lemonade concentrate
1	6-ounce can frozen limeade concentrate
1	cup cranberry juice
1	cup pineapple juice
1	28-ounce bottle of ginger ale

Combine the tea with the lemonade, limeade, cranberry punch, and pineapple juice in a punch bowl. To serve, add the ginger ale and stir. Garnish with lime and lemon slices frozen in either cubes or a small ring.

Friend of WFYI
Anderson

Lemon-Mint Tea

This is a delicious drink for a luncheon or afternoon tea.

2	cups boiling water
6	regular tea bags
3	lemons, cut into ½-inch thick slices
1	cup mint leaves, crushed
2	46-ounce cans pineapple juice
4	cups water
1	cup sugar
1 ½	teaspoons vanilla extract
1 ½	teaspoons almond extract

Pour the water over the tea bags. Add the lemons and mint; cover and let stand 20 minutes. Strain.

Combine tea mixture and remaining ingredients. Serve over ice. Makes about 3 quarts.

Mary Rinck
Indianapolis

Garden Glories

SALADS AND DRESSINGS

Salads nowadays come in as many taste-tempting varieties as there are ingredients with which to make them. No longer mere pallid piles of iceberg lettuce, salads now contain sophisticated blends limited only by the imagination. Crystalline aspics, marinated vegetable melanges, and concoctions of fruit, pasta, and seafood beckon to our palates.

Warm Spiced Fruit Salad

This is a wonderful Christmas dish.

1   29-ounce can pear halves
1   8 ¾-ounce can apricot halves
1   8 ¾-ounce can light sweet cherries
1   13 ¼-ounce can pineapple chunks
¼   teaspoon nutmeg
¼   teaspoon cinnamon
⅛   teaspoon ground cloves
2   tablespoons butter

Preheat oven to 350°F.

Drain fruit, reserving 1 cup of the juices combined. Mix the fruit in a 2-quart casserole dish. Add the spices to the cup of juice and mix well. Pour the juice and spice mixture over the fruit. Dot with butter and bake for 20 minutes. Serve warm.

In memory of June Gerlib
Indianapolis

Four-Fruit Salad

This refreshing salad can be made any time of the year, but it's perfect for Easter!

1   20-ounce can pineapple chunks
½   cup sugar
2   tablespoons cornstarch
⅓   cup orange juice
1   tablespoon lemon juice
1   11-ounce can mandarin oranges, drained
4   apples, unpeeled and chopped
3   bananas, sliced

Drain pineapple, reserving ¾ cup juice. In a saucepan, combine sugar and cornstarch. Add the pineapple juice and orange and lemon juices. Cook and stir over medium heat until thickened and bubbly. Remove from heat; set aside. Combine pineapple chunks, oranges, apples, and bananas. Pour the warm sauce over the fruit, stirring gently to coat. Cover and refrigerate. Serves 12 to 16.

Mary Barker
Waldron

Taffy Apple Salad

1   tablespoon flour
½   cup sugar
2   tablespoons vinegar
1   egg, beaten
1   8-ounce can crushed
     pineapple with juice
4   cups sliced apples
1   cup cashews
1   8-ounce carton frozen
     whipped topping

In a saucepan, combine the flour, sugar, egg, vinegar, and pineapple with juice; cook, stirring constantly, over medium heat about 5 minutes, or until the mixture thickens. Cool and refrigerate overnight. Combine the sauce with the sliced apples and cashews; top with the whipped topping. Serves 8.

Betty Ford
Cicero

Sinful Salad

1   large package (6 ounces)
     strawberry gelatin
1   cup boiling water
3   medium bananas, mashed
     (about 1 cup)
1   cup pecans, chopped
2   10-ounce packages frozen
     strawberries, thawed and
     drained
1   can crushed pineapple,
     drained
1   pint (2 cups) sour cream

In medium bowl, combine gelatin and boiling water. Stir with rubber spatula until gelatin is completely dissolved. Cool. Add bananas, pecans, strawberries and pineapple to gelatin; stir to combine. Divide in half.

Pour half the gelatin mixture into an 8-inch square dish. Refrigerate until set, about 1 hour. Keep the other half of the gelatin at room temperature. Spread sour cream over the set gelatin. Add rest of gelatin. Cover and refrigerate until set, about 1 ½ hours. Makes 12 servings.

Betty Elkins
Ambia

Green Salad with Chicken

Great for a spring luncheon served with muffins and a pretty dessert.

DRESSING

8	tablespoons sugar
2	teaspoons salt
½	teaspoon pepper
8	tablespoons white balsamic vinegar
1	cup vegetable oil
¼	cup poppy seeds

SALAD

4	boneless, skinless chicken breast halves
1 ½	heads iceberg lettuce or combination of iceberg and romaine
3	green onions, sliced
1	small package slivered almonds
1	small box frozen green peas, thawed
1	cup sliced fresh mushrooms
1	3-ounce can crisp Chinese noodles

Combine all dressing ingredients in a blender container and process until well mixed.

Sauté or grill chicken about 6 minutes per side, or until done. Cool and cut into bite-size pieces.

Tear lettuce into a salad bowl. Add the chicken, onions, almonds, peas, and mushrooms. Pour just enough dressing over salad to moisten and top with Chinese noodles. Serves 4.

Friend of WFYI
Knightstown

Southern Sweet Greens

¼	cup salad oil
2	tablespoons sugar
½	teaspoon salt
2	tablespoons tarragon vinegar
1	tablespoon chopped parsley dash pepper
4	teaspoons sugar
¼	cup sliced almonds
¼	bunch romaine lettuce
½	head iceberg lettuce
3	green onions, sliced thinly
½	cup celery, sliced thinly
1	11-ounce can mandarin oranges, drained

Combine the first 6 ingredients and refrigerate.

In a non-stick skillet, combine the almonds and sugar. Cook over low heat, stirring, until the sugar melts and coats almonds. Set aside and let cool.

Tear the lettuce into bite-size pieces; add the onions, celery, and oranges. Toss with the dressing. Add almonds and serve.

Gail McBeath
Indianapolis

Spinach Salad

1	pound small curd cottage cheese
½	tablespoon yellow mustard
1	teaspoon salt
2	tablespoons horseradish
½	cup sour cream
¼	cup sugar
3	tablespoons vinegar
1	pound spinach, washed and patted dry
1	cup white seedless grapes, halved
1	cup pecans, broken

Combine the first 7 ingredients and mix gently. Let stand overnight.

Tear spinach into bite-size pieces and add grapes and pecans. Toss with dressing and serve. Serves 6–8.

Stephanie Hisle
West Lafayette

Rosie's Bleu Cheese Salad

⅔ cup sugar
1 teaspoon salt
1 or more cloves of garlic, pressed
1 ½ cups vegetable oil
1 cup vinegar
1 4-ounce package crumbled bleu cheese
3 tablespoons sesame seeds
8 slices bacon
1 head romaine lettuce

Combine the first 5 ingredients plus half of the bleu cheese in blender container and blend till smooth.

Preheat oven to 350°F. Spread the sesame seeds on a cookie sheet and toast for 10 minutes; let cool. Fry the bacon until crisp; drain and crumble.

Tear the lettuce into bite-size pieces and place in a large bowl; add the bacon, sesame seeds, and the remaining bleu cheese. Pour the dressing over the salad, toss and serve.

Janet Gibson
Indianapolis

Market Salad

½ cup white vinegar
½ cup vegetable oil
½ teaspoon salt
1 teaspoon oregano
2 garlic cloves, minced
½ cup sugar
2 cups cauliflower pieces
2 cups broccoli pieces
2 medium carrots, cut in strips
1 16-ounce can kidney beans, drained
2 cups shredded mozzarella cheese

Combine the first 6 ingredients and set aside.

In a bowl, combine the cauliflower, broccoli, carrots, kidney beans, and cheese. Toss with dressing. Cover and refrigerate for about 2 hours.

Mary Beth Comer
Terre Haute

St. Elmo's Wedge Salad

DRESSING

1	cup cider vinegar
¼	cup plus 1 tablespoon sugar
⅜	cup Gulden's Spicy Brown Mustard
3	tablespoons A-1 Steak Sauce, bold
2	teaspoons kosher salt
1	tablespoon black pepper
1	tablespoon herbes de Provence
⅛	cup minced fresh garlic
1½	cups vegetable oil

SALAD

2	heads crisp iceberg lettuce
½	cup diced tomato
¾	cup crumbled bleu cheese

In a blender container, combine the vinegar and sugar; blend until well mixed and sugar is dissolved. Add remaining ingredients except oil and pulse just until well-mixed.

With blender running on the lowest speed, slowly add oil. Blend until mixture is emulsified, occasionally scraping lid and sides of blender container. Place dressing in a clean glass jar and refrigerate 6 hours or overnight. Makes about 1 pint.

To serve the salad, cut each head of lettuce into 3 wedges, and place wedges on salad plates that have been chilled in the freezer. Divide diced tomatoes and bleu cheese evenly among the servings and top with the salad dressing. Serves 6.

St. Elmo Steak House
Indianapolis

St. Elmo Steak House was founded in 1902 by Joseph Starr. Originally named Joe Starr's Tavern, the nautically inclined Mr. Starr renamed it after the patron saint of sailors—St. Elmo. The electrical discharge, or fire mirage, sometimes seen coming off the masthead of ships was called St. Elmo's Fire.

Long a favorite dining spot for visiting celebrities, St. Elmo Steak House offers a menu famous for its steaks, of course, and its shrimp cocktail, an extensive wine cellar, and the salad featured on this page.

Napa Salad

This salad is always a favorite at family gatherings.

1	cup sugar
1	cup canola oil
½	cup cider vinegar
3	teaspoons soy sauce
4	tablespoons butter or margarine
1	cup almonds, slivered
1	large Napa cabbage, finely chopped
10	green onions, chopped
¾	cup sunflower seeds
2	packages regular ramen noodles, uncooked

For the salad dressing, combine the sugar, canola oil, vinegar, and soy sauce.

In a skillet, melt the butter or margarine; add the almonds and sauté just until lightly browned. Remove from heat and let cool.

Combine the cabbage, onions, sunflower seeds, and almonds in a large bowl.

Crumble the ramen noodles (discard the seasoning packets or reserve for another use). Add the noodles to the cabbage mixture and toss with dressing. Let the salad stand about 20 minutes before serving.

Susan Crocker
Carmel

Cucumber Salad

This is a good summer dish, but is also nice at Christmastime because of the color. It is light and goes well with a heavy meal.

1	3-ounce package lime gelatin
1	cup boiling water
1	cup cottage cheese
⅔	cup mayonnaise
1	medium cucumber, finely chopped
2–3	tablespoons finely chopped onion

Dissolve gelatin in boiling water and let cool. Mix together the cottage cheese, mayonnaise, cucumber, and onion. Add to gelatin and refrigerate until set.

Marsha Grotrain
Flora

Green Summer Salad

Make the dressing ahead and you have a salad that's gourmet in just a few minutes.

⅓ cup sugar
1 teaspoon dry mustard
1 teaspoon salt
⅓ cup salad vinegar
1 cup vegetable oil
1 tablespoon celery seed
1 medium onion, grated
Dash of pepper
1 pound fresh spinach and/or salad greens
1 can mandarin oranges, drained
1 cup cashews
1 cup artichoke hearts
1 cup pitted black olives, sliced
1 cup Swiss cheese, cubed
1 bunch small green onions

Combine first 8 ingredients in blender container or food processor bowl. Process just until well-blended.

Tear spinach and greens into bite-size pieces in a salad bowl. Add remaining ingredients and toss with the dressing. Serves 6–8.

Friend of WFYI
Peru

Beet Salad (Patzaria Salata)

2 1-pound cans cut red beets
 or
2 pounds fresh red beets, cooked, drained and sliced
3 tablespoons garlic, minced
½ cup olive oil
½ cup wine vinegar
Salt and pepper to taste

Combine ingredients and marinate in refrigerator several hours before serving. This salad should be well seasoned, so add a generous amount of salt and pepper. Serves 6–8.

Doris Bowman
Indianapolis

Broccoli Salad

¾ cup mayonnaise
2 tablespoons vinegar or lemon juice
¼ cup sugar
1 large bunch broccoli florets
½ pound bacon, fried and crumbled
½ cup roasted and salted sunflower seeds
½ cup raisins (optional)
1 small red onion, finely chopped

For the dressing, combine the mayonnaise, vinegar or lemon juice, and sugar. Mix well.

Chop broccoli florets into bite-size pieces and put in a salad bowl. Add the bacon, sunflower seeds, raisins, and onion. Pour dressing over salad and mix well.

Judie Carpenter
Indianapolis

Bok Choy Salad

2 packages ramen noodles
2 tablespoons margarine
4 ounces sunflower seeds
4 ounces sliced almonds
1 medium onion, thinly sliced
1 head bok choy, finely sliced
¼ cup soy sauce
¼ cup cider vinegar
¼ cup vegetable oil
½ cup sugar

Cook noodles according to package directions. Drain and let cool. Melt margarine in a skillet and sauté sunflower seeds, almonds, and onion.

In a large salad bowl layer ½ of the noodles and ½ bok choy. Repeat with the other half of noodles and bok choy. Top with the sautéed mixture.

Combine the soy sauce, vinegar, vegetable oil, and sugar in a saucepan. Simmer until sugar is dissolved. Pour the hot dressing over the salad and serve.

Judy Ford
Richmond

One Terrific Green Salad

1	large head lettuce or mixed greens, torn into pieces
1	medium onion, chopped
8	ounces fresh mushrooms, sliced
½	pound bacon, cooked and crumbled
4	ounces sunflower seeds, toasted if desired
½	cup white vinegar
1	tablespoon celery seed
½	cup sugar
1	tablespoon onion, chopped
1	teaspoon dry mustard
1	teaspoon salt
1	cup oil

Layer lettuce, onion, mushrooms, bacon, and sunflower seeds in a large bowl.

Combine vinegar and celery seed in small pan and bring just to a boil. Remove from heat and let cool. Combine sugar, onion, dry mustard, salt, and oil in blender container or food processor and mix. Add the cooled vinegar mixture and process until creamy. Toss with salad greens. Serves 8–10.

Kathy Mulvaney
Carmel

Tomato Aspic

Makes a great summer luncheon!

1 ½	cups boiling water
1	large package lemon gelatin
2	cups V-8 juice
5	shakes of ground cloves
1	tablespoon tarragon vinegar
2	teaspoons sugar
½	teaspoon coarse black pepper
	Dash of Tabasco sauce

Dissolve the gelatin in the boiling water. Add the V-8 juice. Stir well. Add the remaining ingredients and pour into a well-oiled mold. (Double the recipe if using a ring mold.) Chill until set.

To serve, line a serving plate with lettuce leaves and unmold the aspic. Garnish with mayonnaise, or serve with cottage cheese or your favorite chicken salad.

Friend of WFYI
Covington

Perfection Salad

This is a pretty, refreshing, and light salad. It is good with any meat or fish dish.

1	3-ounce package lemon gelatin
1	3-ounce package lime gelatin
2	cups boiling water
¼	teaspoon salt
¾	cup sweet pickle juice or vinegar
1 ¼	cups cold water
½	cup cottage cheese
¼	cup diced celery
½	cup crushed pineapple
2	tablespoons shredded carrots
2	tablespoons diced pimento
¼	teaspoon finely minced green onion

Dissolve gelatin in the boiling water. Add salt, pickle juice and 1 ¼ cups cold water. Chill until syrupy. Stir in cottage cheese and the rest of the ingredients. Pour into a 9 x 13-inch pan and refrigerate until set.

Marie Martin
Greensburg

Cranberry Salad

This will keep for several days and may also be served warm before refrigerated. Great for cold days.

1	pound fresh cranberries
2	cups sugar
2	large boxes cherry gelatin
1 ¾	cup boiling water
1	20-ounce can crushed pineapple
2	apples, diced
2	oranges, peeled and diced
2	stalks celery, diced
1	cup chopped pecans

Combine the cranberries and sugar and cook according to package directions until the berries pop.

Remove from heat and add gelatin and 1 ¾ cups boiling water. Stir until dissolved. Add remaining ingredients; mix well and pour into a 9 x 13-inch dish. Refrigerate until set. Top with whipped topping and serve.

Kendal and Cindy Hammel
Columbus

Shrimp Salad with Curry Dressing

1	tablespoon butter
2	2-ounce packages slivered almonds
1	bunch each romaine, red leaf, and butter lettuce
2–3	stalks celery, sliced
5	green onions, sliced
½	pound cooked shrimp
1	cup vegetable oil
2	tablespoons lemon juice
1	teaspoon Worcestershire sauce
1	garlic clove, minced
1	teaspoon salt
1	teaspoon pepper
1	teaspoon curry powder
1	teaspoon ground superfine mustard

Melt the butter. Add the almonds and sauté until lightly browned. Remove from heat and set aside.

Tear the lettuces into bite-size pieces into a salad bowl. Add the celery, onions, shrimp, and almonds.

Combine the remaining ingredients and blend well. Add to the salad ingredients and toss. Serves 12.

Joan Waits
Oakland

Asparagus-Cucumber Mold

Cool and refreshing. Serve with chicken salad for a summer luncheon.

1	3-ounce package of lime gelatin
½	cup boiling water
1	can condensed cream of asparagus soup
½	cup mayonnaise
⅛	teaspoon white pepper
1	cup chopped cucumber
¼	cup chopped celery
¼	cup onion, diced
¼	cup fresh minced parsley

Dissolve gelatin in boiling water; let cool. Combine soup, mayonnaise, and pepper; stir into the cooled gelatin mixture. Add remaining ingredients, mixing well. Pour into a lightly oiled 4-cup mold and chill until firm. Serves 8.

Friend of WFYI
Shelbyville

Seafood Salad

The best way to very gently and cautiously mix anything that should not be stirred is to use one's hands: Slide your hands very gently down along the sides of the bowl. Pull the ingredients up from the bottom and let them fall on top of each other.

2   pounds cooked crabmeat (canned or frozen)
2   large cooked lobster tails, shelled
3   pounds cooked shrimp (peeled and deveined)
6   cups sliced celery
1   dozen hard-boiled eggs
3 ½ cups mayonnaise

Thoroughly pick over the crabmeat; remove and discard any pieces of cartilage or shell. Cut the crabmeat and lobster tails into bite-size pieces. Place in a mixing bowl and add the shrimp and celery.

Cut the hardboiled eggs into small pieces and add to the seafood mixture. Very gently fold in just enough mayonnaise to hold the mixture together—do not stir! Serves 25.

Gay Burkhart
Zionsville

Lemon Cheese Salad

2   3-ounce packages lemon gelatin
3 ¾ cups boiling water
1   8-ounce package cream cheese, softened
1   teaspoon salt
1   cup finely chopped celery
1   small can crushed pineapple
1   cup chopped pecans
½   pint cream, whipped

Dissolve gelatin in boiling water and let cool. Beat cheese and salt and blend well with gelatin. Add celery, pineapple, and nuts. Fold in whipped cream. Pour into 8 individual molds or one 1 ½-quart mold. Chill until set. Serves 8.

Gay Burkhart
Zionsville

Grilled Tuscan Shrimp Salad

36 shrimp
Olive oil
Salt and pepper to taste
¾ cup Orange Vinaigrette
(recipe follows)
24 cups mixed salad greens
30 large croutons, made from
rustic Italian bread
2 medium fennel bulbs,
trimmed and thinly shaved
2 medium red onions, peeled,
thinly shaved
1 ½ cups cucumber, diced
18 cherry tomatoes, halved
18 Kalamata olives, pitted and
halved
24 orange segments

Skewer shrimp and brush with olive oil. Season with salt and pepper. Place on a grill over a hot fire until shrimp are just cooked through. Set aside. Prepare mixed salad greens and toss with croutons, fennel, red onion and cucumber. Toss with Orange Vinaigrette. Top with shrimp and tomatoes and garnish with olives and orange segments. Serves 6.

Orange Vinaigrette

½ garlic clove
2 anchovy fillets
½ tablespoon capers
½ teaspoon salt
6 tablespoons rice wine
vinegar
¾ cup orange juice
13 tablespoons extra virgin
olive oil
1 shallot, minced
Salt and pepper to taste

Blend garlic, anchovy fillets, capers, salt, rice wine, vinegar and orange juice in blender until smooth. Add the olive oil slowly in a steady stream with the blender running. Fold in the shallots and add salt and pepper to taste.

Joseph Heidenreich, Executive Chef
California Café
Indianapolis

Crab Salad

Excellent served for bridge luncheon with tomato aspic.

2 ½	pounds crabmeat, shredded
10	ounces frozen petite peas (cooked slightly)
1	pound cheddar cheese, shredded
1 ½	cups mayonnaise
½	cup sour cream
2	teaspoons dill
1	tablespoon honey
½	teaspoon pepper

Combine crabmeat, peas, and cheese. Blend the remaining ingredients and fold into the crabmeat mixture. Refrigerate several hours or overnight. Serves 12.

Helen B. Davis
Martinsville

Alene's Coleslaw

My grandmother, Blanche Reed of Lamar, Indiana, always fed us well whenever we visited. I have vivid memories of her hurrying around the kitchen making fried chicken, mashed potatoes with milk gravy, peach cobbler, and more! She got this slaw recipe from her sister-in-law, and it is very good.

1	tablespoon prepared mustard
⅔	cup sugar
⅔	cup mayonnaise or salad dressing
⅓	cup vinegar
⅓	cup salad oil
1	tablespoon garlic salt
1	teaspoon black pepper
1	small head cabbage
1	medium onion
1	green bell pepper
2	celery stalks

Combine the mustard, sugar, and mayonnaise or salad dressing in a bowl. Add the vinegar, salad oil, garlic salt, and black pepper. Blend well.

Chop the cabbage, onion, bell pepper, and celery and combine in a salad bowl. Pour dressing over this and toss until blended.

In memory of Blanche Reed
Lamar

Helen Whetstone's Potato Salad

My mom's potato salad was always a favorite at our supper table and at family reunions, and now in my home this is one of our favored salads.

6	potatoes, boiled and peeled
4	eggs, boiled and peeled
½	small onion, chopped
3	celery stalks, chopped
2	tablespoons sweet pickle relish
	Salt and pepper to taste
1 ½	cups mayonnaise or salad dressing
¼	cup mustard
⅓	cup sugar
1	tablespoon milk

Cut potatoes and eggs into about ¾-inch pieces and combine with next 4 ingredients in a large bowl. Set aside.

In a saucepan, combine the mayonnaise or salad dressing, mustard, sugar, and milk. Cook over medium heat, stirring constantly just until boiling. Remove and pour over the egg and potato mixture. Blend thoroughly, sprinkle with a little celery salt if desired, and let cool. Serves 10–12.

(Substitute macaroni for potatoes for a delightful macaroni salad.)

John Whetstone
The Carpenter Shop, Inc.
Silver Lake

Simple Gans Potato Salad

This is my mother's potato salad and her mother's before, and it takes me back to my childhood days. We ate it whenever we went camping; I associate it with towering redwoods, Saguaro cacti, Canadian rivers and the open road in general. The recipe is designed to be simple and delicious, and variable in size—one potato, one pickle, one egg becomes salad for one. Two potatoes, two pickles, two eggs becomes salad for two.

8	hard-boiled eggs
8	potatoes, boiled
8	sweet pickles, chopped
1	onion, chopped
	Mayonnaise to taste
	Salt and pepper to taste

Cut eggs and potatoes into large chunks. Combine in a mixing bowl and add pickles and onion. Add enough mayonnaise to hold the mixture together and add salt and pepper. Cover and refrigerate overnight. Serves 8.

Dan McCarthy
Rochester

Spirit of the Wood

The Shakers have a saying: Hands to work, hearts to God.

This adage could also be applied to two people living in the northern Indiana town of Silver Lake. They are John Whetstone and his wife, Debbie, who labor to make the simple tools of everyday life.

"Twenty-four years ago, I was sitting in a Christian ethics class, and the teacher was telling us that young men ought to have skills in trades. I had none; I was working in a factory just being a laborer. So I asked the Lord for a skill, and this is what He put in my heart. I asked Him for the tools and equipment, and everything we have is what's been provided.

"When we first started in the woodworking field, we made furniture, millwork windows, doors, all kinds of things out of wood. That was actually my schooling to get to the point where I am today. As of six years ago, all we produce is woodenware.

"We currently produce sixty-three different wooden utensils and employ eight people. From the time it arrives as lumber until it's ready for sale, it takes seventeen different operations to complete a wooden tool.

"We have serving spoons; we have ladles; we have mixing paddles, which are very utilitarian and something you can use every day. We have breadboards, cutting boards, scoops . . . just all kinds of things out of hard maple. That's what we call it in Indiana—in some regions they call it sugar maple. It's close-grained wood, very dense and very heavy. For years, it's been used for rolling pins, butcher blocks, cutting boards. Historically, it's been the wood of choice in the United States for woodenware.

"Many of the pieces we have designed do draw from the European tradition. Some of the designs are just adaptations; we make things just a little bit smaller or we change them a little bit so that we can use them today. We do make some shaker reproductions, and we have scaled them down because the average person is not cooking for hundreds any more. We have welded form and function together—everything looks great, but everything is intended to be used daily.

"Prices for Whetstone utensils range from five to six dollars for simple spoons to around thirty-two dollars for a special spoon or ladle. We're currently preparing a new catalog as well as organizing home woodenware shows similar to Tupperware parties.

"We don't want to produce too many products because we lose our edge in being able to manufacture them. It would become kind of like the ice cream place where there are so many flavors that it's hard for people to decide what they want. And we don't want to change the way we make things. We use modern machines, but people run the machines. And people cut the pieces out and sand them and form them. It's very labor-intensive, and it's definitely a handcrafted product."

Potato Salad

5	pounds russet potatoes
1	leek, diced
6	hardboiled eggs, diced
1	kosher pickle, diced
½	pound bacon
½	clove garlic, minced
2	teaspoons flour
1	bay leaf
½	cup honey
1 ½	tablespoons kosher salt
	Black pepper to taste
1 ½	cups vinegar
1 ½	cups dry sherry
	Fresh parsley

Boil potatoes. Drain and let cool slightly; peel and dice. In a large mixing bowl, combine potatoes and leek. Add eggs and pickle.

Fry bacon until crisp; drain and crumble. Add to the potato mixture.

Pour all but about 1 tablespoon of the bacon drippings from the pan. Add garlic and sauté about 2 minutes, being careful not to burn it. Add flour and blend thoroughly. Add bay leaf, honey, salt, and pepper. Add vinegar and sherry. Heat just to a boil and remove immediately from heat. Discard bay leaf.

Fold about half of the dressing mixture into the potatoes. Continue adding dressing until you reach desired consistency. Garnish with sprigs of fresh parsley.

Betty Musgrave
Monrovia

Corn Slaw

½	cup sour cream
½	cup mayonnaise
¼	cup sugar
¼	cup white vinegar
	Salt and pepper to taste
1	16-ounce can whole kernel corn, drained
3–4	carrots, peeled and chopped
1	each red and green pepper, seeded and chopped
1	small onion, chopped

Combine first 5 ingredients in a large bowl; stir well. Add vegetables; toss gently. Cover and chill overnight. Drain any excess liquid before serving.

Annabelle May
Noblesville

"Champagne" Pasta Salad

Additional vegetables can be added to suit your taste. Also the amounts can be cut in half to serve less. Great for luncheon served as entree.

1   each red, green, yellow, orange pepper, chopped and slivered
1   bunch celery, chopped
1   head broccoli, cut in florets
2   large cans sliced black olives
2   jars pimento, chopped
1   can artichoke hearts
1   box each plain and spinach fettuccine, break in half
1   bag 4-shaped pastas
1   bottle Gerard's Champagne salad dressing
    Salt, pepper and celery salt

Mix vegetables. Drain olives, pimentos and artichoke hearts and add vegetables.

Refrigerate. Break the fettuccine in half; cook it and the shaped pasta according to package directions just until *al dente*, about 10 minutes—don't overcook.

Drain pastas and place in large bowl and mix in vegetables. Add dressing, salt, pepper and celery salt to taste.

Chill and serve. Serves approximately 20.

Nancy Peterson
Zionsville

Lentil Salad

½   pound brown lentils
3 ½   cups water
1   bay leaf
1   small onion, **peeled and whole**
1   small onion, **chopped**
2   tablespoons **fresh chopped parsley**
1   clove garlic, **minced**
1   tomato, **diced**
1   tablespoon **lemon juice**
3   tablespoons **olive oil**
    Salt **and pepper to taste**

Sort and rinse lentils. Drain and place in saucepan. Add water, bay leaf, whole onion. Bring to a boil; reduce heat and simmer partly covered for about 30 minutes. Remove and discard the onion and bay leaf, and drain the lentils.

Place lentils in a mixing bowl, and add the chopped onion, parsley, garlic, tomato, lemon juice, olive oil, and salt and pepper. Serves 4.

Helen Corey
Indianapolis

Pasta Salad

1	pound tri-color pasta
¼	pound each pepperoni, hard salami, and provolone cheese
1	medium onion, chopped
2	green peppers, chopped
3	stalks celery, sliced
1	large tomato (or 2 medium tomatoes), diced
1	15-ounce can black olives, drained
½	cup bottled vinaigrette dressing
¾	cup olive oil
1	tablespoon salt
4	tablespoons sugar
1	tablespoon oregano
1	teaspoon pepper

Cook pasta according to package directions. (Slightly undercook, because it will absorb dressing.) Cut pepperoni, salami, and provolone into bite size strips. Combine with next 5 ingredients and toss together.

Mix the remaining ingredients in covered jar and shake well. Pour over salad and toss. Marinate overnight for best flavor.

Debra Johnson
New Harmony

Hot Bean Salad

1	16-ounce can kidney beans, drained
1	cup sliced celery
¼	pound sharp American cheese, diced
½	cup chopped sweet pickles
¼	cup sliced green onions
½	teaspoon salt
½	cup mayonnaise
⅓	cup crushed Ritz crackers

Preheat oven to 450°F. Combine all ingredients except crackers. Lightly spray a 1 ½- or 2-quart baking dish with non-stick vegetable spray and pour in the bean mixture. (Note: This can be prepared to this stage ahead of time and refrigerated.) Sprinkle with crushed crackers and bake 30 minutes or until bubbly.

Maggie Thomas Newsom
Columbus

Pea Salad

16	ounces frozen peas
1	cup cubed cheddar cheese
2	hard cooked eggs
¼	cup celery
2	tablespoons onion, chopped
2	tablespoon chopped pimento
⅓	cup light mayonnaise
½	teaspoon salt
¼	teaspoon pepper

Cook the peas according to package directions; drain. Combine with the remaining ingredients. Serve chilled.

Sandra James
Oxford

Hot French Fry Potato Salad

Great served with bratwurst!

5	strips bacon, chopped
½	cup onion, chopped
2	tablespoons flour
⅓	cup sugar
1 ½	teaspoons salt
⅛	teaspoon pepper
1	egg, beaten
½	cup vinegar
1	cup water
1	pound frozen french fries
	Parsley flakes

In a large skillet, cook bacon and onions over medium heat until bacon is crispy and onions are tender. Add flour, sugar, salt, and pepper Stir until well-blended and smooth. Add egg and continue cooking, stirring, until egg is softly scrambled.

Add vinegar and water; stir until the mixture thickens. Add the frozen french fries and cook until the french fries are hot. Garnish with parsley flakes and serve immediately.

Sally Ouweneel
Indianapolis

Curried Coleslaw

3 ½	cups shredded cabbage
¼	cup raisins
2	tablespoons diced onion
½	cup mayonnaise
1	tablespoon cider vinegar
1	teaspoon sugar
½	teaspoon curry powder
4	slices bacon, cooked and crumbled

Combine cabbage, raisins, and onion in a large bowl. Set aside. Combine mayonnaise, vinegar, sugar and curry, mixing well. Spoon over cabbage mixture; toss well. Cover and chill. Stir in bacon just before serving. Serves 4–6.

Mary Rinck
Indianapolis

Marinated Tomatoes

Cherry tomatoes are beautiful when served this way.

2	teaspoons salt
1	teaspoon coarse ground black pepper
1	teaspoon paprika
½	teaspoon dry mustard
½	teaspoon dried minced onion
¼	cup vinegar
1	tablespoon ketchup
3	tablespoons fresh lemon juice
1	cup salad oil
6–8	medium tomatoes, or small box of cherry tomatoes Fresh parsley

Combine first 5 ingredients in a blender container or food processor bowl. Add vinegar, ketchup, and lemon juice and process enough to mix. Add the oil gradually while processing.

To easily peel the tomatoes, dip them into boiling water for just a few seconds, and then plunge into cold water. Let the tomatoes cool and place in a large dish or jar and cover with the marinade. Refrigerate about 24 hours. Drain marinade and slice tomatoes (if using large ones) and serve on endive or lettuce leaves. Sprinkle with minced fresh parsley.

Judy Britton
Camden

Herb Salad Dressing

A wonderful use for fresh herbs from your garden—dry them and they are ready to use.

½   teaspoon salt
⅛   teaspoon pepper
¼   cup vinegar
¾   cup walnut oil
½   teaspoon dried ground
      mustard
2   tablespoons various dried
      ground sweet herbs
½   cup cream
½   cup honey (optional)

Combine all ingredients in a lidded jar and shake until well blended. Store in a cool place until use. Add the honey if you prefer a sweet dressing. (This dressing is better if the flavors are allowed to blend a few days.) Pour over greens and mix well.

Friend of WFYI
Vincennes

French Dressing

We hope you like this dressing. Our family uses it all the time.

⅔   cup vinegar
½   cup sugar
1   can tomato soup
1 ½ cups salad oil
1   teaspoon dry mustard
1   teaspoon salt
1   teaspoon paprika
1   teaspoon Worcestershire
      sauce
1   clove garlic, minced

Combine vinegar and sugar in a saucepan, and heat over medium heat until the sugar is thoroughly dissolved. Remove from heat and add remaining ingredients; let cool. Store in the refrigerator in a covered jar.

Virginia Anderson
Frankfort

Summer House

"Thomas Jefferson said, 'Gardening is a symbol of hope and a symbol of religion,' " said Kerry. "If you plant a seed, you're hoping that tomorrow's going to come and that the seed's going to germinate and grow. Eventually, it's going to flower and produce more seed and continue the cycle. Gardening is like life itself."

We were standing near an authentic 1850s summer house that stands on a one-acre plot near North Manchester, Indiana. For the past ten years, Kerry Hippensteel and his mom and brother have been working on this plot to create a living replica of a nineteenth-century Hoosier garden. This floral oasis is their family business, called, appropriately enough, The Summer House.

I looked around at the profusion of herbs, perennials, and everlastings, and decided that Thomas Jefferson was right. I also decided that he would have loved this garden. It's so clearly a labor of love for the Hippensteels.

And I'm sure that Jefferson would have appreciated the story of how The Summer House was originally acquired and how the garden began.

The previous owner didn't want to pay taxes on the structure any more, Kerry explained, and decided to get rid of it.

"My younger brother, Seth, saw this man pouring kerosene on the summer house and about to destroy it [by setting fire to it]. So Seth gets my mother, and she comes up with an agreement that consists of a handshake and a quarter."

Oris Hippensteel and her sons restored the summer house using authentic glass and broad beams, as well as hand-split wood shingles. Then they began on the gardens, which now feature nearly eight hundred varieties of plants.

They're passionate about gardening and about teaching people about gardening. In addition to quoting Thomas Jefferson, Kerry occasionally gets quite poetic on the subject of living and growing things. Instead of thinking of our past as a series of colorless photographic images, Kerry says he views our heritage as rich and vibrant, painted in a remarkable palate of lavenders, lemons, and deep forest greens.

"We try to create color throughout the season," he tells visitors to The Summer House. "It starts in very early spring with tulips and daffodils, and it goes on through the fall. We have a native bamboo that blooms two or three days before frost—kind of a frost indicator."

Through their garden, the Hippensteels provide a living link with the past and offer a chance to pause and reflect and come to a greater understanding of nature, history, and ourselves.

"This garden speaks to you. It *should* speak to you. And if it doesn't, you need to get closer to the earth and put your hands in the dirt once in a while and feel it."

Thomas Jefferson couldn't have said it better.

Spinach Salad Dressing

1   cup salad oil
¾   cup sugar
1   small onion, chopped
⅓   cup ketchup
⅓   cup vinegar
1   tablespoon Worcestershire
     sauce

Mix all ingredients in blender. Serve over stemmed, torn raw spinach, mixed with sliced hard boiled eggs. Garnish with bacon bits.

Given to Marilyn Sherbrooke, Evansville
By Red Geranium, New Harmony

Celery Seed Salad Dressing

Good used with a green salad that includes mandarin oranges or grapefruit sections.

1   cup sugar
2   teaspoons salt
2   teaspoons dry mustard
3   teaspoons celery seed
⅔   cup tarragon vinegar
1 ½   teaspoons lemon juice
2   cups vegetable oil

Place sugar, salt, dry mustard, celery seed, vinegar, and lemon juice in blender container. Blend for one minute. Gradually add the oil, a little at a time, blending well. Store in refrigerator in glass jar until ready to use on your favorite green salad.

Friend of WFYI
LaPorte

Raspberry Vinaigrette

Drizzle over assorted salad greens and top with a few fresh raspberries and pine nuts for a refreshing spring or summer luncheon.

1   cup vegetable oil
½   cup olive oil
¾   cup white vinegar
¾   cup honey
1   teaspoon fresh ground
     pepper
2   cups frozen raspberries
¼   teaspoon salt

Combine all ingredients in blender container and process on medium speed until smooth and well-blended. Makes 5 cups. Store in glass jar in refrigerator.

Friend of WFYI
Fishers

Tarragon Dressing

Great for a crisp garden salad or as a marinade for raw vegetable salad. Use broccoli, cauliflower, celery, green pepper, tomatoes, green peas and green onions marinated for 3 to 4 hours in this dressing and serve on a leaf lettuce for a refreshing summer salad.

½   cup vegetable oil
¼   cup lemon juice
3   tablespoons tarragon
    vinegar
2   tablespoons sugar
2   teaspoons minced onion
1   teaspoon salt
½   teaspoon dry mustard

Combine all ingredients and mix well. Makes 2 cups.

Friend of WFYI
Lafayette

True Bleu Cheese Salad Dressing

1   cup mayonnaise
4   ounces bleu cheese,
    crumbled
3   tablespoons milk
2   tablespoons lemon juice
1   tablespoon onion, finely
    chopped
2   teaspoons sugar
¼   teaspoon Worcestershire
    sauce
¼   teaspoon dry mustard
¼   tablespoon salt

Combine all ingredients and mix well. Store in refrigerator.

Karen Peters
Indianapolis

Caesar Dressing

Your guests or family will be impressed!

1   egg or egg substitute
½   teaspoon garlic salt
½   teaspoon ground pepper
½   teaspoon dry mustard
¾   cup vegetable oil
½   cup Parmesan cheese
1   teaspoon Worcestershire
     sauce
1   tablespoon red wine vinegar
     Dash of lemon juice

In a mixing bowl, beat egg with a whisk. Continue beating and add garlic salt, ground pepper, and dry mustard. Add oil 3 or 4 tablespoons at a time; the dressing will gradually thicken. Add Parmesan cheese and Worcestershire sauce and mix well. Add lemon juice and vinegar.

Toss with romaine lettuce, torn into bite-size pieces, and top with your favorite croutons.

Priscilla Dobbins
West Lafayette

Just Plain Good

SOUPS AND SANDWICHES

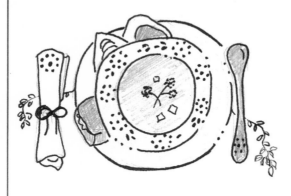

Although it isn't likely that it was an Indiana native who coined the term "tailgate party," Hoosiers have certainly embraced the concept with enthusiasm. Across the state—from Notre Dame in the north to Hanover in the south; from DePauw in the west to Ball State in the east—crisp autumn afternoons find college-football fans enjoying the moveable feasts of flavorful soups and hearty sandwiches.

Galician Bean Soup

Although we have no ties to Spain, this hearty soup from the Spanish province of Galicia has warmed our family through many a damp Hoosier winter.

2 tablespoons olive oil
1 medium onion, diced
1–3 garlic cloves, minced
1 pound smoked sausage
1 medium potato, diced
3 15-ounce cans Great Northern beans
1 bay leaf
1 box frozen chopped mustard greens or kale
Black pepper, freshly ground

In a skillet, heat the olive oil over medium heat and sauté onion until it is translucent. Add garlic and continue cooking until soft. Remove to a large soup kettle. Cut sausage into disks and brown in the same skillet, adding more oil if necessary. Remove with a slotted spoon and add to soup kettle. Add potato, undrained beans, and bay leaf. Heat and simmer, partly covered, for about 35 minutes. Meanwhile, cook greens according to package directions and squeeze dry. Combine with bean mixture, stir until heated through and adjust seasoning with pepper as desired. Serve with sourdough bread.

Sandra Miesel
Indianapolis

Cream of Spinach Soup

3 tablespoons sliced green onion
3 tablespoons butter
3 tablespoons flour
2 cups milk, warmed
1 cup half-and-half
Salt and pepper to taste
¼ teaspoon nutmeg
2 cups fresh spinach, cooked, or 2 10-ounce packages of frozen spinach, cooked and well drained
¼ teaspoon paprika

Sauté onions in butter until soft. Add flour and stir until smooth. Slowly stir in milk and half-and-half until sauce thickens. Add salt, pepper and nutmeg. Put spinach in a food processor or blender and chop into small pieces. Add spinach to cream sauce. Sprinkle with paprika. Reheat to serve. Serves 6.

Friend of WFYI
West Newton

Hot and Sour Soup

4	cups chicken broth
½	cup mushrooms, sliced thin
½	cup bamboo shoots, halved length-wise
½	cup water chestnuts, chopped
2	tablespoons white vinegar
1	tablespoon soy sauce
1	teaspoon sugar
½	teaspoon black pepper
½	pound boneless chicken breast, cooked and cubed
1	tablespoon cold water
1	tablespoon cornstarch
1	egg, beaten
2	tablespoons fresh coriander or parsley

In large saucepan, combine the chicken broth, mushrooms, bamboo shoots, water chestnuts, vinegar, soy sauce, sugar and pepper. Bring to a boil. Simmer, covered, for 10 minutes. Add chicken. Simmer, covered, for another 10 minutes.

Stir cold water into cornstarch. Stir into soup. Pour egg slowly into the hot soup in a thin stream. Stir the soup gently and keep it just simmering (not boiling) so that the egg forms thin threads. Continue cooking soup until it is slightly thickened and bubbly. Remove from heat. Stir in chopped coriander or parsley. Serves 4–6.

Clare C. Rosenbalm
Brownsburg

Hamburger Soup

Quick and easy for a cold winter evening. Serve with a green salad and French bread.

1	pound ground beef
1	cup onion, chopped
2	cans beef bouillon
3	cans water
2	cans tomato soup
2	cups carrots, sliced
1 ½	cups celery, chopped
⅓	cup rice
1	tablespoon basil

Brown ground beef and add chopped onions. Skim off grease. Add the rest of the ingredients and simmer slowly in a heavy pot for 45 minutes or longer. Serve with crackers.

Sandy Christopher
Indianapolis

French Onion Soup

3   medium onions, thinly
    sliced
3   tablespoons butter
2   tablespoons flour
2   cans beef broth
¼   cup half-and-half
    French bread croutons or
    toasted French bread slices
¼   pound Swiss cheese, grated

In a heavy iron skillet, cook onions in butter until slightly browned. Sprinkle with flour and cook over low heat until golden brown. Add broth and bring to a boil, stirring constantly with a wooden spoon, then reduce heat to simmer and cook, uncovered, for 20 minutes. Add hot half-and-half and adjust seasoning. Pour into oven-proof casserole dish or individual oven-proof bowls. Place slice of bread on top; sprinkle generously with cheese. Brown quickly under broiler and serve.

Mary Anne Weiss
West Lafayette

Sawbill Pumpkin Soup

Pumpkins mean autumn to me, so pumpkin soup is a staple of many Fall family get-togethers at our cabin on Sawbill Lake. I have experimented with many different ingredients from sweet to savory but find the curry really enhances the naturally rich taste of pumpkin.

2   tablespoons olive oil
1   large onion, diced
1   tablespoon (rounded) curry
    powder
1   49 ½-ounce can chicken
    broth (for a richer taste, use
    home made)
1   29-ounce can pumpkin
    puree
¾   cup milk or half-and-half
    Salt, pepper, and cayenne to
    taste
    Parsley and sour cream

In a large soup pot, sauté onions and curry powder in olive oil until onions are translucent. Add chicken broth and pumpkin, bring to a boil, then reduce heat and simmer for 15 minutes. Add milk slowly, blending with a whisk, add spices, cook an additional 10 minutes on low. Garnish with sprigs of fresh parsley and dollops of sour cream and serve. Serves 8.

Diane Lupke
Indianapolis

Tomato Soup

We like to grow tomatoes in our garden and use them in lots of interesting ways. Making this soup is one of those ways. Although it does take a bit of time and trouble to make, it is absolutely delicious and well worth the effort.

4 pounds ripe fresh tomatoes
3 tablespoons oil
3 cups onions, chopped
1 cup carrots, sliced
1 garlic clove, chopped
½ teaspoon sugar
2 tablespoons flour
6 sprigs parsley
1 celery stalk with leaves
8 cups chicken broth
 Salt and pepper to taste

Peel and seed tomatoes. Roughly chop. You should have about 6 cups of pulp. In a large saucepan, heat oil and sauté onions until wilted and golden. Add 2 cups of the tomatoes, carrots, garlic and sugar. Cook together, stirring, until the moisture has evaporated and the mixture is thick (about 20 minutes). Whisk in flour and cook 2–3 minutes, stirring to cook flour and make smooth. Tie together the parsley and celery and add to the pan. Add remaining tomatoes and 3 cups chicken broth. Cool 10–15 minutes to release the tomato juices and thicken slightly. Add the remaining broth and simmer 20 minutes. Remove the parsley and celery and lightly process soup in a food processor or food mill. Do not use a blender or process too much or the soup will not have enough texture. Season with salt and pepper. Yields 2 ½–3 quarts.

Susie Marvel
Rochester

Hoosier Chicken Gumbo

I won first prize in the Kokomo Tribune recipe contest with this. It's good enough and easy enough to go to the trouble of fixing it. High school home economics classes prepared the recipes for the judging; so, if they can do it, so can you!

2	tablespoons vegetable oil
2	tablespoons flour
2	slices bacon, diced
1	large onion, coarsely chopped
2	garlic cloves, chopped
1	green pepper half, chopped
1	teaspoon salt
1	teaspoon black pepper
2	teaspoons Worcestershire sauce
1	teaspoon hot pepper sauce
1	quart stewed tomatoes
3	pounds chicken breasts
4	cups water
1	package frozen okra
2	teaspoons filé powder

Combine oil and flour in a Dutch oven. Cook and stir until golden brown over medium heat. Add bacon and cook until browned. Stir in onion, garlic, and green pepper, and cook 4–5 minutes. Add next 6 ingredients and bring to a boil; reduce heat and simmer for 45 minutes until chicken is tender and done. Remove chicken and discard skin and bones. Cut chicken meat into bite-size pieces.

Skim fat from soup. Bring to a boil and add okra. Simmer, stirring occasionally, for 15 minutes. Return chicken to pot and heat through. Stir in filé. Serve in bowls over hot cooked rice. Serves 10.

Patsie Ronk
Galveston

Corn Chowder

5	slices bacon
1	medium onion, sliced thin and separated into rings
2 ½	cups milk
2	cups frozen corn
1	can mushroom soup
1	cup cooked diced potatoes
	Salt to taste

In large pan, cook bacon until crisp. Drain on paper towel. Crumble bacon. Reserve 2–3 tablespoons drippings in pan. Cook onion rings in drippings until tender. Stir in milk, corn, soup, and potatoes. Bring to a boil, reduce heat and simmer for 2–3 minutes. Remove from heat. Season to taste with salt. Top with bacon.

Linda Arnot
Indianapolis

Broccoli-Cheddar Soup

¼	cup onion, chopped
¼	cup butter
¼	cup flour
¼	teaspoon salt
¼	teaspoon pepper
¾	cup chicken broth
1 ½	cups milk
1	cup fresh or frozen broccoli, cooked
½	cup cheddar cheese, shredded

In pan, sauté onion in butter till tender. Stir in flour, salt, pepper. Cook and stir till smooth and bubbly. Add broth and milk all at once, stirring constantly. Bring to a boil till thick as desired. Add broccoli; simmer till heated through, stirring constantly. Remove from heat; stir in cheese till melted.

Barbara A. Fausett
Frankfort

Potato Soup with Rivals

RIVALS

4	eggs, well beaten
2	teaspoons baking powder
3–4	cups flour

SOUP

6	medium potatoes, peeled and diced
1	onion, diced
2	slices bacon, finely diced
	Celery salt and pepper to taste
1 ½	cups milk
2	tablespoons butter

FOR THE RIVALS: Break eggs in a medium bowl. Add the salt and baking powder; mix well with a fork. Add flour, about ¼ cup at a time, mixing until a soft dough forms. (These are good also with bean soup, or clear chicken or beef broth.)

FOR THE SOUP: Place potatoes in a large pan; add water to cover. Add onion, bacon, and seasonings. Cover and bring to a boil. Drop rivals dough in small amounts into the boiling soup and reduce heat to medium-low. Cover the pan and simmer until the rivals are done, about 15–20 minutes.

Heat milk with butter in microwave or saucepan; do not boil. Add the hot milk to the potato mixture and continue cooking about another 5 minutes, adding more milk if soup is too thick. Adjust seasonings as desired and serve.

Mary Anne Weiss
West Lafayette

Beef-Vegetable Soup

2–3	pounds stew beef
1	cup flour
2	tablespoons vegetable oil
8	cups beef stock
2	large tomatoes
2	leeks, chopped
1	medium onion, thinly sliced
3–4	carrots, chopped
2	large potatoes, peeled and diced
1	cup lima beans, green beans, or peas
¼	teaspoon Worcestershire sauce
½	teaspoon lemon juice
	Salt to taste

Cut beef into bite-size pieces and dredge lightly in flour. Heat oil in large pot and brown beef on all sides. Add stock. Peel, seed, and chop tomatoes and add to beef and stock. Add leeks and onion; stir and bring to a boil. Cover pot with loose-fitting lid and simmer for 2 hours. Add carrots, potatoes, and desired vegetable. Cook until meat and vegetables are tender. Add Worcestershire sauce and lemon juice. Season to taste. Serves 8.

Friend of WFYI
Brazil

Home-Canned Tomato Soup

4	quarts tomatoes
½	cup celery, chopped
2	onions, chopped
2	sprigs parsley, chopped
½	teaspoon mixed spice (allspice, cloves)
1	bay leaf, crushed
¼	cup water
2	teaspoons sugar
2	teaspoons salt

Wash ripened tomatoes well. Core and chop. Combine all ingredients in a large pot and simmer until soft. Put entire mixture through a food mill to separate out the peels and seeds from the pulp. Reheat liquid to simmering. Pour liquid into hot, sterile canning jars. Seal and process for 10 minutes at 5 pounds pressure in a pressure canner. Cool. Can be put into pints or quarts. When ready to eat, just heat to boiling and serve.

Ka Freeman
Indianapolis

Curried Zucchini Soup

Zucchini are soft-skinned summer squashes with a mild flavor, pepped up here by a warm spicing of curry powder. Choose small zucchini, less than 6 inches long.

3	pounds zucchini
2	pounds potatoes
1	stick butter
2	onions, chopped
3	garlic cloves, crushed
3	tablespoons curry powder
1	49.5-ounce can chicken broth
	Salt and pepper to taste

Trim zucchini and cut in half lengthwise. Cut each half into ½-inch slices, set aside. Peel and dice potatoes, set aside. Melt the butter in a large pot. Add the onion, garlic, and curry powder. Cook, stirring, 5 minutes. Add the stock and potatoes. Season to taste with salt and pepper, then simmer, uncovered, for 15 minutes. Add the zucchini and simmer for 15–20 minutes. Puree the soup in a blender or processor, then taste for seasoning. Ladle the soup into warmed individual bowls. Serve with garlic toast.

Annabelle May
Noblesville

Potato Soup

2	large potatoes, peeled and cut up
2	medium carrots
1	stalk celery
⅓	cup chopped parsley
1	medium onion, chopped
1	bay leaf
1	tablespoon salt
6–8	teaspoons allspice
2	tablespoons butter or margarine
2	rounded tablespoons flour

Peel and cut up the potatoes and carrots; chop celery. Combine potatoes, carrots, and celery with next 5 ingredients in a large pot. Add 1 quart of water and simmer until vegetables are tender.

Make a roux (*zaklepka*) melting butter or margarine in a small skillet over low heat. Add flour and blend well. Cook, stirring constantly, until browned. Remove from heat and slowly add to soup. Simmer, stirring, for 5 more minutes and serve.

Irene Kimmel
South Bend

Midwest Pride Three-Bean Soup

A hearty meal or Super Bowl party entree!

½ pound mild sausage
½ cup onion, diced
1 14.5-ounce can diced tomatoes, undrained
1 15.5-ounce can kidney beans, drained
1 15.5-ounce can butter beans, undrained
1 15.5-ounce can lima beans, undrained
2 ½ cups water
⅓ cup brown sugar, packed
1 tablespoon spicy brown mustard
1 tablespoon prepared horseradish
1 teaspoon chili powder
½ teaspoon garlic powder
½ teaspoon basil

Cook sausage and onion in large soup pot until sausage is crumbled and no longer pink. Add remaining ingredients. Bring to a boil and stir. Reduce heat and simmer for 1 hour. Serves 6.

Sherri Auckley
Lafayette

Kwas

A hearty Polish soup.

2 ½ pounds spareribs
4 quarts water
¾ cup vinegar
2 tablespoons salt
½ cup sugar
2 jars prunes, junior foods
¾ cups raisins
½ cup flour
  Prune butter (optional)

Cut spareribs into serving pieces; place in large pot and cover with water. Add vinegar, salt, sugar, and prunes. Cook until meat is almost done, about 1 hour. Add raisins and continue cooking until meat is tender, about another 30 minutes. Remove bones and discard.

Mix flour with ½ cup cold water; add to soup and cook until thickened. Prune butter may be added for extra flavor and color.

Serve with potato dumplings or desired noodles.

Pauline Cybulski
South Bend

Chilled Cream of Apricot Soup with Rosemary

2	15-ounce cans apricot halves in heavy syrup
6	4-inch sprigs fresh rosemary
6	whole cloves
2	cups half-and-half

Drain off the apricot syrup into a microwave-proof dish or large measuring cup. Add the rosemary and cloves. Microwave on high for 5 minutes. Stir, then microwave 2 minutes longer. Let cool at least 8 hours or overnight.

In a food processor, purée the apricot halves thoroughly and pour into a bowl. Strain the syrup through a sieve and add to the puréed apricots. Whisk in the half-and-half just before serving.

Marcia Adams
Fort Wayne

Cream of Fresh Mushroom Soup

4 ½	cups fresh mushrooms, sliced
2	tablespoons onion, sliced
4	tablespoons margarine
2 ½	cups water
1 ½	cups chicken broth
¾	teaspoon salt
¼	teaspoon pepper
1	stick margarine
½	cup all-purpose flour
1	quart whole milk

In a kettle, sauté mushrooms and onions in 4 tablespoons margarine. Add water and chicken broth. Simmer until reduced by half. Add salt and pepper. Set aside.

In a separate pan, melt stick of margarine over low heat. Gradually add flour, stirring constantly; cook until bubbly and smooth. Slowly stir in milk. Cook, stirring with wire whisk, until thickened and smooth. Slowly add white sauce to mushroom-broth mixture, stirring constantly. Simmer for 30 minutes. Serve hot.

Bernice Boucher Hopp
Indianapolis

Oven Roasted Tomato and French Bread Soup

2	tablespoons vegetable oil
1	medium yellow onion, finely diced
½	cup Chardonnay
4	quarts vegetable or chicken stock
3	cups roasted tomatoes, diced
6	cloves garlic
2	tablespoons fresh basil
1	tablespoon thyme
4	cups diced French bread
	Salt and pepper to taste

Heat oil in a large stock pot. Add onion and sauté until translucent. Add remaining ingredients and simmer for 45 minutes. Adjust seasonings as desired.

Purée in a blender or food processor. Can be served hot or cold.

Steven J. Oakley, Executive Chef
Something Different and Snax Restaurants
Indianapolis

Gazpacho Anduluz

1	slice country-style bread, about 1 inch thick
2	small cucumbers, peeled, seeded and coarsely chopped
2	pounds very ripe tomatoes, peeled, seeded and coarsely chopped
1	clove garlic, peeled and chopped
2	tablespoons sherry vinegar
½	cup extra virgin olive oil
	Salt to taste
	Juice of 1 lemon
1	cup water

Combine all ingredients in a blender or food processor and purée until nearly smooth. Chill.

If desired, serve finely chopped cucumbers, green pepper, onions, tomatoes, and croutons as garnishes. Cooked shrimp may also be added at serving time. Serves 4.

Nancy H. Hannin
Indianapolis

Taco Soup

Everyone in our family loves this soup. It has to be good—it's from Marcia Adams.

1 ½ pounds ground beef
1   medium onion, chopped
1   1 ¼-ounce package taco
    seasoning
1   1-ounce package dry
    original ranch dressing mix
2   teaspoons cumin
1   10-ounce can Rotel diced
    tomatoes, undrained
1   14-ounce can hominy,
    drained
1   14-ounce can red kidney
    beans, undrained
1   14-ounce can black beans,
    undrained

1   14-ounce can pinto beans,
    undrained
3   14-ounce cans stewed tomatoes
    Shredded sharp cheddar cheese
    Corn chips, broken in pieces

Treat a deep kettle with cooking spray. Add the meat and onion, brown over medium heat until meat is cooked through. Drain off excess fat; stir in dry seasoning mixes and cumin. Add remaining ingredients and stir. Simmer on medium heat, uncovered, for 30 minutes. Garnish with cheese and corn chips or freeze for later use. Makes 12 generous servings.

Suzanne Hall
Fort Wayne

Bun-Steads

1   7-ounce can tuna
1   cup (about ¼ pound)
    shredded American cheese
3   hard boiled eggs, cut up
2   tablespoons chopped green
    bell pepper
2   tablespoons chopped onion
2   tablespoons chopped olives
2   tablespoons chopped celery
½   cup mayonnaise or salad
    dressing
6   round sandwich buns

Preheat oven to 250°F. Drain tuna and put in a mixing bowl. Add the next 7 ingredients and mix.

Split the buns and fill them with the mixture. Wrap in foil and bake for about 30 minutes.

Betty Taylor
Noblesville

Lentil Soup

We had some form of soup served with hamburgers almost every weekend for Saturday or Sunday supper. This and split pea were our family favorites.

1	whole ham shank
1	pound lentils
2	cups chopped onion
2	cups carrots
2	cups celery
	Salt and pepper to taste
1	8-ounce package link sausages

Put the ham shank in a large pot and add about 3 ½ quarts of water. Bring to a boil, reduce heat, and simmer for 6–8 hours. Remove shank from the stock. Cut the meat from the bone into bite-size pieces and refrigerate. Discard bone.

Refrigerate stock until the fat rises to the top and hardens. Remove the fat and discard. Bring stock to a boil and add the lentils, onion, carrots, and celery. Reduce heat to low and simmer for about 2 hours, or until lentils are tender. Add the salt and pepper.

Brown the sausages in a skillet, drain, and slice. Add sausage slices to each bowl of soup and serve. (Note: This soup is best when made ahead and flavors are allowed to blend. It also freezes very well. Split peas may also be substituted for the lentils.)

Gay Burkhart
Zionsville

Ayres Open-Faced Sandwich

This is a sandwich as I remember it from the L. S. Ayres Tea Room.

Rye bread
Ham
Turkey or chicken
Swiss cheese
Tomatoes, sliced
Lettuce leaf
Thousand Island dressing
Eggs, hard-boiled
Ripe olives

For each person, top a slice of rye bread with the next 5 ingredients in order as listed. Cover with Thousand Island dressing and garnish with a slice of hard-boiled egg and a ripe olive.

Gay Burkhart
Zionsville

Spicy Sausage Sauerbraten Sandwiches

This is great served with red cabbage, cole slaw or hot German potato salad and garlic dill pickles.

1 ¼	pounds bulk pork sausage
¼	pound ground beef
¼	cup onion, minced
1 ½	teaspoons salt
1	egg, beaten
1	cup red burgundy wine
½	cup cider vinegar
1	tablespoon sugar
¼	teaspoon ground ginger
1	bay leaf, very finely crumbled
6	kaiser buns, sliced
6	tablespoons apple butter Lettuce leaves or shredded lettuce

Mix sausage, beef, onion, salt, and egg; shape into patties. Heat a skillet over medium heat and cook the patties until brown, about 5 minutes per side. Remove patties from skillet; drain off fat.

In the same skillet combine wine, vinegar, sugar, ginger and bay leaf. Cook 5 minutes. Return the patties to the skillet; cover and cook about 10 minutes longer, or until done. Spread each bun with apple butter. Place patty on apple butter; spoon sauce over patty. Garnish with lettuce. Serves 6.

Sherman House Restaurant and Inn
Batesville

The Sherman House in Batesville welcomed its first guests on November 9, 1852, and over the past century has evolved from a coaching tavern to the unique and popular hostelry it is today. It received its current name to commemorate General Sherman's contributions to Northern victory in the Civil War, and several priceless prints of the Sherman era hang in the inn's lounge. It remains a favorite stopping place for travelers in southern Indiana with an extensive menu offering selections ranging from steaks and chicken dishes to Old Vienna favorites and Grilled Ostrich Madeira.

Pork Loin on Pepper Biscuits

3–4 pounds pork loin roast
½ cup brandy
⅛ cup soy sauce
1 cup brown sugar
Pepper Biscuits (recipe follows)

Combine brandy, soy sauce, and brown sugar. Pour over the roast and marinate 6 hours or overnight, turning several times.

Preheat oven to 350°F. Remove the meat from the marinade and place in a roasting pan. Roast uncovered approximately 20–30 minutes per pound or 160–178°F inside temperature on meat thermometer. Slice and serve on Pepper Biscuits.

Pepper Biscuits

2 cups flour
4 teaspoons baking powder
½ teaspoon salt
½ teaspoon cream of tartar
1 tablespoon pepper
2 tablespoons sugar
½ cup shortening (all purpose)
⅔ cup buttermilk

Preheat oven to 425°F. Mix all dry ingredients together. Cut in shortening with a pastry cutter. Add buttermilk and stir until ball is formed. Turn out on floured surface and knead about 30 seconds. Pat out until a ½ inch thick. Cut any size using a biscuit cutter. Place on ungreased baking sheet approximately 1 ½ inches apart. Bake 8–10 minutes.

Sue Kobets
Illinois Street Food Emporium
Indianapolis

Sloppy Joes for a Crowd

5 pounds ground beef
3 cups ketchup
5 tablespoons brown sugar
5 tablespoons cider vinegar
5 tablespoons dry mustard
5 teaspoons Worcestershire sauce
2 ½ teaspoons salt

Brown ground beef and drain. Add remaining ingredients and mix well. Cover and simmer for 30 minutes; uncover and simmer another 30 minutes.

Jeanne Jerden
Bloomington

Rump Roast Sandwiches

Great for after-football parties or for tailgate.

	15-pound rump roast
1	tablespoon crushed peppercorns
1	tablespoon garlic powder or ½ garlic clove, crushed
1	tablespoon rosemary
1	tablespoon marjoram
2	tablespoons salt
2	tablespoons minced chives
2	tablespoons oregano
3	medium onions, minced fine
7	cups liquid (all meat drippings and 2 packages au jus gravy mix)

Preheat oven to 350°F. Place meat in large pan and roast to rare, or 140°F on a meat thermometer. Slice meat thinly, but do not shave (a meat cutter can do this for you).

Combine remaining ingredients in a large pot and blend well. Bring sauce to a boil, add meat and simmer for an hour. Serve with minibuns.

Betsy Carpenter
West Lafayette

Kraut Relish Sandwiches

½	cup sugar
½	cup vinegar
1	16-ounce can sauerkraut
1	cup diced celery
1	cup diced green pepper
½	cup diced onion
1	2-ounce jar pimento, drained and chopped
1–2	pounds sliced ham
1–2	pounds sliced salami
1	pound thinly sliced Swiss cheese
	Rye bread of choice

Heat sugar and vinegar till sugar is dissolved; cool. Combine undrained sauerkraut, celery, green pepper, onion, and pimento. Mix with the vinegar mixture. Chill for several hours. Butter slices of rye bread (I use German black bread). Stack slices of ham, salami and thin-sliced Swiss cheese on slice of bread; top with ¼ cup of the drained relish. Close the sandwich with another slice of buttered bread. Insert a toothpick with an olive to hold together. Serves 12.

Betsy Carpenter
West Lafayette

Pizzaburgers

1	pound lean ground beef
½	cup chopped onions
1	6-ounce can tomato paste
1	teaspoon salt
1	teaspoon oregano
1	teaspoon thyme
¼	teaspoon garlic powder
6	buns, split, toasted, and buttered

In skillet, brown beef and cook onion until tender but not brown. Add tomato paste and seasonings. Simmer uncovered about 15 minutes. Spoon hot meat mixture between bun halves. For extra taste treat, slip mozzarella cheese slices on top of each bun. Makes 6 servings.

Nancy Lugar Fogle
Indianapolis

Corned Beef Sandwich Squares

2	tubes crescent rolls
8	ounces kosher corned beef, chopped
1	cup mayonnaise
3	tablespoons pickle relish
1	tablespoon minced onion
1	teaspoon Worcestershire sauce
8	ounces shredded cheddar cheese
4	ounces shredded Swiss cheese
1	egg white Sesame seeds

Flatten one tube of crescent rolls in bottom of 9 x 13-inch baking dish. Cover with corned beef. Mix mayonnaise, relish, onion, Worcestershire sauce and cheese. Spread over corned beef. Top with second tube of crescent rolls. Beat egg white slightly and brush on top of crust. Sprinkle with sesame seeds. Bake as directed on crescent roll tube or until golden brown. Cool to set. Cut in squares to serve.

Friend of WFYI
Richmond

Fire House Café's Famous BLT Soup

½   pound bacon
3   cups whole milk
2   heaping teaspoons
    cornstarch
1   head lettuce, finely chopped
2   medium-size tomatoes,
    finely chopped
    Salt, pepper, and garlic salt
    to taste

Cook bacon until crispy, and finely chop. Set aside with drippings. In large saucepan heat milk over medium heat.

Mix the cornstarch in 1 cup of cold water and add to the milk; cook, stirring constantly, until thickened. Add bacon, drippings, lettuce, tomato, season to taste. Simmer 5 minutes, serve immediately. Serves 6.

Old # 3 Fire House Café
Fort Wayne

Queenie and Her Ten

Queenie, a Dalmatian, was the mascot at Fire Station #5 at 1405 Broadway. On April 17, 1951, she gave birth to ten pups. The firefighters knew a photographer at the newspaper and they called him. Mom was placed on the seat of the pumper and the ten pups were tucked into fire boots so just their heads and upper bodies stuck out. This was such a cute photo that it was picked up by the national news media and sent nationwide.

For a great sandwich, stack the following:

Braunschweiger, cream cheese, and red onion on marble bread. Serve with celery, carrot sticks and dill dip.

Old # 3 Fire House Café
Fort Wayne

Knights of the Nozzle

"The fire fighters who have worked in this station, some of the experiences they've had, some of the bigger fires that have been fought here—those are the things that really hit home when you look back on it," says Ron Hamm, historian at Fort Wayne's Firefighters Museum.

In 1893 the mayor of Fort Wayne cut the ribbon on the city's newest pride and joy: Fire Station Number 3. At a total cost of fifty-three hundred dollars, the engine house featured one hose wagon, one chemical wagon, six men, and four horses.

In those days, fire fighters often worked thirty days straight. It was a very low-paying and dirty job. The breathing apparatus and the clothing weren't specialized and weren't at all protective. "In fact," explains Hamm, "you'd be lucky if you had any sort of special clothing at all."

When an alert citizen sounded the alarm on a convenient fire box (telephones weren't prevalent at the time), the men of Fire Station Number 3 responded immediately. The horses were released from their stalls and hitched to the wagon, the gear was gathered and stowed on board, the manual gate was lifted, and the truck rolled out—all in less than a minute. The public applauded the valiant efforts of the fire fighting team at Number 3, and the *Fort Wayne Gazette* called them "The Knights of the Nozzle."

"It amazes me that they were able to do the job they did with the meager resources they had available to them," says Hamm. "A lot of places back East were destroyed by fire, and these men were actually able to keep the city of Fort Wayne from burning to the ground."

Fire Station Number 3 continued to serve as an active fire station until 1972. Today the structure has been converted into a Firefighters Museum and a café. When he's not out battling blazes himself, Fort Wayne Assistant Fire Chief Ron Hamm is one of the volunteers who helps operate the facility.

The Firefighters Museum features some rare pieces of equipment, such as an 1848 hand pumper, one of the first fire engines in Fort Wayne. The engine was operated by several men pumping large handles up and down rapidly to create enough pressure to activate the hoses. The handles often oscillated at alarming rates—sometimes as many as sixty or more strokes per minute. If a fire fighter did not hold on tightly, the sheer force of the pumper could throw him many feet into the air.

It's this and many other colorful pieces of history that ignite Ron Hamm's passion and paint a vivid portrait of an important part of the Hoosier heritage.

"You tend to go back to your boyhood dream, when you see the fire fighters on the trucks— that's what every child wants to be. By coming here, you can be placed in that position. You can put yourself in the seats, and you can imagine what it was like hanging on to that tailboard when it was twenty degrees below zero outside. It's a lot of nostalgia and a lot of history."

Blue Ribbon Baking

BREADS AND MUFFINS

Treasured family recipes for yeast breads, muffins, and coffeecakes are honored each year at county fairs across Indiana. Winners proceed to the State Fair, held every August in Indianapolis, in hopes of wider acclaim.

Hot Pepper Corn Bread

3 cups self-rising flour
3 teaspoons sugar
½ teaspoon garlic powder
1 cup cream style corn
1 ½ cups grated sharp cheddar
   cheese
½ cup vegetable oil
2 ½ cups milk
¼ cup grated onion
3 eggs, beaten
¼ cup red or green pepper,
   finely chopped

Preheat oven to 450°F. Mix all ingredients together. Bake in well-greased iron skillet for 25–30 minutes.

In memory of Iva Dickey
Judy Britton
Camden

Molasses Brown Bread

For a superb luncheon, serve shrimp salad a la brown molasses bread. I tested quite a few recipes before reaching one that satisfied an almost duplicate to brown bread I had in a restaurant in Plymouth, Maine. Start your luncheon with corn chowder.

1 cup flour
1 teaspoon baking soda
½ teaspoon salt
½ teaspoon cinnamon
1 egg
1 cup bran cereal
½ cup raisins
2 tablespoons shortening
⅓ cup molasses
¾ cup hot water

Preheat oven to 350°F. Grease 2 loaf pans. Stir flour, soda, salt and cinnamon together. Set aside. In a large bowl, beat egg well. Mix in bran, raisins, shortening and molasses. Add water and stir until shortening is melted. Mix in dry ingredients until well blended. Fill 2 greased bread pans about ⅔ full. Bake about 45 minutes. Makes 2 loaves.

Helen Corey
Indianapolis

Grace Matthews' Famous Zucchini Bread

Every summer Mom bakes and bakes . . . and bakes loaves of zucchini bread. She reminds me of a squirrel preparing for winter. She enjoys the success of this recipe, and all recipients of her gift loaves enjoy the results of her pleasure. I tease her a lot during the "baking season," but I delight in her annual production. This is great as a dessert bread, a snack, or a brunch addition.

1	cup vegetable oil
2	cups sugar (or 1 ½ cups if less sweetening desired)
3	eggs
3	cups flour
2	teaspoons cinnamon
2	teaspoons baking soda
1	teaspoon salt
1	teaspoon vanilla
2	cups grated zucchini
1	cup raisins
1	cup crushed pineapple

Preheat oven to 350°F. Grease and flour 2 large loaf pans or one 10-inch tube pan.

Mix oil, sugar, and eggs together until light. Add all dry ingredients that have been sifted together. Add the vanilla and zucchini. Stir in raisins and crushed pineapple. Mix lightly but thoroughly.

Pour batter into baking pan(s) and bake for 1 hour or until the bread tests done in center when a pick is inserted and comes out clean.

Marcella J. Taylor
Indianapolis

Refrigerator Rolls

1	package yeast
1	cup warm water
¼	cup sugar
½	teaspoon salt
1	egg, well beaten
3 ½	cups flour (approximately)

Dissolve yeast in water. Mix sugar, salt, beaten egg and yeast mixture together. Add about half of flour; beat with mixer for 3 minutes. Remove from mixer and stir in the rest of the flour. Put in a greased bowl and cover with a damp cloth. (Can store for a week or more.) About 1 ½ hours before baking, take out the amount of dough you want. Roll out and cut or make in balls. Put in greased pan. Let rise until double. Bake at 400°F until golden.

Audra Comer
Scottsburg

Dilly Bread

This is easier than the length of the recipe would suggest.

2 tablespoons yeast
½ cup warm water
2 cups creamed small-curd cottage cheese, heated to lukewarm
4 tablespoons sugar
2 tablespoons margarine, melted
2 teaspoons salt
2 unbeaten eggs
2 tablespoons minced instant onion
4 tablespoons dill seed
½ teaspoon baking soda
4 ½ cups flour

In a bowl, stir yeast into warm water. (Be careful that water is not hot.) Set aside for a few minutes for the yeast to soften.

In a large mixing bowl, combine the cottage cheese, sugar, melted margarine, salt, eggs, onion, dill seed and baking soda. Add just enough flour to make stiff dough, beating well after each addition. (You can use mixer at low speed until dough gets too stiff, or use a dough hook if your mixer has one.) Cover and let rise in a warm place for about 1 ½ hours or until doubled. Punch dough down and turn into a well-greased large tube pan. Let rise again about 1 hour, or until doubled. Bake in a preheated oven at 350°F for 1 ½ hours or until brown.

Brush the top of the bread with butter and sprinkle with a bit of salt (coarse salt if you have it). Let cool in pan on wire rack. When cool, remove from pan, wrap in foil. (This freezes very well.) To reheat, leave in foil and heat in a hot oven.

Gay Burkhart
Zionsville

Salt Rising Bread

This is a very old process for bread-making as used by pioneer women, who did not always have access to yeast or a bread starter. It results in a firm-textured bread which retains an aroma similar to sourdough and is excellent for toasting. I experimented with modern measurements, finally developing this recipe which results in loaves that taste and look like the ones my great-aunt baked when I was a child. It is time- and labor-intensive, but worth the trouble!

Mix together in small glass or pottery bowl:

⅓	cup corn meal, stoneground from whole corn, *not* degerminated
¼	teaspoon salt, kosher or other salt without additives
¼	teaspoon baking soda
⅔	cup warm milk

Place bowl in warm place overnight. Avoid drafts or cold utensils when making this bread. Mixture will be bubbly and have a strong odor when it is ready to be used. Early next morning, pour the starter into a 4-quart glass or pottery bowl and add the following ingredients:

2	cups warm milk
¼	teaspoon salt
¼	teaspoon baking soda
4	cups flour

Beat until batter is smooth. Cover bowl with plastic wrap and place in warm place until batter has risen. It should reach the top of the bowl. This will take several hours, as the rising process follows the development of natural or "wild" yeast from the fermentation of the corn meal starter. When the dough mixture has risen, turn it onto a large bread board or into a large dough bowl (at least 8-quart size). Add the following ingredients, using just enough flour to knead to a good bread dough consistency:

1	quart warm milk
5	teaspoons salt
4	pounds unbleached flour (or more as needed for a smooth consistency of dough)

Shape into loaves and place in greased bread pans. Place in warm place, covering tops with a lightly dampened cloth to prevent the surface from drying out during the rising. (A light-weight linen or smooth cotton cloth is preferred, not terry cloth.) Once again, you cannot predetermine the length of time it will take for the dough to rise to the top of the pans due to the natural action of the yeast. It can take one hour or several.

Preheat oven to 350°F and bake loaves for 30 to 40 minutes, depending on size. Recipe makes 4 large loaves or 8 small (1-pound) loaves.

Donna C. Almon
Indianapolis

Yeast Rolls

1   package dry yeast
1   tablespoon sugar
⅓ cup warm water
1   cup milk
1   stick butter or margarine
3   eggs
1   teaspoon salt
3 ½ cups flour

Combine yeast and sugar in warm water; let stand 5–8 minutes. Scald milk, remove from heat and add butter. Let cool.

Beat eggs slightly and add to cooled milk. Add yeast mixture. Add salt and flour, 1 cup at a time, until mixture forms a soft ball. (The amount of flour needed will depend on the humidity.)

Cover dough and refrigerate. Let rise at least 4 hours. (It will keep up to 1 week in refrigerator.)

Remove from refrigerator and punch down. Place dough on a floured surface and roll into a rectangle ¼ inch thick. Spread with melted butter and cut dough into 1 ½-inch strips. Cut each strip into 2-inch pieces and fold buttered sides together. Place in a greased 9 x 13-inch pan. Lightly brush tops with melted butter and let rise until double, 45–60 minutes.

Preheat oven to 400°F. Bake 15–20 minutes or until golden brown. Makes 2–3 dozen rolls.

Anne Pantzer
Indianapolis

Historic Homecoming

Nestled amid the rolling hills of southern Indiana, a piece of history hides beneath a leafy canopy. Just south of Salem, Beck's Mill stands as a majestic reminder of our past.

The Beck family first came to this area in 1804. They became friends with the local Native American tribes, and many of the tribe members are buried on Beck property.

Beck's Mill was one of the first mills established in the region, and for many years it remained the only mill within a forty-mile radius. Local folklore tells that customers used to come down the creek on skates in the wintertime to have their grinding done. Sometimes they would have to stay all night or even two or three days. During its heyday, the mill ran twenty-four hours a day.

When other families moved into the area, they built their houses around the mill. Soon Beck's Mill became a small town, with the mill as the hub of the town, the main gathering place.

Joyce Allen grew up in Louisville and came to this area when she and her late husband, Larue, were courting in the 1930s. From her very first visit, Joyce fell in love, not only with her future husband, but also with the land and its heritage.

"I've been a lot of places," Joyce says, "but this is home. It's quiet here. It's beautiful. There's no season of the year that there isn't beauty."

The mill that stands today was built in 1865. Its weathered remains belie its significance to the pioneer families of long ago. But to Joyce Allen and many others, Beck's Mill is alive with vivid memories, a scenic backdrop for historic homecomings.

"There are so many people who write, who come, and I am the historian of this place. I really do like sitting down and talking with people about Beck's history as I know it. They come looking for something—where their grandparents or great-grandparents came from—and they go away feeling good about it, because they got in touch with their heritage."

Cheese Garlic Biscuits

These are so good! They are just like the ones at a famous seafood restaurant.

2   cups biscuit baking mix
⅔   cup milk
½   cup shredded cheddar cheese
¼   cup butter or margarine, melted
¼   teaspoon garlic powder

Preheat oven to 450°F. Stir together baking mix, milk and cheese to get a soft dough. Beat vigorously with a wooden spoon about 30 seconds. Drop by spoonfuls onto ungreased baking sheet. Bake for 8–10 minutes or until golden brown. Meanwhile, stir together melted butter and garlic powder. Brush over biscuits as soon as they are done. Serve warm. Makes about one dozen biscuits.

Beverly Reynolds
Brownsburg

Magic Biscuits

I always make these for Sunday dinner. Make them before leaving for church, cover with plastic wrap, and place in refrigerator. After coming home, remove from refrigerator, let rise for 30 to 45 minutes and bake. Nice to have hot bread!

2   packages dry yeast
¼   cup warm water
5   cups all-purpose flour
1   teaspoon salt
4   tablespoons sugar
1   cup shortening
2   cups buttermilk
½   teaspoon baking soda
4   teaspoons baking powder
2   tablespoons butter, melted

Place all ingredients except butter together and mix until a soft dough forms. Turn dough onto a lightly floured board and knead about 10–15 times. Form rolls and put into lightly-greased pans. (Biscuits may be refrigerated at this stage.)

Brush tops of biscuits with melted butter and let set for 30 minutes. Bake in preheated 350°F oven until golden brown, about 30–45 minutes. (These can also be made into dough-nuts by adding 1 egg for each package of yeast.)

Wayne Johnson
Indianapolis

Amish Rolls

1 ½ cups milk
2 teaspoons salt
½ cup sugar
½ cup butter
2 packages yeast
½ cup warm water
3 eggs
6 cups flour

Preheat oven to 350°F. Scald milk; add salt, sugar, and butter. Let cool to lukewarm. Dissolve yeast in warm water in a large bowl. Add milk mixture to yeast; stir in eggs and 3 cups of flour. Add remaining 3 cups flour to make a soft dough. Turn out on a floured surface and knead. Let rise 1 hour or until doubled. Shape into rolls and let rise. Bake 15–20 minutes.

Kay Hunter
Vincennes

Applesauce Bread

2 ½ cups hot applesauce
1 cup margarine
2 cups sugar
3 teaspoons baking soda
1 ½ teaspoons cinnamon
½ teaspoon allspice
½ teaspoon salt
4 cups sifted flour
1 pound box raisins (golden or dark)
1 cup chopped pecans (optional)

Preheat oven to 325°F. Grease 2 large loaf pans (or 3 medium, or 5 small pans).

Melt margarine in the hot applesauce. Add sugar, baking soda, cinnamon, allspice, and salt and allow to cool. When cooled, add flour, raisins and nuts. Mix well.

Pour into prepared pans. Bake until tester inserted in center comes out clean. Baking time will depend on how thick your applesauce is. When cool, wrap in heavy foil and refrigerate. You may frost these with plain white icing if you wish. Flavor can be varied by using English walnuts or black walnuts instead of pecans.

Tina M. Miller
Otterbein

The Pumpkin Man

Have you ever pondered the pumpkin? Each autumn, this plump orange gourd is a common sight in the Hoosier state. Pumpkins are so common, in fact, that you probably haven't given them much thought.

Charlie Williams has given quite a bit of thought to pumpkins. For thirty-six years he's raised pumpkins and other vegetables on his farm just west of Ligonier. But to Charlie, the pumpkin is more than a crop. It's a work of art.

You see, Charlie is the caretaker of Pumpkin Fantasyland, the nation's largest—and only—display of pumpkin art. "I guess that's my creative talent," explains Charlie. "I can see a face or something to make out of a pumpkin, and that's what I do."

It all started more than a quarter of a century ago. Charlie was ringing up a customer's order at the country market when suddenly he had an epiphany. "I was at the counter in the market, and a lady brought up two butternut squash and laid them on the counter. And the way they were lying there, I saw the character Snoopy from the comic strip *Peanuts*."

Since then, Charlie has created his famed pumpkin Snoopys. They're part of an expansive display of more than three thousand sculpted squash. With the amber gourd as his canvas, Charlie has immortalized some of the biggest names in history. In the Hall of Presidents, for example,

Honest Abe shares the spotlight with Nixon, Carter, and Clinton.

And Charlie continues to add to the Fantasyland. Each year he creates a display that serves as a snapshot of his experiences over the past twelve months. One year's theme was vacations, with many of the vegetables highlighting a trip Charlie and his wife, June, had taken.

"Vacations was a theme I thought up in California," Charlie says. "My wife and I were celebrating our fiftieth anniversary. So I decided, through my pumpkins, to share our vacation with everybody else."

Memories of the Williams' California trip were captured in a virtual pageantry of pumpkins. An ensemble of jolly jack-o'-lanterns recreated the couple's experiences at the Rose Bowl Parade, aboard the Delta Queen, their excursion to Disneyland, and their visit to the San Diego Zoo.

Charlie Williams says that his collection of pumpkin art reaps an endless harvest of joy and happiness.

"It's not money that counts. It's the happiness we get in our lives. If I can create something that makes people smile, then that's the reward I get."

Pumpkin Bread

6	cups oil
8	cups sugar
16	eggs
8	cups pumpkin
12	cups flour
4	teaspoons salt
8	teaspoons baking soda
8	teaspoons baking powder
4	teaspoons cinnamon
2	teaspoons ginger
2	teaspoons cloves

Preheat oven to 350°F. Grease and flour 10–12 small loaf pans.

Blend well the oil, sugar, and eggs. Add the pumpkin. Sift the dry ingredients together and add to the pumpkin mixture. Mix just until well-blended. Pour into the prepared loaf pans and bake for 45 minutes.

Charlie and June Williams
Fashion Farm Restaurant, Ligonier

Persimmon Date Nut Bread

Another persimmon favorite of Hoosiers.

2 ½	cups sugar
1	cup oil
4	eggs
⅔	cup water
2	cups persimmon pulp
1	cup dates, chopped
½	cup pecans, chopped and toasted
3 ½	cups flour
1	teaspoon salt (or less)
2	teaspoons baking soda
½	teaspoon cinnamon (optional)
¼	teaspoon cloves (optional)

Preheat oven to 350°F. Grease and flour 2 loaf pans.

Combine all ingredients, mixing just until well-blended. Pour into prepared pans and bake 1 hour or until done. Remove bread from pans to cool on a rack.

Rose Worland
Indianapolis

Persimmon Nut Bread

If one lives in Indiana for any length of time, one will eat native persimmons in some form, probably in pudding. Persimmons ripen around the time of the first frost and fall to the ground when ripe. I have recently enjoyed harvesting persimmons from my own trees, one male and one female, a requirement to get any fruit.

1	cup persimmon pulp *
½	cup granulated sugar
½	cup brown sugar, packed
2	eggs, lightly beaten
2 ½	cups all-purpose flour
1	tablespoon baking powder
½	teaspoon salt
½	cup butter, melted
1	cup chopped walnuts

Preheat oven to 325°F. Grease a loaf pan.

Combine pulp, sugar, and eggs in a bowl. Into another bowl sift together flour, baking powder, and salt. Add flour mixture alternately to pulp mixture with butter and combine well. Fold in walnuts and pour into prepared pan. Bake 1 hour or until tester comes out clean.

* Persimmon pulp can be purchased. If making your own, wash the persimmons and remove the flower caps before rubbing the persimmons through a colander to remove the pits.

Marian K. Towne
Indianapolis

Strawberry Bread

3	cups flour
1	teaspoon soda
1	teaspoon salt
1	tablespoon cinnamon
2	cups sugar
4	eggs, beaten
1 ¼	cups oil
2	cups frozen strawberries, thawed and undrained
1 ¼	cups chopped nuts

Preheat oven to 350°F. Spray 2 large loaf pans with non-stick spray.

Sift dry ingredients together in a large bowl. Combine separately the eggs, oil, strawberries and nuts. Make a well in the dry ingredients and add liquid ingredients. Stir just enough to moisten. Bake 1 hour or until done.

Annie DiSalvo
Indianapolis

Excellent Banana Bread

This is the best banana bread recipe I've ever tasted. This also tastes great with pineapple cream cheese.

3	ripe or overripe bananas (4 if small)
1	cup sugar
1	egg
1 ½	cups flour
¼	cup butter, melted
1	teaspoon baking soda
1	teaspoon salt
½	cup walnuts, chopped (optional)

Preheat oven to 325°F. Butter a loaf pan. (Omit buttering pan if using pan with non-stick surface.)

Mash bananas with fork. Stir in remaining ingredients. Pour into prepared loaf pan. Bake for 1 hour or until done when tester inserted near center comes out clean.

Laura Padfield
Columbus

Cheesy Corn Muffins

Carol's State Fair winner!

1	cup all-purpose flour, sifted
¼	cup sugar
3	teaspoons baking powder
½	teaspoon salt
¾	cup cornmeal
1	cup milk
¼	cup cooking salad oil
1	egg, well beaten
3	ounces sharp process American cheese, shredded (¾ cup)
	Poppy seeds

Preheat oven to 425°F. Grease muffin tins or line with paper liners.

Sift together first 4 ingredients; stir in cornmeal. Add remaining ingredients, stirring just till cornmeal mixture is moistened. Fill muffin pans two-thirds full and sprinkle with poppy seeds. Bake for 15 minutes. Makes 12 muffins.

Carol Lumsden
Indianapolis

Poppy Seed Bread

Excellent—a family favorite for years!

3   cups flour
2 ½ cups sugar
1 ½ teaspoons salt
1 ½ teaspoons baking powder
3   eggs
1 ½ cups milk
1   cup plus 2 tablespoons vegetable oil
2   tablespoons poppy seed (or more, if desired)
1 ½ teaspoons vanilla extract
1 ½ teaspoons almond extract
1 ½ teaspoons butter flavoring
1 ½ tablespoons butter

Preheat oven to 325°F. Grease and flour 2 large loaf pans. Mix all ingredients together and pour into prepared pans. Bake for 1 hour or until golden. Top should spring back when lightly tapped.

Annie DiSalvo
Indianapolis

Aunt Daisy's Breakfast Muffins

Best served warm with soft butter and strawberry preserves!

1 ½ cups sugar
2 ½ cups flour
2 ½ teaspoons soda
2   teaspoons salt
4   cups raisin bran cereal
2   eggs, beaten
½   cup vegetable oil
2   cups buttermilk
1   cup blueberries or nuts (optional)

Sift together sugar, flour, soda, salt. Add raisin bran cereal. Beat two eggs until fluffy. Add these to cereal mixture with vegetable oil and buttermilk. Mix thoroughly. Cover and store in refrigerator overnight. Preheat oven to 350°F. Line muffin pans with paper liners. Add blueberries or nuts, if used, to batter and fill muffin pans ¾ full; bake 25 minutes. Makes 24 muffins.

Diana Davis
Indianapolis

Nashville House Fried Biscuits

2 ⅔ packages dry yeast
½ cup warm water
1 quart milk
¼ cup sugar
½ cup lard or shortening
6 teaspoons salt
8 cups flour

Add yeast to warm water. Add other ingredients, using more flour if needed to make a workable dough (no kneading is required). Cover and set in a warm place; let dough rise (but do not let dough rise too high).

In deep fryer, heat oil to just slightly over 350°F. (Note: if oil is too hot, the biscuits will overcook on the outside and be soggy in the center.) Shape dough into biscuits and drop into hot oil; fry until puffy and golden.

This recipe will make about 7 dozen biscuits. They can be frozen individually and stored in plastic bags.

Nashville House
Nashville

Scenic Brown County is the setting for the Nashville House, renowned for savory home cooking, antique collectibles and gadgets, and old-fashioned hospitality. Built on the site of the first hostelry in the county (which was destroyed by fire in 1943), visitors come from far and wide to savor the Nashville House's hickory-smoked meats, oven-fresh baked goods, candies—and of course, the ever-popular fried biscuits and jam.

Zucchini Muffins

A great way to use zucchini from the garden. Can freeze and have ready for a morning coffee or afternoon tea.

2	cups sugar
1	cup oil
3	eggs
2	teaspoons vanilla
3	cups flour
½	teaspoon baking soda
¼	teaspoon baking powder
1	teaspooon cinnamon
1	teaspoon salt
1	cup raisins
1	cup coconut
1	cup chopped nuts
2	cups unpeeled zucchini, grated and well drained
1	teaspoon cinnamon
3	tablespoons sugar
1	stick butter, melted

Preheat oven to 350°F. Grease muffin tins.

Mix sugar and oil until foamy. Beat eggs and vanilla together and add to the above mixture. Sift flour, soda, baking powder, cinnamon and salt together and add to the mixture. Stir in raisins, coconut, nuts, and zucchini. Mix well. Fill greased muffin tins three-fourths full. Bake 10–15 minutes for small muffins, 20–25 minutes for large muffins.

Combine the cinnamon and sugar. While the muffins are still hot, dip the tops in melted butter, then in the cinnamon-sugar mixture.

Carol Hillis
Culver

Perfect Corn Bread

1	cup sifted all-purpose flour
¼	cup sugar
4	teaspoons baking powder
¾	teaspoons salt
1	cup yellow corn meal
2	eggs
1	cup milk
¼	cup shortening, softened

Preheat oven to 425°F. Grease a 9-inch square pan.

Sift flour with sugar, baking powder and salt; stir in corn meal. Add eggs, milk and shortening. Beat with a rotary or electric mixer until smooth, about 1 minute. Pour into prepared pan and bake 20–25 minutes.

Sister Leta Zeller
Poseyville

Lemon Tea Bread

Always keep a couple of loaves in the freezer. They make nice hostess gifts tied with a pretty ribbon.

1 cup shortening
2 cups sugar
4 eggs, beaten
3 cups flour, sifted
2 teaspoons baking powder
1 teaspoon salt
1 cup milk
1 cup nuts, chopped
Grated peel of 2 lemons
½ cup sugar
Juice of 2 lemons

Preheat oven to 350°F. Grease and flour 2 small loaf pans.

Cream shortening and sugar together. Add beaten eggs. Sift dry ingredients together and add to the shortening and egg mixture alternately with milk. Add nuts and lemon peel. Divide batter evenly in the two pans. Bake until tester comes out clean, for about 1 hour.

In a saucepan, heat the ½ cup sugar and lemon juice over low heat until sugar dissolves. While loaves are still warm, poke holes in bread and pour the lemon-sugar mixture over each loaf. Cool and remove from pans. Freezes well.

In memory of Gail Browne
Indianapolis

The Main Event

ENTRÉES

When they think of Indiana's culinary tradition, most people probably imagine old-fashioned farm cooking. Yet the state's central location earned it the nickname Crossroads of America, and Indiana has historically been home to a diversity of cultures and backgrounds. The Hoosier culinary tradition ranges from German to African to Irish to Russian to Indonesian, and still includes good Midwest country cooking.

Pioneer Beef Stew

2	pounds beef stew meat, cut into 1-inch pieces
2	tablespoons solid white shortening
4	cups boiling water
3	large onions, sliced
1	tablespoon salt
½	teaspoon pepper
1	tablespoon paprika
¼	cup dried or fresh parsley
6	carrots, cubed
4	medium potatoes, cubed
1	medium can tomato puree
½	cup water
¼	cup flour

In a heavy Dutch oven, thoroughly brown stew meat in shortening. Add 4 cups boiling water, one sliced onion, salt, pepper, paprika, and parsley. Cover and simmer for 2 hours or until meat is tender and just about falling apart. Add carrots, potatoes, the remaining onions and tomato puree. Cover and simmer for 1 hour more, or until vegetables are done. Thicken if needed (shake in separate container ½ cup water with ¼ cup of flour). Slowly add to stew until desired thickness. Cook 5 minutes more, stirring often and carefully so not to break up vegetables. Serves 6–8.

Mary Ellen Knific
Zionsville

Stew in the Crockpot

Dinner's ready when you come home from Little League.

1	pound stew meat
5	medium potatoes
3	carrots
2	ribs celery
1	medium onion
2	15-ounce cans tomato sauce
1	teaspoon salt
⅛	teaspoon pepper

Cut stew meat into bite-sized pieces. Peel potatoes and cut into eighths. Dice onion. Clean carrots and slice. Chop celery. Put meat, potatoes, carrots, celery, onion, tomato sauce, salt and pepper into crockpot. Stir until mixed. Cook, covered, for 8 hours on low. Serves 6.

Rose M. Rosenbalm
Brownsburg

Grandma Dyer's Beef Stew

I do not know how old this recipe is, but it was first put in writing by my great-grand-mother Arnold in 1910. My grandmother, Ruth Dyer, passed it down to my wife and me when we got married. This is the recipe we use to make 40-gallon batches for our church and our Annual Open House every "weekend before Thanksgiving" at our copper shop in Knightstown. We've fed about 16,000 folks with this recipe since our Open House began in 1988 and can't recall a single complaint. (Maybe because it's free?)

36	46-ounce cans tomato-vegetable juice
60	pounds stew beef
60	pounds potatoes, cut into bite-size pieces
20	pounds celery, chopped
20	pounds carrots, chopped
4	pounds onions, chopped
4	pounds green peppers, chopped
2	handfuls seasoned salt
2	heaping tablespoons black pepper
8	boxes instant or minute regular (not pearl) tapioca

Get your 40- or 50-gallon stew pot. (My stew pot is an apple butter kettle that we tin-lined and made a lid for.) Start your fire—rather smartly the first hour; slow coals the remainder. (I lay up a wall of old bricks around the outside all the way up to the rim to create an oven-like environment.) Pour in the juice, and add the stew beef. As beef and juice boil rapidly, add remaining vegetables and seasonings.

At the fourth hour mark, gently lift the lid and stir in tapioca. (To stir the stew, we carved a small canoe paddle out of a board.)

This recipe is supposed to be slow-cooked on a low fire and isn't at its best until 10 or 12 hours, although it's done enough to swallow at 8 hours if you like crunchy vegetables. However, if the fire is too hot and you have to stir constantly, the vegetables will turn to mush.

Serves eight hundred to twelve hundred guests, depending on the dipper.

Michael Bonne
The Coppersmith
Knightstown

Salisbury Steak with Onion Gravy

1	10-ounce can French onion soup
1 ½	pounds ground beef
½	cup fine dry bread crumbs
1	egg, fork beaten
	dash salt and pepper
1	tablespoon all-purpose flour
¼	cup ketchup
¼	cup water
1	teaspoon Worcestershire sauce
½	teaspoon mustard

In bowl, combine ⅓ cup soup with ground beef, crumbs, egg, salt and pepper. Shape into oval patties. In frying pan, brown patties. Drain off fat and remove patties; keep warm. Gradually blend flour into remaining soup, mixing until smooth. Add remaining ingredients, blending well. Add to frying pan and heat to boiling, stirring to loosen brown bits. Cover and cook 5 minutes, stirring occasionally. Add patties to gravy in pan, cover and simmer 15 minutes. These freeze well. Serves 6.

Laura Padfield
Columbus

Beef Stroganoff

2	pounds beef sirloin or tenderloin
4	tablespoons butter
1	medium onion, chopped
1	teaspoon salt
1	teaspoon pepper
2	tablespoons flour
1 ¼	cups beef consommé
1	teaspoon chervil
2	tablespoons tomato paste
½	pound fresh mushrooms, halved, or one 14-ounce can button mushrooms
½	cup sour cream

Cut the beef into thin strips about 1 ½ inches long. Melt the butter in a large skillet. Add the beef and sauté over medium heat until browned. Add the onion, salt, and pepper and cook about 2 minutes more. Blend in flour, and add the consommé and chervil.

Reduce heat to low, and cover and cook until meat is tender. Add the tomato paste and mushrooms. (Note: If using fresh mushrooms, sauté in small amount of butter before adding.) Cook 10 minutes longer. Just before serving, stir in sour cream. Serve with buttered noodles.

Mary Foster
Lafayette

Quick Corned Beef and Cabbage

Great with peppered corn bread. Add 1 tablespoon red pepper flakes to your favorite cornbread recipe.

1   tablespoon canola oil
1   tablespoon butter
1–2 onions, sliced thin
1–2 garlic cloves, minced
1   can corned beef in chunks
1   medium head of cabbage, sliced
1   can cream of chicken soup
1–2 bay leaves
1   can sliced mushrooms
    Salt and pepper to taste

Heat the oil and butter over medium heat; add the onion and sauté 3–5 minutes. Add the garlic, corned beef, and cabbage and cook another 5 minutes. Add the soup, bay leaves, mushrooms, salt, and pepper. Cover and cook until cabbage is tender. Remove bay leaves and serve.

Bettylou Schultz
Muncie

Beef Chop Suey

3   pounds stir-fry beef
2   pounds pork tenderloin, cut into small chunks
6   large onions, sliced
½   cup oil
1   large can Chinese vegetables, drained
2   small cans sliced water chestnuts
2   cans bean sprouts
4   tablespoons molasses
    Soy sauce to taste
2   tablespoons cornstarch
⅓   cup cold water

Brown meat in oil. Sauté onions in oil and add to meat. Add all other ingredients except cornstarch and bring to a boil. Reduce heat to simmer and cook approximately 1 ½–2 hours until meat is tender. Thicken with cornstarch and water mixture. Serve with white or fried rice.

Susan McBeath
Indianapolis

Steak Caesar

3	tablespoons flour
½	teaspoon each salt and pepper
2	4-ounce beef tenderloin medallions
¼	cup olive oil
1	tablespoons fresh garlic, minced
3	tablespoons burgundy wine
¾	cup beef stock
1	teaspoon chopped fresh chives

Combine flour and salt and pepper. Lightly dredge beef in the seasoned flour. Reserve the flour.

Heat olive oil in a cast iron skillet over medium heat. Add beef and sauté until brown.

Reduce heat to medium-low and add reserved seasoned flour. Stir mixture constantly until it turns a deep mahogany brown. Add the garlic and wine and cook 2 minutes more. Stirring constantly (whisking works best), slowly add the stock until the mixture is blended and shiny. Continue cooking over low heat until the liquid is reduced by a third. Top with fresh chopped chives. Serves 2.

Red Geranium
New Harmony

The Red Geranium Restaurant opened in the summer of 1960 as a tea room on the patio of the Barrett Gate House. Its popularity led it to move to larger quarters in 1993, and now includes the Grapevine Bar, the Garden Room, and the Tillich Room, allowing it to accommodate a wide range of tastes. Located in historic New Harmony, The Red Geranium's menu includes regional as well as Continental favorites, and is famous for its home-made baked specialties.

Sauerbraten

3	pounds round or shoulder roast
½	cup vinegar
½	cup water
1	onion, thinly sliced
2	bay leaves
3	whole cloves
1	teaspoon salt
	Dash of pepper
4	tablespoons vegetable oil
	Flour

Place beef in a bowl. Combine all remaining ingredients except oil and blend. Pour over meat and marinate 24 hours.

Heat oil in a large, heavy pot or Dutch oven. Remove meat from the marinade and brown thoroughly. Add 1 cup of water to marinade and pour over meat. Bring to a boil; reduce heat to low, cover, and simmer 3 hours or until meat is tender. Remove meat. Make gravy from juices in pan by mixing with oil and flour. Serves 6.

Heather Yarbrough
Jasper

Authentic German Sauerbraten

5	pounds top or bottom round beef roast
½	cup chopped onion
1	cup chopped carrots
1	cup chopped celery
1	cup red wine vinegar
1	cup red wine
⅔	cup water
½	cup red current jelly
1	cup crushed ginger snaps
½	cup brown sugar
½	cup sugar
2	bay leaves
⅔	tablespoon peppercorns
1 ½	tablespoons pickling spice
⅔	tablespoon ginger
½	tablespoon cinnamon
1	teaspoon nutmeg

Combine all ingredients except beef in saucepan; cook over high heat to boiling. Reduce heat and simmer for 1 hour. Let cool and pour over beef. Marinade for 5 days.

Preheat oven to 300°F. Place meat with marinade in roasting pan and roast for 4–5 hours or until very tender. Strain marinade from meat and reserve. Cut or pull meat into serving size portions.

Melt 2 tablespoons butter in skillet over medium heat; add ¼ cup flour and cook until smooth and golden brown. Strain spices from marinade and heat until boiling. Add flour and butter mixture to marinade and cook until thickened. Ladle over warm meat.

Dan McMichael
Indianapolis

Chinese Beef Casserole

½   cup uncooked minute rice
1   cup boiling water
½   teaspoon salt
1   pound ground round
1 ½   cups chopped onion
1 ½   cups chopped celery
1 ½   cups chopped green pepper
1   can cream of mushroom
     soup
3   tablespoons soy sauce

Preheat oven to 350°F. Mix together rice, water, and salt. Set aside. Brown meat. Add onion, celery, green pepper, soup and soy sauce. Combine with meat mixture and rice mixture. Blend gently. Turn into 9 x 13-inch casserole dish. Cover with foil and bake for 30 minutes. Remove foil and bake another 10 minutes.

Gail McBeath
Indianapolis

Layered Enchiladas

½   cup butter, melted
2   tablespoons flour
1 ½   cups milk
2   cups sour cream
2   pounds ground sirloin
1   onion, chopped
½   green pepper, chopped
¼   teaspoon coriander
½   teaspoon chopped garlic
1   10-ounce can chili without
     beans
½   teaspoon hot pepper sauce
¼   cup picante sauce
1   teaspoon Worcestershire
     sauce
1   tablespoon chili powder
½   cup ripe olives, chopped
12–15   corn tortillas, quartered
2   cups shredded cheddar or
     Mexican cheese

Preheat oven to 375°F.

In a small saucepan combine butter and flour and mix well. Slowly add milk and cook until thickened and smooth. Cool, then add sour cream.

Sauté ground sirloin, onion and green pepper. Drain, then add remaining ingredients except tortillas and cheese.

Spread a little of the sour cream mixture in the bottom of an oiled 9 x13-inch baking dish. Place half of the tortilla quarters over sauce and follow with half of meat mixture, half of white sauce, and half of cheese. Repeat layers and bake for 20 minutes. Serves 6–8.

Linda Lugar
Carmel

Mo-Meatballs

The children and grandchildren always ask for "mo-meatballs." Delicious!

1 ½ pounds ground beef
16 saltine crackers, crushed
1 cup milk
1 egg, beaten
½ teaspoon each salt and pepper
1 teaspoon oregano
⅛ teaspoon garlic powder
1 small onion, chopped
3 tablespoon margarine
¼ cup vinegar
⅓ cup sugar
¾ cup water
½ cup ketchup
1 tablespoon mustard
1 tablespoon Worcestershire sauce

Preheat oven to 400°F. Mix first 4 ingredients. Add salt and pepper, oregano, and garlic powder. Shape into meatballs. Place on cookie sheet and bake 20 minutes.

Sauté onions in margarine. Add remaining ingredients. Boil 15 minutes. Place meatballs in casserole dish. Pour hot sauce mixture over. Cover and bake for 30 minutes.

Freeda Murphy
Indianapolis

Twin Meat Loaves

This was often our "Sunday dinner" and my mother still brings it to every family reunion.

1 sleeve soda crackers (or approximately 1 cup bread crumbs)
1 cup milk
1 medium onion
2 eggs
1 teaspoon each of salt, pepper, and sage
4 ½ pounds ground beef
½ pound ground pork
½ cup ketchup
3–4 bacon slices

Preheat oven to 350°F. Place all ingredients except the meats in a blender or food processor and pulse till onion is minced and crackers are crumbs. Add to ground meats. Mix well, form into two loaves or place into two loaf pans. Cover with ketchup and bacon slices and bake for 90 minutes. Makes 2 loaves. Each loaf serves 6–8. Freezes well.

Rita Bulington
Lafayette

Ground Beef Casserole

This was a recipe from Mother's aunt, who was raised by my grandmother and was much like a sister to my mother.

1   8-ounce package wide
    noodles, cooked and
    drained
1   pound ground beef,
    browned and drained
1   8-ounce can tomato sauce
1   cup cottage cheese
8   ounces cream cheese
⅓   cup chopped green onions
1   tablespoon chopped green
    pepper
2   tablespoons melted butter

Preheat oven to 350°F. Grease a 2-quart casserole dish. Cook noodles and drain. Brown meat and drain. Add tomato sauce to meat and stir. Remove from heat. Combine cottage cheese, cream cheese, green onions and green pepper. Spread half the noodles in the bottom of the casserole dish. Cover with the cheese mixture, then remaining noodles. Pour melted butter over noodles. Add ground beef mixture on top. Bake 30 minutes. Can be made ahead.

Gay Burkhart
Zionsville

Don Schlundt's Chili

This was a favorite of my dad's at IU tailgate parties on crisp autumn days.

2   pounds lean ground beef
1   green pepper, finely
    chopped
1   small onion, finely chopped
1   cup celery, finely chopped
1   large can tomatoes
1   can tomato soup
3   tablespoons chili powder
2   tablespoons sugar
1   can Hormel hot chili beans
    Salt and pepper to taste

Brown ground beef. Sauté green pepper, onion, and celery. Add to ground beef. Add tomatoes with juice, tomato soup, chili powder and sugar. Simmer ½ hour. Add chili beans, salt and pepper and simmer another ½ hour. To serve, top with shredded cheese, chopped onions and a dollop of sour cream. Serves 6.

Lysa Spicer
Carmel

Hoosier Meatloaf

I call these little meatloaves "Hoosier" because I know a lot of Hoosiers who like them!

1	pound very lean ground beef
2	slices bread, torn into small pieces
⅔	cup milk
1	egg
¼	cup finely chopped onion
¾	teaspoon salt
¼	teaspoon each of dry mustard, sage, celery salt, garlic salt, coriander, sweet basil (all are optional—add what you like!)
4	slices onion
4	tablespoons ketchup
4	tablespoons brown sugar
4	slices lemon or 4 teaspoons lemon juice

Preheat oven to 325°F. Mix first 6 ingredients in large bowl, adding seasonings as desired. Divide into four loaves. Place meatloaves in 8-inch square or round baking dish and flatten slightly.

On each meatloaf, place a slice of onion, 1 tablespoon ketchup, 1 tablespoon brown sugar, and one slice of lemon or 1 teaspoon lemon juice. Bake 1 hour. Serves 4.

Terry McVicker
Hartford City

Mom's Best Meatloaf

Best baked with a light layer of ketchup on top. Some like a few slices of bacon on top, too. This was one of our family favorites, and many friends asked Mom for her recipe.

1 ½	pounds ground beef
1	egg, beaten
1	medium-size onion, chopped
1	10 ¾-ounce can tomato soup
1 ½	cups of finely crushed Ritz crackers
½	teaspoon salt
¼	teaspoon black pepper

Preheat oven to 350°F. Place all the ingredients in a bowl and mix thoroughly. Shape into a loaf and place in a 1 ½-quart oven-proof casserole dish. Bake for one hour. Serves 4–6.

Jennifer Lee Meyer Maxfield
Indianapolis

Italian Meat Roll

2	pounds lean ground beef
2	eggs
1	cup bread crumbs
½	teaspoon garlic salt
1	teaspoon parsley flakes
¼	teaspoon salt
¼	teaspoon pepper
1	large jar pasta sauce
1	large package shredded mozzarella cheese

Preheat oven to 400°F. Mix ground beef, eggs, bread crumbs and spices in a mixing bowl to form a meatloaf consistency. On waxed paper, press the meatloaf mixture into a large rectangle about ½ inch thick. Spread half of pasta sauce over meatloaf and cover with shredded cheese. Roll the mixture at the short side of the rectangle and seal the ends as you go along to hold in the cheese.

Place meat roll in a baking dish, seam side down, and bake 40 minutes. Remove from oven and pour remaining pasta sauce over meat roll. Return to oven for 15 minutes. Slice and serve with pasta. Serves 8.

Kelcy Santuro
Indianapolis

Texas Red Chili

2	ounces beef suet or vegetable oil
3	pounds lean beef, coarsely cubed (¾-inch)
2	tablespoons chili powder
1	tablespoon cumin seed/ powder
1	tablespoon oregano
1	tablespoon salt
½	tablespoon cayenne pepper
2	cloves garlic, minced
1	quart beef stock or broth
¼	cup corn meal
¼	cup of water

Fry suet in pot until crisp. Then add beef, about 1 pound at a time, and brown, stirring as it cooks. Remove each pound after browning. When all meat is browned, return it to pot and add seasoning and beef stock or broth. Cover and simmer 1 ½ to 2 hours. Skim off fat. Combine cornmeal with cold water and stir thoroughly into chili. Simmer 30 minutes. Makes about 2 quarts.

Dick Ouweneel
Indianapolis

Chop Suey Philippine

This is excellent served over white rice.

1 bunch broccoli
½ head cauliflower
1 pound pork or boneless
skinless chicken breast
2 teaspoons olive oil
1 clove of garlic, sliced
1 medium white onion, sliced
and cut in half
1 pound raw shrimp, peeled
1 14.5-ounce can chicken
broth
4 teaspoons soy sauce
½ pound snow peas
2 medium zucchini, cut
diagonally
2 medium carrots, sliced
thinly
1 stalk celery, cut in diagonal
1-inch slices
1 each green red pepper, cut
into 1-inch squares

1 pound fresh mushrooms,
sliced
1 tablespoon cornstarch
1 tablespoon water

Cut florets from broccoli and cauliflower.
Discard stems or reserve for another use.

Cut pork or chicken into strips. Heat olive oil
in wok and sauté garlic until light brown. Add
onions, pork or chicken, and shrimp. Sauté
for 5 minutes and add half of the chicken
broth, cover and simmer until the pork is
tender. Add the remaining broth and soy
sauce and bring to a boil. Add vegetables and
mix well.

Mix cornstarch with 1 tablespoon of water
and add to pan. Cook just until vegetables are
crisp-tender and liquid thickens slightly.

Levie Barrientos
Indianapolis

Chicken Pecan Fettuccine

6	boneless skinless chicken breast halves, cut up
¼	cup butter or margarine
2	cups sliced mushrooms
½	cup chopped onion
2	garlic cloves, minced
¼	cup water
2	tablespoons all-purpose flour
2	cups half-and-half
2	tablespoons instant chicken bouillon granules
¼	cup grated Parmesan cheese
⅓	cup chopped pecans, toasted
8	ounces fettuccine, cooked toasted pecans, optional

Melt butter in medium skillet. Add chicken pieces; cook to brown lightly. Remove from pan; set aside. Add mushrooms, onion and garlic. Cook until tender. Add water and chicken, cover and cook 10 minutes. Remove chicken pieces; set aside. Blend flour with 2 tablespoons of half-and-half. Stir to blend. Add flour mixture, remaining cream and bouillon to vegetable mixture. Cook until thick. Stir in cheese and pecans; add chicken and heat thoroughly. Cook fettuccine according to package directions until tender but firm. Drain thoroughly. Spread on large serving platter. Top with chicken and sauce. Sprinkle with toasted pecans. Serve immediately. Serves 6.

Friend of WFYI
Indianapolis

Chicken Breast Surprise

You'd never guess that sauerkraut is in the recipe!

4	boneless skinless chicken breast halves
1	can shredded sauerkraut, drained well
1	8-ounce package sliced Swiss cheese
1	small bottle Thousand Island dressing

Preheat oven to 350°F. Layer the sauerkraut, chicken and cheese. Pour dressing over top. Bake for 45 minutes to 1 hour. It should be kind of brown on top. Serve with mashed potatoes, a green vegetable, and cranberry salad. Can be baked day before and reheated in microwave. Serves 4.

Bobbie Darnell
Indianapolis

Chicken Pot Pie

This was a great favorite for the First Presbyterian Church suppers.

1   large chicken (or 2 small)
4   tablespoons melted butter
2   cups plus 3 tablespoons
      flour
1 ½   teaspoons salt
¼   teaspoon pepper
4   cups warm chicken stock
1   cup cream
2   teaspoons baking powder
1   egg, well beaten
1 ⅓   cups milk

Cut up chicken and place in a large pot with enough water to cover. Bring to a boil; reduce heat and cook, covered, about 1 ½ hours or until the meat slips from the bones. Remove chicken from the pot; discard skin and bones and cut meat into bite-size pieces.

Put chicken in a 9 x 13-inch baking dish. Mix 3 tablespoons melted butter, 3 tablespoons flour, ½ teaspoon salt, and pepper together. Add chicken stock and cream. Pour mixture over the chicken; set aside in a warm place.

Preheat oven to 400°F. Combine remaining flour, salt, and butter with baking powder and egg; stir in milk. Pour over the chicken mixture and bake 45 minutes or until light brown. Serves 6–8.

In memory of Frances Petro Schnaiter
Martinsville

Glazed Apricot Chicken

We like to serve this with a bowl of brown and wild rice and, on the side, a dish of mushrooms sautéed in butter.

½   cup mayonnaise
½   cup apricot preserves
1   1 ¼-ounce package onion
      soup mix
4   boneless skinless chicken
      breast halves

Preheat oven to 350°F. Mix mayonnaise, preserves, and soup mix. Place chicken in 9 x 13-inch pan or baking dish. Spread mixture over chicken. Bake 30 minutes or until cooked through. Makes 4 servings.

Retha Kaye Naylor
Frankton

Hoosier Hen Loaf

This recipe was served in the 1930s and 1940s by the Ladies of Little Eagle Creek Christian Church. It was very popular with the various organizations which they served, such as Lions Clubs. Also, this dish was very economical for them as all the ladies lived on farms and had their own poultry. The proceeds from this project were donated by the ladies to help build the present church building.

6–7 pound stewing chicken
½ pound soda crackers
6 boiled eggs, chopped
4 raw eggs, beaten
1 quart chicken broth
Salt and pepper to taste

Preheat oven to 350°F. Grease a 9 x 13-inch pan. Cook the chicken until tender and remove meat from bones. Cut meat crosswise of the grain with kitchen shears into ½-inch cubes. Do not use skin. Roll the crackers and add to chicken. Add the chopped boiled eggs. Beat the raw eggs with rotary egg beater and add to chicken mixture. Add the quart of broth and season with salt and pepper to taste. Turn into pan and bake for 45 minutes to 1 hour. Cut into squares and serve warm. Garnish with sprig of parsley if desired. Serves 12–15.

Wanda H. Essex
Westfield

Chicken Florentine

I like to serve this with wild rice.

3 packages frozen chopped spinach, thawed and squeezed
8 boneless skinless chicken breast halves
1 cup mayonnaise
2 cans cream of chicken soup
1 tablespoon lemon juice
1 teaspoon curry powder
1 cup grated cheddar cheese

Preheat oven to 350°F. Spread well-drained spinach in 9 x 13-inch pan. Put chicken on top. Mix remaining ingredients, except cheese, and spread on top of chicken. Add cheese last. Bake for 1 ½ hours.

Carol "Kayo" Walker
Indianapolis

Chicken-Crescent Roll-Ups

This can be served at breakfast as well as lunch time.

2   8-count tubes of crescent rolls
1   8-ounce cream cheese, softened
¼   cup margarine, softened
¼   cup milk
2   cups cooked and chopped chicken
2   tablespoons finely chopped onion
2   ribs celery, chopped
1   10-ounce can cream of chicken soup
½   cup milk

Preheat oven to 350°F. Separate crescent roll dough into 8 rectangles. Beat cream cheese, margarine and ¼ cup milk in mixing bowl until light and fluffy. Stir in chicken, onion and celery. Spread mixture evenly on each rectangle. Roll to enclose filling. Place in non-stick 9 x 13-inch baking dish. Bake for 18 to 20 minutes or until lightly browned. Mix soup and ½ cup milk; heat. Spoon over roll-ups and serve immediately. Serves 6–8.

Susie Warner
Goshen

Chicken Rice Casserole

3   cups cooked chicken, chopped
1   can cream of chicken soup
1   8-ounce can water chestnuts, sliced
1   cup chopped celery
1   cup cooked peas
3   boiled eggs, chopped
2   cups cooked rice
2   teaspoons lemon juice
1   teaspoon salt
1   cup mayonnaise

1   tablespoon onion, chopped
    sliced almonds
2   tablespoons margarine
2   cups crispy rice cereal

Preheat oven to 350°F. Grease 9 x 13-inch casserole dish. Combine all ingredients except the almonds, margarine, and rice cereal, and mix well. Pour into a casserole dish. Put sliced almonds on top. Melt margarine and mix with the rice cereal. Pour over the top. Bake for 40 minutes.

Grace E. Farlow
Frankfort

The Swiss Connection

Picture the rolling Alpine landscape, dotted here and there with small farms. The occasional quaint little village appears, with its narrow streets, picturesque shops, and McDonald's.

McDonald's? Okay, this isn't Switzerland. We're in Indiana, in a small town that takes great pride in its heritage. We're in Berne, where the heritage is Swiss.

In the early years of the nineteenth century, Berne was known as a Swiss settlement. Since then, people from diverse backgrounds have settled in and around Berne, but the core of the community is still Swiss. In fact, a Swiss-German dialect is still spoken by a number of the older citizens.

The majority of the early Swiss settlers were Mennonite farmers and tradesmen who built farms and started businesses using the skills they had brought with them. (Even today, Berne is known as a furniture-manufacturing center.) Sadly, much of the legacy of those pioneers has been lost over the years. That is why the Swiss Heritage Village was created.

"The village has about twenty-one acres, including about six acres of woods," says Merle Inniger of the Swiss Heritage Village. "We've brought in twelve buildings which are authentic: they were constructed in the nineteenth century, and each one tells a story about the early settlers who came to Berne."

There is a cheese house where visitors can learn how cheese was made in the 1860s, and a schoolhouse, built in 1881 and used as a school until 1940. There is the Lugenbill house, built in

1848 and featuring a half-timber construction that is distinctly Swiss. The house is home to many artifacts donated by people in the area.

"We look on ourselves as an educational society," Inniger says of the Heritage Village.

Not all the Swiss settlers arrived in Berne in the 1800s. Immigration continued well into the twentieth century. Walter Zuercher's father and grandfather were accordion makers, and they came to America in 1922.

"There were dirt streets when we came," Zuercher remembers, "and some places had no sidewalks."

There have been many changes in the more than seventy years that have passed since the Zuerchers arrived in Berne, but Walter and his friends still have fun speaking Swiss.

In fact, Berne remains firmly linked to Switzerland. A few years ago, someone got the idea to decorate his place of business in the Swiss manner. The idea spread, even to the local post office. Swiss pride is everywhere, but there is no arrogance or sense of superiority. Like the original Swiss settlers, the people of Berne remain peaceful, polite, and courteous.

Chicken Scallopini Swiss Style

This is excellent served with Sour Cream Mashed Potatoes (page 146).

4	boneless skinless chicken breasts
¼	cup vegetable oil
¼	cup flour
	Salt and pepper to taste
8	slices of tomato
12	slices of Swiss cheese
1	small tomato, cut in thin strips
2	tablespoons minced fresh parsley
4	sprigs fresh rosemary

Cut each chicken breast in half. Slice each half diagonally twice so that you have 3 pieces per half. Heat oil in skillet. Dust each piece of chicken breast with flour, salt and pepper and sauté in the oil until well done. Broil tomato slices. Fan the sautéed chicken breasts on the serving dish or individual plate. Cover with broiled tomato slices. Place a slice of Swiss cheese over this and broil until cheese begins to melt. Garnish top with thin strips of fresh tomato, chopped parsley, and a sprig of rosemary. Serves 4.

Rolf Meisterhans, owner and executive chef
Chef Rolf's Cafe, Carmel

Chicken Artichoke Casserole

A delightful bridge luncheon entree.

1	can cream of chicken soup
¾	cup mayonnaise
2	tablespoons lemon juice
3	tablespoons sherry
½	teaspoon salt
½	teaspoon pepper
1	14-ounce can artichokes
3	cups cooked chicken, diced
¼	cup celery, diced
½	cup onion, diced
1	can water chestnuts, sliced
4	hard-boiled eggs, sliced
2	cups potato chip crumbs

Preheat oven to 350°F. Blend soup, mayonnaise, lemon juice, sherry, salt and pepper. Drain liquid from artichokes and rinse in cold water. Drain on paper towels and cut in half. Combine chicken, celery, onion, water chestnuts and artichokes. Blend together gently. Fold chicken mixture into soup and mayonnaise mixture. Pour half of this into a 2-quart oblong utility dish and place sliced eggs over mixture. Add remaining mixture and sprinkle potato chip crumbs over top. Bake for 30 minutes. Serves 8.

Vivian Gobens
Martinsville

Chicken Lasagna

1   stick butter
2   garlic cloves, crushed
½   cup flour
1   teaspoon salt
2   cups chicken broth
2   cups milk
2   cups shredded mozzarella cheese
1   cup grated Parmesan cheese
½   cup onion, chopped
1   teaspoon dried basil
1   teaspoon dried oregano
¼   teaspoon pepper
8   ounces lasagna noodles, uncooked
2   cups cottage cheese
2   cups cooked chicken, diced
1   10-ounce package frozen spinach, cooked and drained

Melt butter in 2-quart saucepan. Add garlic. Stir in flour and salt. Cook, stirring constantly, until bubbly. Remove from heat. Stir in broth and milk. Return to the heat and bring to a boil. Reduce heat to simmer and cook 1 minute, stirring constantly. Stir in mozzarella and ½ cup of Parmesan cheese, onion, and seasonings. Cook over low heat until mozzarella is melted.

Preheat oven to 350°F. Spread 1 ½ cups of sauce in an ungreased 9 x 13-inch baking dish. Top with 3 or 4 noodles, making sure they overlap. Spread ½ cup cottage cheese over noodles, then another 1 ½ cups of cheese sauce over that. Place 3 or 4 noodles on top of the second layer of sauce, followed with remaining cottage cheese. Top with chicken, spinach, 1 ½ cups of cheese sauce, 3 or 4 noodles, and the rest of the sauce. Sprinkle the remaining ½ cup Parmesan over all. Bake uncovered 35–40 minutes. Test center to make sure it is set up. Cook longer if needed. Let stand 15 minutes before cutting.

Marge Salisbury
Muncie

Easy Chicken Enchiladas with Sour Cream and Wine

Serve with citrus or fruit salad and Mexican rice or refried beans. You can usually serve one per person; they are really filling.

FOR EACH PERSON HAVE
1	medium flour tortilla
½	boneless chicken breast, uncooked
	Sprinkle of oregano
	Small sprinkle of sage
	Dash pepper
½	slice jack cheese
½	slice cheddar cheese
½	canned whole green chili, cut in half, or 1 teaspoon minced green chilies

TOPPING
1	can cream of chicken soup
8	ounces light sour cream
4	ounces white wine
	Shredded jack and cheddar cheese
	Sliced green chilies
	Fresh cilantro

Preheat oven to 350°F. Place a chicken breast in middle of tortilla. Sprinkle with seasonings, cover with a half slice of each cheese and a green chili half. Roll tortillas. Place seam down in one layer in rectangular casserole dish. (They seem to "grow" while cooking, so leave some room between, even if it means using more than one pan.) They can be refrigerated at this stage.

Mix soup, light sour cream, and white wine. Spoon mixture over each tortilla. Bake 45 minutes. Sprinkle with shredded cheese and bake 15 minutes longer. Top with sliced chilies on each enchilada. Garnish with cilantro and serve.

Char Lugar
Indianapolis

Grilled Chicken and Linguine
with Italian Sun-Dried Tomatoes

5	boneless skinless chicken breast halves
¼	cup low-sodium soy sauce
4	ounces pineapple juice
½	8.5-ounce jar sun dried-tomatoes with olive oil and herbs
1	can pasta ready sauce
½	fresh tomato, chopped
½	fresh yellow tomato, chopped
½	pound linguine Freshly grated Parmesan cheese

Pound chicken until flattened. Marinate chicken in a mixture of the pineapple juice and soy sauce for 2–3 hours in the refrigerator. Remove from marinade and grill chicken breasts for 4–6 minutes or until no longer pink in center. Remove from grill and slice chicken into ½-inch strips. Cut up sun-dried tomatoes and mix with chicken, pasta ready sauce and chopped tomatoes. Pour small amount of juice from the sun-dried tomatoes over this and heat in a large frying pan on stove or in microwave on medium high for 10 minutes. Cook linguine *al dente* and drain well. Serve chicken mixture over linguine and sprinkle with Parmesan cheese. Serves 4–5.

Mary Ellen Knific
Zionsville

Chicken Green Bean Casserole

Good for luncheons.

1	can mushroom soup
½	cup milk
1	teaspoon salt
1	can chop suey vegetables
1	small can water chestnuts
1	small can mushrooms, sliced
3	cups cooked chicken, cut up
2	packages frozen green beans

⅓	cup cheddar cheese, grated
1	cup french fried onions

Preheat oven to 350°F. Blend soup, milk and salt. Drain chop suey vegetables, water chestnuts, and mushrooms. Fold in all ingredients except onions. Place in 12 x 7 x 2-inch baking dish. Bake for 45 minutes. Top with onions and bake 10 more minutes. Serves 4–6.

Betty Ford
Cicero

Oriental Chicken Casserole

A good casserole that has been served at many luncheons, many family reunions, and my daughter's shower. Everyone always asks for the recipe.

1   4-ounce can sliced mushrooms
¼   cup butter
¼   cup chopped onion
¼   cup flour
1   teaspoon salt
    dash pepper
½   teaspoon curry powder, if desired
1   tall can (1 ⅔ cups) evaporated milk
2   cups cooked cut-up chicken
1   pound fresh or 1 10-ounce package frozen cut asparagus, cooked*
1   3-ounce can chow mein noodles
1   cup shredded cheese

Preheat oven to 350°F. Drain mushrooms, reserving liquid. Melt butter, add mushrooms and onion. Cook over medium heat until onion is transparent. Remove from heat; blend in flour, salt, pepper, and curry powder. Add water to mushroom liquid to measure ½ cup. Slowly add to mushroom mixture and heat, stirring constantly. Blend in evaporated milk. Cook and stir over medium heat until thickened. Add chicken, cooked asparagus, and noodles, tossing lightly to mix. Put into buttered 1 ½-quart casserole dish. Top with shredded cheese. Bake for 20 to 30 minutes until heated through and cheese is melted. Serves 5–6.

* You can substitute a 14-ounce can French cut green beans, if desired.

Martha Larson
Indianapolis

Chicken Divan for a Crowd

This was one of Mother's absolute favorite dishes for entertaining. She used it often, always to rave reviews.

40	boneless skinless chicken breast halves
4	bunches broccoli, cooked or steamed until just shy of tender crisp, separated into small stalks
12	tablespoons minced onion
5	sticks butter
2 ½	cups flour
14	cups broth
3 ½	cups cream
8	tablespoons mustard
5	12-ounce cans Parmesan cheese

Preheat oven to 350°F.

In batches, lightly sauté the chicken breasts over medium-high heat until just about half-done, about 4 minutes per side. (Be careful to not fully cook the chicken, as overcooking will cause it to be tough.)

Spray 2-inch deep individual casserole dishes with oil. Lay one or two stalks of broccoli, florets at opposite ends if using more than one, in casserole and place half a chicken breast on top.

Melt butter in large pan and sauté onions until just transparent. Remove from heat and add the flour, stirring quickly and thoroughly with a whisk. Put back on heat and cook over low heat for 2-3 minutes, to remove taste of raw flour. Again remove from heat and whisk in the chicken broth. Return to heat and cook until it starts to thicken and slowly add the cream and mustard. Pour sauce over broccoli and chicken in casserole and sprinkle heavily with Parmesan cheese. Bake for 30 minutes, more if this has been prepared ahead and refrigerated.

Gay Burkhart
Zionsville

Chicken Perigord Style

¼ cup margarine
8 boneless skinless chicken breast halves
¼ pound mushrooms, sliced
2 ½ tablespoons flour
⅛ teaspoon salt
1 cup chicken broth
1 tablespoon milk

Cut each breast into 3 large pieces. Brown chicken on all sides, a few pieces at a time, in 3 tablespoons margarine in a large skillet or Dutch oven over medium heat. Remove chicken and drain. Add remaining margarine to skillet and brown mushrooms until golden, about 5 minutes. Remove mushrooms, drain well. Add flour and salt to the skillet drippings over medium heat until blended. Gradually stir in chicken broth and milk until mixture is thickened. Place chicken and mushrooms in sauce. Reduce heat to low. Cover and simmer 25 minutes. Serve over potatoes or rice. Serves 4.

Susie Marvel
Rochester

Chicken Tetrazzini

1 8-ounce package spaghetti
1 package gravy for chicken
¼ cup milk
¼ cup cooking sherry
2 cups cooked chicken, cubed
1 can cream of chicken soup
Salt and pepper to taste
1 cup cheddar cheese, shredded
1 cup frozen peas
Parmesan cheese

Preheat oven to 350°F. Cook spaghetti according to package. In a greased 8-inch square pan put spaghetti on bottom. Mix all other ingredients and pour over spaghetti. Sprinkle top with Parmesan cheese. Bake 45 minutes and let stand 15 minutes before serving.

Teresa Lugar
Carmel

Moroccan-Style Chicken

2   teaspoons olive oil
½   teaspoon salt
1   medium onion, thinly sliced
1   teaspoon spice mixture
     (recipe follows)
1 ½ teaspoons brown sugar
½   teaspoon pepper
1   cup low-sodium chicken
     broth
2   carrots, cut into 1-inch
     pieces
1   large potato, cut into 1-inch
     chunks
1   whole chicken breast,
     skinned and boned, cut into
     1-inch pieces
¼   cup raisins
1   15-ounce can garbanzo
     beans, drained and rinsed
2   cups couscous or rice

Preheat oven to 350°F. In a large nonstick skillet heat the oil; add onion and salt, cover and cook 8 minutes on low heat. Add spice mixture, brown sugar, and pepper. Cover and cook another 15 minutes. Add chicken broth, carrots, and potatoes. Bring to a boil; reduce heat and cook until vegetables are just tender, about 15 minutes. Add chicken breast pieces, raisins, and garbanzo beans. Place in an 8 x 8-inch baking dish coated with cooking spray. Cover and bake for 30 minutes, stirring halfway through cooking time. Serve over couscous or rice. Makes 2 generous servings. Leftovers can be frozen. Variations: Use ½–¾ pound of lamb chunks in place of chicken. Replace garbanzo beans with green beans, adding the green beans with the carrot and potato.

SPICE MIXTURE
5   teaspoons cumin seeds
5   teaspoons coriander seeds
2 ½ teaspoons whole allspice
5   teaspoons ground nutmeg
2 ½ teaspoons ginger
1 ¼ teaspoons cayenne
1 ¼ teaspoons cinnamon

Place all spices in grinder and blend to a fine powder. Store in an airtight container.

Becky Schneider
Indianapolis

Baste and Turn

Baste and turn, baste and turn.

There was perhaps nothing my grandfather loved more than standing over a hot grill on a sultry summer day, basting chickens and telling stories to "his boys." My grandfather was a coach—football, basketball, baseball, track, you name it. Whatever sport the local high school sponsored, he coached. "His boys" were members of his teams, all gathered to share good food with good friends. Later, "his boys" consisted of my father and his buddies, and later still, my friends and me. The "Coach" ladled out his own brand of down-home wisdom as liberally as he basted those chickens. "Life is like a basketball game," he would start with a smile. "You'll always be a winner, as long as you never take your eye off the ball." We all knew what he meant.

As we gulped our backyard gourmet barbecued chicken, buttered corn on the cob, and homemade ice cream, he kept us enthralled with mythical stories of great teams and famous players who once studied under the Old Master. He never had much money growing up. His father died when he was young. To survive, his mother ran a boarding house for boys in a tiny town in southern Illinois. The barbecue sauce she used was her own concoction, based on the few ingredients she had in the kitchen.

The "recipe" (if you can call it that) consisted of two sticks of margarine, two cups of vinegar, one cup of water and three tablespoons of salt (health-conscious types may want to cut down on the liberal amount of salt . . . my grandfather was never much for those health-conscious types, anyway). This sauce can baste four whole (quartered) chickens, with plenty of sauce left over for dippin'. (You should always save the leftover sauce for dippin' at the table—it's a rule.)

The Coach would heat the sauce over the stove for a few minutes, then soak each "bird" (as he called it) thoroughly before placing it on the grill. (Folks with microwaves may want to heat the chickens for 6–8 minutes on HIGH before putting them on the grill . . . though my grandfather was never much for microwaves, either.) Cook for 35–40 minutes while constantly basting and turning (Coach's rule: Always turn with tongs. Do not pierce the chicken with a fork and "let all those good juices get away.")

Summers come and summers go. My grandfather's last was in 1996. Several weeks before he passed away, he sat in a lawn chair telling stories and watching as my father and I went about the hot but pleasurable task of basting and turning, basting and turning. His last days were spent just the way he always liked it, with good food and good friends.

Nowadays I stand over my own grill, basting and turning, as my young son plays in the backyard with the dog. Someday I'll pass this simple little recipe on to him, along with a liberal dose of stories about his great-grandfather. One day he, too, will learn to baste and turn, and, hopefully, learn never to take his eye off the ball.

Todd Gould
Senior Producer
WFYI

Roast Leg of Lamb

This recipe is really quite easy, but makes an elegant presentation. Serve with roasted potatoes and fresh asparagus for a spring treat.

1	6–6 ½-pound leg of lamb
½	teaspoon ground rosemary
1	clove garlic, mashed
1	tablespoon soy sauce
½	cup Dijon mustard
4	tablespoons olive oil
½	cup sliced carrots
½	cup sliced onions
2	garlic cloves
2	cups brown lamb stock or beef bouillon

Preheat oven to 350°F. Meat should be at room temperature. Lay lamb on rack in roasting pan with its least presentable side up. Mix rosemary, garlic, soy sauce, and mustard in a small bowl with a wire whisk. Beat in the oil by droplets to make a thick mayonnaise-like sauce. Paint the lamb with mustard sauce, coating on all sides. Reserve 2–3 tablespoons of sauce to flavor the drippings after roasting.

Insert a meat thermometer in the thickest part of the meat. Place carrots, onions and garlic cloves over the meat. Roast for 1 hour 30 minutes or until meat thermometer reads 140°F for medium rare—pink and juicy. No basting or turning is needed. Remove to warm platter and let stand for 20 minutes before carving.

Remove fat by spooning it out of the pan. Pour in stock or bouillon and boil rapidly for several minutes, scraping up juices and mashing vegetables into liquid with wooden spoon. Remove from heat, stir in reserved mustard sauce and strain into warm bowl.

Judie Carpenter
Indianapolis

Roast Loin of Veal with Fresh Herbs

This roast loin of veal fits into today's demand for lighter and yet delicious party menus. It's easy, and the emerald green spiral of herbs add flavor and eye-appeal without a lot of calories or cholesterol. A boneless, lean pork loin can be substituted by having your butcher spiral cut the loin to make a plank which is re-rolled after being filled with the herb mixture; increase cooking time 15 minutes per pound.

4	shallots, peeled and chopped
3	tablespoons chopped fresh basil
2	tablespoons chopped fresh oregano
2	tablespoons fresh thyme
2	tablespoons chopped fresh rosemary
3	cloves garlic, chopped
1	tablespoon kosher salt
1	tablespoon freshly ground pepper
	Zest of 1 lemon
1	6- or 7-pound loin of veal, boned with flank
¼	cup canola oil

In small ceramic bowl, combine first 6 ingredients. Set aside.

Cut the round tenderloin from the flat meat; and rub both pieces well with salt and pepper mix and lemon zest. Place the flat loin piece of veal on a clean work surface and cover with herb-garlic mixture. Place round tenderloin on top of the flat loin and roll both together; secure by tying with butcher's twine. Rub oil over surface and season with salt and pepper.

Preheat oven to 400°F. In a large sauté pan, heat the remaining oil almost to the smoking point. Add the meat and brown on all sides. Place meat in a roasting pan along with the drippings from the sauté pan and roast uncovered about an hour, until meat thermometer reads 150°F. Remove and let rest 10 minutes; remove twine, slice and serve. Serves 10.

Marilyn Hanson McCormick
Vincennes

Sausage and Noodle Casserole

A family favorite—especially with my grandsons.

2   cups noodles, cooked
1   pound pork sausage
½   cup chopped onion
½   cup chopped celery
1   4-ounce can mushroom stems and pieces, drained
     Salt and pepper to taste
1   cup shredded mozzarella cheese
¼   cup Parmesan cheese
2   tablespoons milk

Cook noodles according to package directions. Combine sausage, onion and celery in a 2-quart casserole dish. Microwave at high 7–9 minutes, stirring to break up meat after half the cooking time. Drain. Stir in noodles, mushrooms, salt and pepper. Add the shredded cheese, 2 tablespoons of the Parmesan cheese, and milk. Cover. Microwave at high 5–7 minutes or until cheese melts, stirring after half the time. Sprinkle with remaining Parmesan cheese before serving. Serves 4.

Beverly Reynolds
Brownsburg

Baked Squash with Sausage

2   small acorn squash, cleaned and halved
4   tablespoons pure maple syrup
2   tablespoons butter
8   ounces bulk hot Italian sausage

Preheat oven to 350°F. Wash squash, cut in half, and remove seeds. Mix syrup, butter and sausage. Put ¼ of mixture in cavity of squash. Place squash on baking sheet and bake for 30–40 minutes or until fork-tender. Serves 4.

Wayne Johnson
Indianapolis

A Special Occasion

Hoosiers have always been known for their warm and gracious hospitality. An elegant dinner enhanced by candlelight, beautiful roses, and a gourmet menu mark such special occasions as a birthday, an anniversary, or a holiday celebration. Creating that elegant mood for family, friends, or that "special someone" is worth the effort.

Wonderfully elegant meals are the hallmark of a special occasion, whether it's dinner for two or twenty. This memorable menu includes Chicken Scallopini Swiss Style (page 104), Sour Cream Mashed Potatoes (page 146), Steamed Snow Peas, and European Rolls. A bow to Rolf Meisterhans, executive chef and owner of Chef Rolf's Café in Carmel. (Photo by Matthew Musgrave)

After-Theater Supper

Indiana is known for its wonderful theaters—professional and amateur, small community and summerstock—as well as marvelous symphony, pops, and chamber orchestras, ballet, opera, jazz festivals . . . and the list goes on and on. Inviting friends for a late-night supper served buffet-style is a beautiful way to enjoy the final curtain of a theater performance.

A dramatic after-theater supper stars Oven Roasted Tomato, French Bread, and Basil Soup (page 61), with a supporting cast of Potato, Leek and Prosciutto Gratin (page 145), Grilled Asparagus with Morel Vinaigrette (page 160), and Chocolate Espresso Mousse (page 219). Applause to Steven J. Oakley, executive chef at Something Different and Snax Restaurants in Indianapolis. (Photo by Matthew Musgrave)

Ham Roll-Ups

Mother made a note that the cost of this recipe in 1955 was $14 and in 1980 it was $49.78.

11	cans asparagus, carefully drained
88	thin (not shaved) slices of ham
½	gallon milk
1	cup flour
4	pounds American cheese, grated or cubed

Preheat oven to 350°F. Roll 3 or 4 stalks of asparagus, depending on thickness, in a slice of ham. Repeat with all and arrange in a large baking dish. Blend flour and milk together until smooth. Put into large pan and add cheese. Heat until cheese is melted, stirring frequently enough to keep it from sticking to the bottom of the pan.

Pour cheese mixture over ham roll-ups. Bake for 30 minutes. (If made ahead and refrigerated, will need to be heated for 45 minutes or so.) Cover with plastic wrap or foil until served. Serves 44.

Gay Burkhart
Zionsville

Ham and Beans

Plan ahead! This takes 2 days.

1	pound navy beans
1	pound ham, cut into ½-inch cubes
1	medium onion, chopped
1	large carrot, finely grated
1	stalk celery, finely chopped
1	teaspoon liquid smoke
1	teaspoon salt
	Black pepper to taste
	Pinch of habañero pepper
4	cups water

Pick through the beans and discard rocks, dirt, etc. Rinse the beans and put in a large pan. Cover beans with water and soak for 8 hours. Change water and soak for another 8 hours.

Drain beans and combine with remaining ingredients in crockpot. (Another cup or 2 of water may be added for soupy beans.) Cook on low setting for 24 hours. Serve with hot cornbread and chopped onions. Servings: Not nearly enough.

John Rosenbalm
Brownsburg

Ham with Cranberry-Honey Glaze

1   8-pound fully cooked ham
     half, well-trimmed
¾   cup frozen cranberry juice
     cocktail concentrate, thawed
     and undiluted
2   cups sparkling mineral
     water
     Cranberry-Honey Glaze
     (recipe follows)

Place ham in a large ziplock plastic bag. Pour cranberry concentrate and mineral water over ham. Seal bag and place ham in a large pan. Chill 8 hours, turning occasionally.

Preheat oven to 325°F. Remove ham from marinade; reserve marinade. Place ham on a roasting rack that has been coated with cooking spray and place rack in shallow roasting pan. Roast 2 hours, basting occasionally with marinade. Remove ham from oven and coat with Cranberry-Honey Glaze. Bake uncovered an additional 15 minutes. Let stand 10 minutes before serving. Serve with Cranberry-Honey Glaze. Serves 18.

Cranberry-Honey Glaze

1   12-ounce package whole
     cranberries
½   cup honey
¼   cup water
2   tablespoons grated orange
     rind
2   teaspoons chopped
     crystallized ginger

Combine all ingredients in a medium saucepan; place over medium high heat and bring to a boil. Reduce heat and simmer 10 minutes, uncovered, stirring occasionally.

Barbara Acton
Plainfield

Annie's Glazed Pork Roast

1 4-pound boneless pork loin roast
Salt and pepper
1 16-ounce can whole berry cranberry sauce
¼ cup lemon juice
3 tablespoons brown sugar
2 tablespoons corn starch

Preheat oven to 450°F. Season meat with salt and pepper to taste and place in shallow roasting pan. Roast 20 minutes; reduce oven temperature to 325°F and continue roasting for 1 hour.

Meanwhile, combine remaining ingredients in a small saucepan. Simmer until thickened and clear, about 5 minutes. Spoon half the mixture over the roast; return meat to the oven and continue roasting, basting occasionally, for 1 more hour or until meat thermometer reads 155°F. Spoon remaining sauce over meat and return to oven for 5 minutes more.

Remove roast from oven; let stand for 10–15 minutes. Bring pan juices/sauce to a boil and spoon over meat to serve.

Annie Watts Clonc
Roachdale

Grilled Pork Chops
with Ginger Soy Sauce Marinade

6 center cut pork chops (1 ½-inches thick)
1 beef bouillon cube
⅓ cup hot water
1 teaspoon ginger
1 teaspoon salt
1 tablespoon brown sugar
¼ cup soy sauce

Dissolve the bouillon in hot boiling water. Combine ginger, salt, brown sugar and soy sauce and add to bouillon. Marinate chops in mixture for 3 hours, turning occasionally. Remove chops and grill, brushing frequently with marinade. Turn after grilling 15 minutes and continue brushing with marinade. Do not overcook. Meat should be moist when ready to serve. Discard marinade. Serves 6.

Joan Bossert
Liberty

Tenderloin Supreme

4   pork tenderloin slices, butterflied
1   6-ounce jar sliced mushrooms, drained
4   bacon slices
½   pint sour cream
1   can mushroom soup
    Paprika

Preheat oven to 275°F.

Butterfly tenderloins by cutting them down the middle lengthwise about ⅔ to ¾ of the way through, so the meat lies flat. Arrange the mushrooms lengthwise on half of each of the tenderloins. Fold the meat over the mushrooms and wrap a bacon slice around each tenderloin to secure.

Mix sour cream and soup. Place tenderloins in a baking pan and pour the soup mixture over them and sprinkle with paprika. Bake uncovered for 3 hours.

David Hunter
Vincennes

Sweet and Sour Pork

Worth the effort, and a meal in itself with a crisp salad and good rolls.

2 ¼   pounds lean pork, cut into 1-inch cubes
1   egg
¼   cup cornstarch
¼   cup chicken stock
2   teaspoons salt
¼   cup flour
1   cup sugar
4   tablespoons cornstarch
½   cup soy sauce
1   dash Tabasco
1   cup vinegar
2   teaspoons Worcestershire sauce
1   cup pineapple juice
2   carrots, cooked and sliced thin
2   bell peppers, sliced
¾   cup sweet pickles, sliced
2   cups pineapple chunks, well drained

Make a batter of egg, cornstarch, chicken stock, salt and flour. Dip pork into batter. Fry in hot vegetable or peanut oil until golden brown. Keep in warm oven.

Blend next 7 ingredients and cook until thickened. When ready to serve add carrots, bell peppers, pickles, and pineapple chunks. Heat thoroughly. Add pork and serve over steaming white rice.

Friend of WFYI
Morgantown

Hog Heaven

This is delicious and can be prepared the night before serving. Broiling rather than grilling yields good results also.

4	pieces pork center loin chops
¾	cup bourbon
¼	cup soy sauce
¼	cup brown sugar, packed
3	tablespoons Dijon mustard
1	tablespoon Worcestershire sauce
1	large yellow onion, sliced

Combine bourbon, soy sauce, brown sugar, mustard and Worcestershire with a whip. Add sliced onion to marinade and pour over chops. Marinate pork chops overnight in the refrigerator, turning a few times. Grill pork over medium-hot coals until cooked through (Fletcher suggests medium, which is still juicy). Serve with Bourbon-Onion-Apple Topping (recipe follows). Serves 4.

Bourbon-Onion-Apple Topping

2	large yellow onions, sliced
1	tablespoon vegetable oil
2	medium apples, peeled and sliced
¼	cup bourbon
¼	cup brown sugar
2	tablespoons Dijon mustard

Sauté onion in oil until translucent. Add apple slices and sauté 4 minutes longer. Mix last 3 ingredients together and add to pan. Continue cooking until apples and onions are glazed.

Fletcher Boyd
Fletcher's Restaurant
Atlanta

Grilled Country Ribs

6–8 pounds country-style pork ribs
1 bay leaf
1 onion, quartered
1 teaspoon each salt and pepper
½ teaspoon thyme
1 cup ketchup or barbecue sauce
1 cup apricot or peach jam
½ cup chopped onion (optional)
½ cup brown sugar, packed
¼ cup mustard
3 tablespoons Worcestershire sauce
2 tablespoons lemon juice
1 tablespoon minced garlic or 1 teaspoon garlic powder
⅛ teaspoon hot pepper sauce

Place ribs in large kettle and with just enough water to cover; add bay leaf, onion, salt, pepper, and thyme. Bring to a boil; cover and simmer 45–60 minutes or until tender. Remove ribs to shallow dish; cover with plastic wrap and refrigerate.

In saucepan, combine remaining ingredients; simmer uncovered 20–30 minutes, stirring occasionally.

Coat grill rack with vegetable cooking spray and preheat grill. Trim fat from ribs; brush with sauce. Grill ribs over hot coals, turning and brushing frequently with sauce, just until heated through, about 5–8 minutes.

Anne Watts Clonc
Roachdale

History on Rails

Lowell Sasser is a storyteller and a time traveler. He spins yarns that transport listeners to the rough and rugged days of early train travel.

"If you're not familiar with your past, how are you going to engage in your future?" Lowell asks. "History means life, and it's a livelihood for me. I can't get too interested in mechanical things, or something else like that. It's just history that's really taken me, and I went on from there."

History has taken Lowell Sasser to the Whitewater Valley Railroad, a sixteen-mile route from Connersville to Metamora. As vintage 1920 passenger cars rumble along the tracks, Lowell's narrative—accented by a rendition of "I've Been Working on the Railroad" on his harmonica—takes passengers back to Indiana's pioneer days.

He begins: "You can tell this was quite a woodland area at one time. It had all kinds of problems. To be a pioneer back in those days in any area of the United States, it was rough, very rough . . ."

At a stately ten miles per hour, the Whitewater locomotive chugs across Indiana farmlands. Passengers enjoy the view as Lowell continues his story: "There once were these three pioneer ladies who lived in this town up yonder . . ."

Lowell is a volunteer. In fact, they're all volunteers. From the engineer to the brakeman, every crew member devotes his or her time to the preservation of this special chapter of Hoosier history.

Lowell provides background information as his listeners experience history firsthand.

"Back in the early days, some folks devised this line as a mode of transportation from Cleveland to Cincinnati to Chicago to St. Louis, with daily stops at quaint hamlets along the way. They called it 'The Big Four' . . ."

Retired from the Connersville Fire Department nearly two decades ago, Lowell is free to pursue his passion for historic train travel. He's laughed and joked his way through nearly thirteen hundred journeys aboard the Whitewater Valley Railroad. He believes people shouldn't waste away their lives by doing nothing. Like trains, they should keep going. For Lowell, the railroad is more than a hobby. It's a way of life.

Grilled Summer Garden Pork Medallions

1 tablespoon garlic salt

2 tablespoons sugar

2 tablespoons fresh oregano, chopped

1 teaspoon black pepper, fresh cracked

5 pounds pork tenderloin

¼ cup olive oil

1 tablespoon garlic, fresh chopped

2 small onions, sliced

1 each red and green peppers, sliced ⅛ inch

1 zucchini, sliced ¼ inch

1 small yellow squash, sliced ¼ inch thick

1 small eggplant, peeled, quartered and sliced

1 14.5 ounce can diced tomatoes, drained

1 cup white wine, Riesling preferred

1 tablespoon fresh basil, chopped

2 tablespoons fresh oregano, chopped

Salt and pepper to taste

Blend garlic salt, sugar, oregano and black pepper into a dry rub. Slice pork into 4-ounce medallions and sprinkle with the dry rub. Cover and refrigerate for at least 30 minutes.

Heat oil in a large pot and sauté garlic and onions until lightly browned. Add peppers, zucchini, yellow squash and eggplant. Gently sauté an additional 5 minutes, stirring occasionally. Add diced tomatoes, wine and herbs. Simmer for 10 minutes and adjust the seasonings with salt and black pepper.

Preheat grill to high heat. (If using a charcoal grill, the coals should be white and ash covered.) Position rack at least 5 inches above the coals. Place medallions on grill; cover the grill if possible. Turn medallions every 4–5 minutes until fully cooked (155°F with no pink color).

Place sautéed vegetables in a casserole dish. Shingle the grilled medallions down the middle and garnish with fresh herbs. Serves 10.

Chef Carl Behnke
Department of Restaurant, Hotel,
Institutional & Tourism Management
Purdue University
West Lafayette

Grilled Salmon

This recipe was given to me by Pargo's Restaurant in Nashville, Tennessee. I liked it so well each time I have dined there.

1	cup soy sauce
½	cup brown sugar
½	cup bourbon
½	cup Jack Daniel's
1	teaspoon Worcestershire sauce
¾	cup water
	Juice of one lemon
6–8	salmon fillets or steaks

Mix first 7 ingredients together. Marinate salmon fillets or steaks no more than 4 hours. Grill until done, about 6 minutes per side, and enjoy.

Geneva E. Parker
Indianapolis

Sizzlin' Grilled Salmon

⅓	cup packed light brown sugar
¼	cup chicken broth
2	tablespoons soy sauce
1	teaspoon white vinegar
1	clove garlic, minced
¼	tablespoon ginger
1	tablespoon cornstarch
6	salmon fillets, ½ pound each (skin on)
	Juice of ¼ lemon
2	tablespoons butter, melted

Mix first 7 ingredients in a small sauce pan over medium-high heat until bubbly and thick. Set aside.

Place salmon on grill, skin-side up, over medium-high heat. Grill 4–6 minutes on each side or until salmon turns to a light pink. Combine lemon juice and melted butter and use to baste salmon during grilling. With skin side down, brush lightly with glaze. Turn glazed side over onto grill and allow to sizzle on grill for 1 minute. Serve with rice and grilled vegetables. Serves 6.

Mike and Janice Crabtree
Sellersburg

Grilled Salmon Napoleon

A great summer grill entrée to delight your guests. Prepare everything except the salmon ahead of time. When ready to serve, assemble individual plates or on a large platter for a beautiful presentation.

3	cups mashed potatoes
½	cup arugula
1	teaspoon shallots
1	tablespoon chardonnay
6	6-ounce salmon fillets, grilled
2	tablespoons vegetable oil
1	teaspoon salt
1 ½	cups Grapefruit Sauce (recipe follows)
24	potato chips
12	grapefruit sections
4	tablespoons chives, finely chopped

Prepare mashed potatoes using your favorite recipe. Sauté arugula and shallots in the chardonnay. Season with salt and pepper.

Oil and salt salmon fillets. Grill until just fully cooked but not over-cooked, about 6 minutes per side.

Ladle ¼ cup of Grapefruit Sauce on each plate. With a pastry bag pipe ½ cup mashed potatoes in a wide zigzag in the center of the sauce. Top with 4 potato chips and a small amount of the sautéed arugula. Place salmon on top, pipe a small rosette of potatoes in the center of the fish. Place 2 grapefruit segments in the potatoes. Sprinkle chopped chives onto the sauce. Serves 6.

Grapefruit Sauce

1	quart grapefruit juice
½	cup sugar
1	shallot, minced
2	pounds butter, diced and kept chilled until needed

In a non-reactive pan, combine grapefruit juice, sugar, and shallot. Bring to a boil and cook until liquid is reduced by half.

Add the cold diced butter a little at a time over low heat, whisking constantly, adding more butter as the last of the previous is just melting. As butter is added the sauce becomes thicker. Hold at 90 degrees. A higher heat will cause the sauce to separate, thus losing its velvety texture. Makes 1 quart.

Joseph Heidenreich, Executive Chef
California Café
Indianapolis

"Barbecued" Shrimp

This is a peel 'em and eat 'em dinner. Messy—have plenty of napkins and large bowls on the table for disposing of shells. Serve with crusty French bread for sopping up the juices, which are delicious. A large, hearty salad and a dessert complete the meal.

5   pounds fresh (green) whole (or headless) shrimp, unpeeled

1   bunch celery with leaves, chopped into 1- to 2-inch chunks

3–4   cloves garlic, chopped

6   lemons, cut in half

1   pound butter, cut into tablespoon-size chunks

½   ounce cracked pepper

3   tablespoons Worcestershire sauce

1–2   tablespoons salt

Preheat oven to 350°F. Wash shrimp and place in a large, shallow pan. Add celery and garlic. Squeeze lemons over top and put halves on top. Dot with butter and sprinkle with remaining seasonings. Bake, stirring frequently to get bottom shrimp to the top. They are ready when all shrimp are pink and opaque. Serve with plenty of juices from pan. Serves 10–15.

Gay Burkhart
Zionsville

Angel Hair Pasta with Shrimp and Feta Cheese

1   pound shrimp, cooked, shelled, and deveined

1   pound feta cheese, rinsed, dried, and crumbled

6   scallions, finely chopped

4   teaspoons fresh oregano

4   tomatoes, peeled, seeded, and coarsely diced
     Salt and freshly ground pepper to taste

1   pound angel hair pasta, cooked and drained

Combine all ingredients except pasta. Let stand at room temperature 1 hour or more. Add pasta to mixture and toss. (Can be refrigerated at this point, then brought to room temperature before serving.) Serves 4.

Friend of WFYI
Culver

Salmon Loaf

3 cups salmon (2 cans, flaked)
¼ cup cornflakes
¼ cup cracker crumbs
¼ cup cornmeal
½ cup onions, chopped
¼ cup celery, chopped
¼ cup red sweet pepper, chopped
½ teaspoon salt
1 teaspoon black pepper
½ teaspoon garlic salt or powder

Juice of ½ lemon or 1 tablespoon bottled lemon juice
2 eggs

Preheat oven to 375°F. Grease a loaf pan. Mix all ingredients thoroughly and tightly pack into the loaf pan. Bake for 45 minutes or until brown. Serves 4 to 6.

Joyce K. Allen
Beck's Mill
Salem

Simple and Delicious Salmon Cakes

These cakes are so easy, crispy and delicious! This recipe is good with side dishes of creamed peas and macaroni and cheese.

Vegetable oil
1 12-ounce can pink salmon
1 small box cornbread mix
1 egg
1–2 tablespoons onion flakes
Salt and pepper to taste

In a heavy skillet heat about a half inch of the vegetable oil on medium-high heat. Mix remaining ingredients together well. Drop by rounded tablespoons in hot oil and brown on both sides. Serves 4–6.

Anita Coffey
Indianapolis

Herbed Crab and Pasta

½   cup butter
½   cup flour
4   cups half-and-half
3   cups milk
3   cups Parmesan cheese
2   tablespoons butter
3   cups frozen stir-fry
     vegetables
3   cups crab meat
¼   teaspoon dill weed
1 ½   teaspoons garlic salt
1   tablespoon minced parsley
16   ounces cooked angel hair
     pasta
     Broccoli florets
     Tomato wedges

Melt ½ cup butter in saucepan over medium heat. Stir in flour, blending well. Add half-and-half, milk, and Parmesan cheese. Cook until sauce thickens, about 10–15 minutes.

Melt 2 tablespoons of butter in skillet. Add stir-fry vegetables, crab meat, dill weed, garlic salt, and parsley. Sauté until vegetables are crisp-tender.

Arrange cooked pasta on plates. Top with cheese sauce and crab and vegetable mixture. Garnish with broccoli florets and tomato wedges. Serves 6–8.

Hamilton House
Shelbyville

In 1830, John Hamilton and his family emigrated from Ireland to the United States, ultimately settling in Shelbyville. In 1853 they built the home where the family continued to live until 1932. It was placed on the National Register of Historic Places in 1979. For fine dining in a historic setting, the Hamilton House offers dining accommodations ranging from private dinners to banquet facilities for business and special occasions.

Shrimp Newburg

Can be served in a chafing dish for a lovely buffet entree.

3	tablespoons butter
½	pound fresh mushrooms, sliced
3	pounds shrimp
2	10-ounce cans shrimp soup
1	10-ounce can mushroom soup
½	cup half-and-half
⅓	cup sherry
2	teaspoons dry mustard
¼	teaspoon pepper
4	tablespoons Parmesan cheese, freshly grated
	Fresh parsley, chopped

Preheat oven to 350°F. Sauté mushrooms in butter. Place mushrooms and shrimp on bottom of 9 x 13-inch casserole dish. Combine soups, half-and-half, sherry, dry mustard and pepper and heat through. Pour over shrimp and mushrooms. Sprinkle Parmesan cheese on top. Bake 30 minutes. Serve with white rice cooked in chicken bouillon cubes. Sprinkle fresh chopped parsley on top.

Friend of WFYI
New Castle

Lively Lemon Fish Roll-Ups

⅓	cup butter
⅓	cup bottled lemon juice
2	teaspoons salt
¼	teaspoon pepper
⅓	cup rice, cooked
1	10-ounce package frozen chopped broccoli, thawed
1	cup sharp cheddar cheese, shredded
8	fish fillets (about 2 pounds)
	Paprika

Preheat oven to 375°F. In small saucepan, melt butter, stir in lemon juice, salt and pepper. In medium bowl combine rice, broccoli, cheese and ¼ cup lemon sauce. Divide among fillets. Roll up and place seam-side down in shallow baking dish. Pour remaining sauce over roll-ups. Sprinkle with paprika. Bake for 25 minutes.

Mary Foster
Lafayette

Old Fashioned Tuna Bake

A fruit or vegetable salad is a simple accompaniment for a delightful meal with little effort. I have used this recipe since 1940.

¼	pound medium-size noodles
1	medium onion, minced
2	tablespoons butter or margarine
1	15-ounce can tomatoes
½	teaspoon garlic salt
1	teaspoon salt
¼	teaspoon pepper
½	cup parsley, minced
1	bay leaf, crushed
1	small can chunk-style tuna
½	pound processed American cheese, sliced

Preheat oven to 350°F. Cook noodles according to package directions; add minced onions; drain. Add butter. Combine tomatoes, garlic salt, salt, pepper, parsley and bay leaf. In 8 x 8-inch baking dish, place half of noodles; then half of tuna, then tomato mixture. Top with half of cheese. Repeat layers, ending with cheese. Bake uncovered for 40 minutes. Serves 4.

Lucille E. Peterson
Indianapolis

My Fake Lasagna

This meatless one-dish meal is my own original recipe. Tastes like the real thing!

1	cup bread crumbs, buttered
2	cups diced tomatoes
1 ½	cups dry elbow macaroni
1	regular size jar of spaghetti sauce
2	cups sliced potatoes
1	can cheddar cheese soup
½	teaspoon oregano
1	teaspoon parsley leaves
	Salt and pepper to taste

Preheat oven to 350°F. Line bottom of 9 x 13-inch baking dish with buttered crumbs. Layer on diced tomatoes. Cook elbow macaroni till tender. Drain and layer onto tomatoes. Cover with spaghetti sauce. Add sliced potatoes, and cover with cheese soup. Sprinkle on oregano, parsley leaves, salt and pepper. Bake for about 35 minutes.

Barbara Fausett
Frankfort

Stuffed Italian Shells

1	package large macaroni shells
1	pound ricotta cheese
½	pound mozzarella cheese, cubed
½	pound Parmesan cheese, grated
2	eggs
1	tablespoon parsley flakes
	Salt and pepper to taste
1	large jar spaghetti sauce (or make your own sauce)

Preheat oven to 350°F. Cook shells in boiling water for 9–11 minutes. Drain. Mix cheeses, eggs, parsley flakes, salt and pepper in large bowl until well blended. Line bottom of large rectangular pan with some sauce. Stuff each shell with cheese ingredients and place in pan. Pour the rest of the sauce over the stuffed shells and sprinkle with Parmesan cheese. Bake 30–40 minutes. Serves 6–8.

Betty Ford
Cicero

Side Delights

VEGETABLES AND SIDE DISHES

Indiana gardens are justly renowned for juicy tomatoes of all sizes, for savory yellow and white corn, for tender zucchini and other squashes, for peppers in both sweet and fiery varieties, and for . . . well, Indiana gardens are justly renowned! And Hoosier cooks are renowned for their creative treatment of this bounty in a wide variety of delectable side dishes.

Reunion Baked Beans

This recipe easily adapts for outdoor grill. Cook over indirect heat with a low/medium fire. For smaller gatherings, decrease quantities proportionately to fit your needs. Cut cooking time by approximately 1 hour. Because moisture in beans may vary, ketchup may be added if mixture sets up too fast.

1	gallon quality canned pork and beans
3	pounds smoked sausage, cut up
2	large onions, diced
2	large Granny Smith apples, unpeeled and chopped
3	garlic cloves, minced
1	cup brown sugar, firmly packed
1	tablespoon black pepper, coarsely ground
1	tablespoon Cajun hot sauce*
1	tablespoon Worcestershire sauce*

Preheat oven to 275°F. Pour canned beans into a large baking pan or dish. Cut sausage lengthwise into fourths, and then slice into ½-inch lengths and add to beans. Dice onions. Core apples (do not peel) and coarsely chop. Add onion and apples to the beans. Add remaining ingredients and mix well. Bake uncovered until mixture thickens, approximately 4 hours. Serves 30–40.

* If this is a bit too spicy, substitute both ingredients with ¼ cup of steak sauce.

Jack Anderson
Dayton

Broccoli Casserole

1   cup rice
4   cups water
2   packages frozen chopped
     broccoli
1   large onion, chopped fine
2   stalks celery, chopped
2   tablespoons butter
1   can cream of chicken soup
1   can cream of mushroom
     soup
1   medium-size jar pimento,
     chopped
1   large jar Cheez Whiz

Preheat oven to 350°F. Cook rice in water according to package directions. Cook broccoli according to package directions. Sauté onion and celery in butter. Mix all ingredients together. Add soups, pimento and Cheez Whiz. Season to taste. Bake for 30 minutes or until there are bubbles in the middle.

Sandra James
Oxford

Broccoli Cheddar Casserole

2   packages chopped broccoli
¼   cup onions, chopped
6   tablespoons butter
2   tablespoons flour
½   cup water
1   cup grated cheddar cheese
3   eggs, well beaten
½   cup bread or cracker crumbs

Preheat oven to 325°F. Cook broccoli just until tender; drain and put in a mixing bowl.

Melt 4 tablespoons of butter in skillet and sauté onion until translucent. Stir in flour, blending well. Add water and cook over low heat until mixture thickens and comes just to a boil. Blend in cheese.

Add cheese mixture to broccoli. Add eggs and mix gently until blended. Turn mixture into a greased 1 ½-quart casserole. Sprinkle with bread or cracker crumbs and dot with remaining butter. Bake for 30 minutes.

Judy Yarbrough
Jasper

Broccoli Fondue

2 loaves French bread, cut into 1 ½-inch squares
2 sticks butter or margarine
1 medium onion, chopped
1 cup sliced mushrooms
2 packages chopped broccoli
2 cans cream of mushroom soup
12 ounces garlic cheese
1 teaspoon salt
¼ teaspoon pepper
  Dash Tabasco sauce
1 tablespoon Worcestershire sauce
1 ½ cups slivered almonds

Cut bread and let sit to dry out a bit. Melt 2 sticks of butter or margarine in 2-quart saucepan. Sauté onion and sliced mushrooms. Add broccoli, soup and cheese and simmer till well mixed. Season with salt, pepper, Tabasco sauce, and Worcestershire sauce. Heat thoroughly. Add slivered almonds, stirring well. Keep hot in a fondue pot over heat. Using fondue forks, dip bread into fondue pot and enjoy.

You can substitute cheddar cheese for the garlic cheese if you sauté 3–4 cloves of garlic, minced, with the mushrooms and onion.

Kate Esterline
Indianapolis

Broccoli Lima Bake

1 package frozen chopped broccoli
1 package frozen fordhook lima beans
1 can cream of mushroom soup
1 cup sour cream
1 package dry onion soup mix
1 can sliced water chestnuts
3 cups crispy rice cereal
1 stick butter or margarine

Preheat oven to 350°F. Cook vegetables until barely tender. Blend soup, sour cream, onion mix and stir into vegetables. Add water chestnuts. Spoon into buttered casserole dish. Top with crispy rice cereal browned lightly in butter. Cover loosely with foil and bake for 30 minutes. This can be prepared 24 hours ahead of time and baked just before serving. Serves 8.

Lois Frye
Indianapolis

Marinated Carrots

A wonderful accompaniment for a roast or grilled meat. Refreshing taste!

2	cans small carrots or 1 package fresh baby carrots
1	medium sweet onion, sliced thin
½	cup vegetable oil
½	cup vinegar
½	cup sugar
¼	teaspoon dry mustard
¼	teaspoon paprika
¼	teaspoon salt
1	teaspoon celery seed

Drain the carrots. (If using fresh carrots, cook just until tender and drain.) Place in covered container. Add onions.

Combine marinade ingredients and pour over carrots and onions. Let stand overnight in refrigerator. Serve cold.

In Memory of Ann Bond
Indianapolis

Company Carrots

Wow 'em with this easy dish!

2 ½	pounds carrots, sliced
1	tablespoon minced onion
¾	cup mayonnaise
1½	tablespoons horseradish
	Salt and pepper to taste
½	cup crushed saltine crackers
2	tablespoons margarine
2	tablespoons chopped fresh parsley
½	teaspoon paprika

Preheat oven to 375°F. Cook carrots in boiling, salted water, just until tender. Reserve ½ cup of the cooking liquid. Sauté the onion.

Grease a 9 x 13-inch baking dish and put carrots in bottom. Combine mayonnaise, cooled carrot liquid, onion, horseradish, and salt and pepper. Pour over carrots. Sprinkle with cracker crumbs, and dot with margarine. Sprinkle top with parsley and paprika. Bake for 25 minutes.

Judy Ford
Richmond

Swiss Green Beans

2	9-ounce packages frozen French-cut green beans
2	tablespoons butter
2	tablespoons flour
1	teaspoon salt
¼	teaspoon pepper
1	teaspoon sugar
1	teaspoon onion, grated
1	cup sour cream
2	6-ounces packages grated Swiss cheese
2	cups crushed cornflakes
2	tablespoons butter, melted

Preheat oven to 375°F. Cook green beans in small amount of water for 3–5 minutes. Drain thoroughly. Melt butter. Add flour, salt, pepper, sugar and onion. Mix thoroughly over low heat. Gradually add sour cream, stirring constantly. Fold in beans. Heat thoroughly. Pour into greased 1 ½-quart casserole dish. Top with grated cheese. Combine cornflakes and butter for topping and spread over cheese. Bake 20 minutes.

Friend of WFYI
Rushville

Crunchy Green Beans

A different way to serve green beans. Easy but can be doubled and taken to pitch-in dinners at your next church or family get-together.

2	10-ounce packages frozen French-cut green beans
1	16-ounce can sliced water chestnuts, drained
1	20-ounce can bean sprouts
1	cup fresh mushrooms, sautéed in butter
1	10 ¾-ounce can cream of mushroom soup
¼	cup sharp cheddar cheese, shredded
1	3-ounce can french fried onions

Preheat oven to 375°F. Cook green beans in salted water 3–5 minutes. Drain. Arrange in buttered baking dish layers of beans, water chestnuts, bean sprouts, mushrooms and soup. Repeat until all is used. Top with cheese. Bake for 20 minutes or until bubbly. Top with french fried onions and bake 10 minutes more.

Friend of WFYI
Greensburg

Corn with Black Beans and Jalapeño Chilies

½ cup dried black beans, rinsed

2 cups water

1 cup chopped onion

1 bay leaf

3 whole cloves

2 cups chicken stock or canned low-salt broth

2 teaspoons butter or margarine

1 tablespoon seeded and chopped jalapeño peppers

½ teaspoon chili powder

½ teaspoon ground cumin

⅛ teaspoon ground cloves

2 cups frozen whole kernel corn, thawed and drained, or kernels from 2 large ears of corn

Salt and freshly ground pepper to taste

Place beans in heavy large saucepan. Add enough cold water to cover by 3 inches and let stand overnight.

Drain beans. Return to saucepan. Add 2 cups water, onion, bay leaf and whole cloves. Bring to boil. Reduce heat, cover and simmer about 1 hour until beans are tender, stirring occasionally. Drain well. (Can be prepared a day ahead. Cover and refrigerate.)

Boil stock in heavy medium saucepan until reduced to ¼ cup, about 20 minutes. Melt butter in heavy medium skillet over medium heat. Add jalapeños, chili powder, cumin and ground cloves and sauté 1 minute. Add stock and cook 1 minute. Add corn and sauté 2 minutes. Add beans and stir until heated through. Season with salt and pepper. Spoon onto plates and serve. Serves 4.

Char Lugar
Indianapolis

Three-Corn Casserole

½ cup butter

1 cup sour cream

1 egg

1 16-ounce can whole corn, drained

1 16-ounce can cream style corn

1 9-ounce package corn muffin mix

Preheat oven to 350°F. Mix butter, sour cream, and egg. Stir in both cans of corn. Blend in corn muffin mix. Pour into well-greased 1 ½-quart casserole dish. Bake for 45 minutes.

Thelma Ritchie
Geneva

Scalloped Corn

2 ½ cups finely crushed Ritz or Town House crackers
½ cup butter, melted
2 whole eggs, well beaten
¾ cup half-and-half
1 teaspoon salt
½ cup sugar (or less if you do not like too much sweetness)
1 14 ¾-ounce can whole kernel corn, drained
1 14 ¾-ounce can cream-style corn

Preheat oven to 375 °F. Place cracker crumbs in a large bowl and pour melted butter over them. Mix well, and reserve 1 cup of the crumbs for sprinkling over the top of the corn mixture before baking. Combine eggs with half-and-half; add salt and sugar and blend well. Add all of this to remaining crumbs in the bowl. Add all the corn and mix well. Pour into a well-buttered 3-quart casserole or other baking dish. Put the reserved crumbs over the top. Bake for approximately 25 minutes or longer until set and nicely brown.

Geneva E. Parker
Indianapolis

Rice Dressing

This is a prize-winning recipe and can be served with poultry and eggplant dishes.

2 cups long grain rice
6 tablespoons clarified butter
½ cup slivered almonds
½ pound ground beef
4 cups boiling water
1 teaspoon salt
¼ teaspoon each of cinnamon, allspice, nutmeg and pepper

Rinse rice thoroughly in warm water and drain. Melt butter in cooking vessel. Add ½ cup slivered almonds. Stir until light brown. Add the ground beef and sauté until beef is no longer pink. Add rice and stir gently about 2 minutes. Add the boiling water and the seasonings. Cover and cook on low fire until absorbed, about 25 minutes. Serves 8.

Helen Corey
Indianapolis

Country Green Beans

These have a wonderful old-fashioned flavor just like Grandmother's green beans. Serve them for Sunday dinner with fried chicken, mashed potatoes, and chicken gravy.

1	6-pound can cut green beans, including liquid
	or
3	pounds fresh green beans, cleaned and snapped
¼	large onion
1	teaspoon salt
2	tablespoons brown sugar
½	cup diced jowl bacon

Place beans in a large kettle. (If using fresh green beans, add just enough water to barely cover.) Add onion, salt, brown sugar, and jowl bacon.

Bring beans to a boil. Reduce heat to low and simmer, covered, for 4–6 hours, stirring occasionally. (The long, slow cooking improves the flavor.)

Remove onion and discard before serving.

Kopper Kettle Inn
Morristown

The Kopper Kettle Inn in Morristown has long been a favorite stop on Route 52 since 1849. The large, quaint house is a veritable art museum housing a collection of antique furnishings and artifacts from all over the world. Former owner Mrs. Robert Vredenburg purchased a collection of antique copper kettles which she displayed in the inn, which explains its name. The restaurant offers an outstanding selection of heartland favorites daily, and a champagne brunch on Sundays.

Eggplant Roll-Ups

2   medium onions, chopped
½   cup olive oil
4   garlic cloves, minced
2   teaspoons salt
1   teaspoon pepper
2   bay leaves
1   teaspoon dried oregano
1   teaspoon dried basil
1   6-ounce can tomato paste
1   15-ounce can tomato sauce
3   cups water
¼   cup brown sugar
2   medium eggplants
1   teaspoon salt
½   teaspoon pepper
8   ounces mild cheddar cheese, shredded
5   small bunches fresh basil leaves
8   ounces mozzarella cheese, cut into ½- inch sticks

In 2-quart cooking pan, sauté onions in olive oil until tender. Add garlic, salt, pepper, bay leaves, oregano, and basil. Add tomato paste, tomato sauce, water and brown sugar. Simmer 1 hour. Remove and discard bay leaves.

Slice eggplants lengthwise and sprinkle them with salt. Let set for 30 minutes. Preheat oven to 400°F. Brush a baking tray lightly with olive oil. Dry the eggplant slices with paper towels and brush each slice with olive oil. Place the eggplant on the prepared tray and bake until tender and browned lightly, about 15 minutes. Turn and bake on the other side for 10 minutes and remove from oven.

Reduce the oven heat to 375°F. Spread ⅓ of the sauce in bottom of 8 x 10-inch baking dish.

Sprinkle eggplant slices with cheddar cheese. Place a basil leaf at narrow end of each slice and place a mozzarella stick on top of the basil leaf. Roll the eggplant slices and place them side-by-side in the baking dish. Top the rolls with the rest of the tomato sauce and bake about 20 minutes until hot and bubbly. If you like , you can top the tomato sauce with shredded mozzarella before baking. Serve with Rice Dressing (page 140) or pasta. Serves 8.

Helen Corey
Indianapolis

Elegant Stuffed Eggplant

Beautiful served at a holiday dinner on a pretty tray, garnished with parsley and surrounded with small baked apples or crabapples. This recipe was from the Old Stone Inn in Simpsonville, Kentucky, and it has been served to my family for 40 years.

1   large eggplant
½   cup water, boiling
½   teaspoon salt
¼   cup onion, chopped
1   tablespoon butter
1   tablespoon parsley, chopped
1   10 ½-ounce can cream of mushroom soup
1   teaspoon Worcestershire sauce
1   cup crumbled Ritz crackers
1   tablespoon butter
1 ½ cups water

Preheat oven to 375°F. Slice off one side of eggplant. Remove pulp to within ½-inch of skin. Place pulp in ½ cup boiling water to which ½ teaspoon of salt has been added. Cook 10 minutes or until tender. Drain thoroughly. Cook onion in butter until tender. Add eggplant pulp, parsley, mushroom soup, Worcestershire sauce, and all of cracker crumbs except 2 tablespoons. Fill eggplant shell with mixture. Place in baking dish. Dot with 1 tablespoon butter. Sprinkle crumbs on top. Pour 1 ½ cups of water in bottom of baking dish. Bake for 1 hour.

Diana Davis
Indianapolis

Eggplant Parmesan

1   eggplant, peeled and cut into ½-inch slices
¾   cup buttermilk
1 ½ cups Italian flavored bread crumbs
¼   cup olive oil
4-6 ounces provolone cheese
¼   cup Parmesan cheese
3   cups spaghetti sauce (canned or homemade)

Preheat oven to 400°F. Dip eggplant slices in buttermilk and coat well with bread crumbs. Place on baking sheet spread with olive oil. Bake 20–30 minutes till crumbs are crisp and eggplant is softened. Turn once in the middle of baking. Pour spaghetti sauce in 9 x 13-inch dish. Place eggplant slices in sauce and cover with slices of provolone cheese and sprinkle with Parmesan cheese. Lower oven temperature to 350°F and bake 30 minutes or until sauce is hot and cheese is golden.

Nancy Brandenburg
Indianapolis

English Pea Casserole

½   cup butter
⅓   cup celery, chopped
⅓   cup onions, chopped
⅓   cup green pepper, chopped
1   can cream of mushroom
      soup
¼   cup milk
3   cups cooked peas
8   ounces sliced water
      chestnuts, drained
1   small can of pimento,
      drained and sliced
1   cup crushed cheese crackers

Preheat oven to 350°F. Sauté celery, onion and green pepper in butter until tender. Add soup and milk. Mix well. Place peas, water chestnuts, and pimento in buttered 1 ½-quart casserole dish. Mix all lightly and sprinkle cracker crumbs on top. Bake 25–30 minutes.

Virginia Davis
Greenfield

Portuguese Potato Casserole

6   medium potatoes, peeled
1   cup commercially prepared
      roasted red bell peppers
3   cloves garlic, minced
5   tablespoons olive oil
1   cup minced parsley (flatleaf
      Italian is best) or ½ cup
      minced fresh cilantro and ½
      cup parsley
1   mild or hot fresh chili
      pepper, minced
½   teaspoon salt
1   tablespoon lemon juice
3   fresh tomatoes, peeled and
      sliced (Romas are good)
1   cup shredded Colby or
      other mild cheese

Preheat oven to 400°F. Boil potatoes until done. While potatoes are cooking make a puree of the bell peppers, 2 cloves of minced garlic and 3 tablespoons of the olive oil in a blender or food processor. When potatoes are done, drain and slice them. Lay slices in a buttered, shallow heat-proof casserole dish. Spread puree on potatoes. Mix together parsley, the remaining garlic and olive oil, chili pepper, salt, and lemon juice. Sprinkle half of this mixture over the potatoes. Top with sliced tomatoes. Sprinkle remaining parsley mixture over tomatoes; then top with shredded cheese. Bake 30–40 minutes. Let stand 5 minutes before serving. Serves 4

Sandra Miesel
Indianapolis

Country Potatoes

8 medium potatoes
1 can cream of chicken soup
½ cup butter
1 ½ cups cheddar cheese, grated
1 pint sour cream
⅓ cup minced onion or dry
  onion soup
TOPPING (optional)
1 cup cornflake crumbs
2 tablespoons butter

Cook potatoes in skins. Cool, peel, and grate. Heat soup, butter, and cheese until melted. Add sour cream and onion. Combine with potatoes and pour in large casserole dish. Refrigerate overnight.

Preheat oven to 350°F. Mix topping ingredients and sprinkle over potatoes. Bake uncovered for 45 minutes.

Susan Sturges Stewart
Greensburg

Potato, Leek, and Prosciutto au Gratin

3 pounds Idaho potatoes,
  peeled and thinly sliced
1 quart milk
1 teaspoon nutmeg
  Salt and pepper to taste
1 leek, diced (about ½ cup)
1 ounce prosciutto, chopped
1 tablespoon sage
1 tablespoon thyme
1 cup cream
1 cup grated Parmesan cheese

Cook potatoes, milk, nutmeg, salt and pepper until potatoes are soft. Drain potatoes and place in oval 9 x 13-inch casserole.

Preheat oven to 350°F. Mix leek, prosciutto, sage, thyme and cream together and pour over potatoes. Season to taste with salt and pepper. Sprinkle with cheese and bake for 40–45 minutes.

Steven J. Oakley, executive chef
Something Different and Snax Restaurants
Indianapolis

Sour Cream Mashed Potatoes

This is excellent served with Chicken Scallopini Swiss Style (page 105) and steamed snow peas.

8	Idaho potatoes
½	cup heavy cream
½	cup sour cream
½	cup (1 stick) butter or margarine
	Salt and pepper to taste
½	teaspoon nutmeg
1	tablespoon vegetable oil
1	tablespoon diced onion
1	tablespoon diced red onion
1	tablespoon diced leek
1	tablespoon diced scallions
2	tablespoons chopped garlic

Peel potatoes and cut into large chunks. Place in a pan with enough water to cover; bring to a boil and cook until the potatoes are soft.

Drain the potatoes well and mash until all lumps are removed. Add the heavy cream, sour cream, butter, salt, pepper and nutmeg. Whip until fluffy.

In a skillet over medium-high heat, heat the oil and add both kinds of onions, leeks, scallions, and garlic. Sauté for 3 minutes. Add to mashed potatoes and mix well. Serves 4–6

Rolf Meisterhans, owner and executive chef
Chef Rolf's Cafe
Carmel

Potato Balls

Finely chopped, cooked carrots or beef is very good for a filling as well.

1	egg white
4	cups mashed potatoes
3	tablespoons cream cheese, softened
⅔	cups of peas, cooked
1	whole egg, beaten
1	cup cracker crumbs
½	cup vegetable oil

Beat the egg white until soft peaks form. Mix potatoes with cream cheese and the beaten egg white. Form into balls. Let sit until a little firm. Scoop out inside and fill with peas, cover the opening with scooped-out potatoes and press closed. Dip in beaten egg and roll in cracker crumbs. Fry in oil until brown.

David Hunter
Vincennes

Potatoes au Gratin

8–9 large Idaho potatoes,
     unpeeled
1   cup green onions, chopped
1   cup stuffed olives, chopped
2   cups mayonnaise
1   pound processed American
     cheese, cubed
¾   pound bacon, fried and
     crumbled

Boil potatoes until tender. Cool, peel and slice.

Preheat oven to 350°F. Mix all ingredients except bacon, and pour into greased 9 x 13-inch pan. Sprinkle crumbled bacon on top. Bake for 30 minutes. This can be prepared the night before baking.

Tonya Beuligmann
Poseyville

Two-Layered Scalloped Potatoes

This was my mother's delicious potato recipe. It was originally prepared in a wood /coal burning oven.

4   medium potatoes, peeled
     and sliced ⅛ inch thick
2   large onions, peeled and
     sliced ¼ inch thick
1 ½ tablespoons all-purpose
     flour
¼   teaspoon salt
¼   teaspoon garlic powder
     pinch of pepper
3   tablespoons of butter
     Milk
4   slices uncooked bacon

Preheat oven to 425°F. Peel and slice potatoes and onions. Layer half of them in a large, deep casserole dish. Combine the flour, salt, garlic powder, and pepper. Sprinkle half of this mixture over the potatoes and onions. Dot with 1 ½ tablespoons of butter. Repeat layering the potatoes, onion, and flour mixture and butter. Pour just enough milk over the layers to cover. Arrange the bacon slices on top and bake for 1 hour, or until sauce has thickened.

JoAnne M. Bell
Marion

Baked German Potato Salad

This is equally good served warm or cold.

6	cups boiled red potatoes, sliced ⅛-inch
1	cup bacon, cut in small pieces
1	cup onion, chopped
1	cup celery, chopped
3	tablespoons flour
½	teaspoon pepper
1	teaspoon salt
1 ½	cups water
⅔	cup sugar
⅔	cup cider vinegar
2	teaspoons celery seed
⅓	cup minced parsley

Boil potatoes and slice. Place in an oiled baking dish.

Preheat oven to 375°F. In a skillet, sauté the bacon; add the onion and celery and sauté until translucent. Add the remaining ingredients. Blend well and simmer until the mixture is slightly thickened. Pour the mixture over the potatoes. Bake 45 minutes.

Agatha Glosson
Spencer

Glazed Sweet Potatoes

A holiday favorite for your family and guests!

7	medium sweet potatoes
¼	cup margarine
¼	cup half-and-half
½	teaspoon salt
¼	cup bourbon
1	teaspoon vanilla
1	teaspoon nutmeg
¼	cup margarine
½	cup brown sugar
½	teaspoon salt
¼	cup water
1	cup chopped pecans

Preheat oven to 350°F. Cook sweet potatoes in boiling water until done. Peel potatoes and mash. Add margarine, cream, salt and bourbon. Stir in vanilla and nutmeg. Put into casserole dish.

In separate pan, melt margarine and add sugar, salt and water. Stir and cook until glaze consistency. Add pecans and pour on top of casserole. Bake for 30 minutes or until bubbly and warm.

Friend of WFYI
Vevay

Yellow Summer Squash au Gratin

It's almost like a dressing to accompany your favorite outdoor grill chops. Something different and yummy, too!

2	pounds yellow squash, sliced
½	cup green onions, chopped
1	cup dairy sour cream
½	teaspoon salt
1	can cream of mushroom soup
1	8-ounce package herb-seasoned stuffing mix
1	package (½ cup) slivered almonds
½	cup margarine, melted

Preheat oven to 350°F. Cook squash in boiling water until almost tender. Drain. Sauté onion in small amount of butter. Combine squash, onion, sour cream, salt and soup. Combine stuffing mix and seasoning packet with margarine and almonds. Press half of the stuffing on the bottom and sides of a 2-quart casserole dish. Pour squash mixture into casserole dish and spread remaining stuffing over top. Bake for 30 minutes.

Friend of WFYI
Merrillville

Stuffed Acorn Squash

1	acorn squash
1	10-ounce package chopped frozen spinach, thawed and squeezed dry
1	egg
3	ounces cream cheese, softened
⅓	cup bread crumbs
¼	cup milk
½	pound Italian bulk sausage (mild or hot), cooked and drained
½	cup onion, chopped and sautéed
	Salt and pepper to taste

Cut acorn squash in half and remove seeds. Cook in microwave oven until just softened. Remove softened squash, leaving ¼-inch rim. Mash softened squash.

Preheat oven to 350°F. Thoroughly mix spinach, egg, cream cheese, bread crumbs, and milk. Combine the spinach mixture, sausage, onion, and mashed squash and mix well. Place in squash halves. Bake 30–45 minutes until thoroughly heated.

Nancy Brandenburg
Indianapolis

Zucchini-Tomato Stir Fry

2 tablespoons olive oil
2 medium onions, sliced
4 medium zucchini, sliced
2 large tomatoes, cut into wedges
4 ounces fresh mushrooms, sliced
½ teaspoon garlic salt
½ teaspoon thyme
¼ teaspoon pepper

Pour oil in wok or large skillet and heat until it starts to smoke. Add onion to skillet and stir-fry for 2 minutes. Add zucchini; stir-fry 6 to 8 minutes. Add remaining ingredients and stir-fry 2 minutes longer. Serves 8.

John Rinck
Indianapolis

Stuffed Zucchini

4 zucchini
4 green onions, chopped
1 14-ounce jar spaghetti sauce
1 8-ounce package shredded mozzarella cheese

Preheat oven to 350°F. Cut zucchini in half lengthwise and scoop out pulp. Mix pulp with onions and spaghetti sauce. Stuff back into zucchini. Place zucchini in a baking dish, top with cheese and bake until zucchini is tender and stuffing is bubbly, about 30 minutes. Serves 8.

Judy O'Bannon
Corydon/Indianapolis

Greek Spinach and Cheese Casserole

3 eggs, beaten
6 tablespoons flour
1 package chopped frozen spinach, thawed and well drained
1 teaspoon salt
2 cups cottage cheese
2 cups cheddar cheese, grated
¼ teaspoon pepper

Preheat oven to 350°F. Beat eggs and flour until smooth. Mix in rest of ingredients and bake uncovered in 1 ½-quart casserole dish for 1 hour. Let stand a few minutes. Six generous servings.

Sally Davis
Muncie

Broiled Tomatoes

These may be prepared ahead of time and refrigerated until time to broil. Very tasty and pretty.

3	large tomatoes
	Salt and pepper
	Garlic powder or garlic salt
	Basil
	Sugar
4	green stuffed olives, chopped
2	slices bacon, diced

Preheat oven to 425°F. Cut tomatoes in half and arrange in a baking pan. Sprinkle tomatoes with salt, pepper, garlic, basil, and sugar to taste. Top with olives and bacon and bake 10 minutes. Heat broiler and broil tomatoes for an additional 3–5 minutes.

Barbara Acton
Plainfield

Fried Green Tomatoes

This southern Indiana favorite can be enjoyed all summer. It is especially popular at the end of the season when the green tomatoes have to be picked because a freeze will kill the tomato plants. Some folks even enjoy this with firm, ripe tomatoes.

4	green tomatoes
1	tablespoon salt
1	egg
½	cup water
1	cup cornmeal
1	cup flour
1	teaspoon salt
½	teaspoon pepper
½	teaspoon paprika
	Cooking oil

Slice tomatoes about ⅛ to ¼ inch thick and place in a bowl. Sprinkle 1 tablespoon of salt over the tomatoes and add just enough water to cover. Refriger-ate for about 1 hour.

Batter is made in two parts. The first is made by beating the egg with ½ cup water. The second part is made by mixing dry ingredients in a flat pan such as a pie pan.

Pour about ¼ inch oil in a skillet and heat over medium heat. The oil should cover the bottom of the skillet but not deep enough to cover tomato slices. Dip the tomato slices in the egg mixture then coat both sides with flour/cornmeal mixture. Fry until golden brown and crispy. Place on paper towels to drain.

Margaret Rapp
Poseyville

Cabbage au Gratin

This is a family-gathering favorite. I usually double the recipe for a holiday occasion. There is hardly ever any left over.

1	medium head of cabbage, coarsely shredded
½	cup water, salted and boiling
3	tablespoons butter
3	tablespoons all-purpose flour
1 ½	cups milk
½	cup dry bread crumbs

Preheat oven to 325°F. Cook cabbage 9 minutes in boiling, salted water. Drain cabbage well and place in buttered 1 ½-quart casserole dish. Melt butter in saucepan; stir in flour and salt; cook over low heat 1 minute. Stir in milk gradually; cook over medium heat, stirring constantly, until thickened and bubbly. Pour sauce over cabbage and sprinkle bread crumbs over top. Bake for about 15 minutes or until crumbs are browned. Serves 6.

Grace Matthews
Indianapolis

Cabbage and Orzo

1	16-ounce package orzo style pasta
¼	cup butter or margarine
1	medium head cabbage, sliced thin
1	shallot, sliced thin
1	garlic clove, minced
1	tablespoon fresh basil, minced
1	tablespoon fresh thyme, minced
1	tablespoon fresh oregano, minced
	Salt and pepper to taste

Cook orzo *al dente* and drain. In frying pan, sauté cabbage with butter or margarine until tender. Add shallot and garlic. Continue to sauté until tender. Add spices and mix thoroughly. Then add prepared orzo and heat through. Salt and pepper to taste.

Mary Ellen Knific
Zionsville

Easy-but-Good Rice

When you are tired of potatoes, try this with a marinated grilled chicken breast for a change.

1	stick margarine
1	cup regular rice
1	can onion soup
1	can chicken broth
1	can water chestnuts, sliced
1	can mushrooms
1	package slivered almonds

Preheat oven to 350°F. Combine all ingredients in a buttered 1 ½-quart baking dish. Stir well and bake for 1 hour.

Friend of WFYI
Rising Sun

Almond Raisin Rice

Serve with your favorite lamb or pork chops. It's even delicious served under a shrimp newburg casserole.

1	cup white rice
2 ½	cups chicken broth
½	teaspoon salt
1	tablespoon butter
⅓	cup seedless golden raisins
¼	teaspoon sugar
⅓	cup chopped or slivered almonds, toasted
1	tablespoon chopped parsley

Combine rice, broth, salt, butter, raisins and sugar in pan. Bring to a boil, cover and reduce heat. Cook on low for 20 minutes. Remove from heat. Add almonds and parsley.

Friend of WFYI
Lawrenceburg

Vegetable Frittata

This dish is most attractive and unusual. I like to serve it with any charbroiled meat, such as grilled sirloin or chicken.

3 medium summer squash
3 medium zucchini
1 each red, yellow, and green bell peppers
3 tablespoons olive oil
1 large onion, thinly sliced
3 cloves garlic, minced
8 ounces fresh mushrooms, sliced
6 large eggs
¼ cup heavy cream
2 teaspoons salt
2 teaspoons fresh ground pepper
2 teaspoons Mrs. Dash
8 ounces cream cheese, crumbled into small bits
2 cups grated Swiss cheese
2 cups stale French bread crumbs (do in processor)
1 tablespoon balsamic vinegar

Preheat oven to 350°F. Grease the bottom and sides of a 9- or 10-inch spring-form pan.

Cut the summer squash and zucchini into ¼-inch slices. Cut the peppers into ¼-inch strips; reserve 12 red pepper strips to place on top of frittata. Heat oil in a large deep pan over medium-high heat. Add onion, garlic, summer squash, zucchini, peppers, and mushrooms; sauté, stirring carefully so you don't break up the vegetables, until they are crisp-tender. This will take 20–25 minutes.

While the vegetables are cooking, whisk the eggs and cream together in a large bowl. Season with salt, pepper, and Mrs. Dash. Stir in the cream cheese, Swiss cheese, bread crumbs and vinegar. Add the egg mixture to the vegetable mixture and gently combine together. Pour into the prepared pan and pack the mixture in tightly. Arrange red pepper strips on top in a pinwheel pattern. Place the pan on a baking sheet to catch any leaks. Bake until it is puffed, golden brown and firm to the touch, about 50–60 minutes. If the top is getting too brown, cover it with a sheet of aluminum foil.

Makes 8 vegetarian entree servings or 12–14 buffet servings as a meat accompaniment.

Serve the frittata hot, at room temperature, or cold. It can also be reheated at 350°F oven until warmed through, about 15 minutes. This keeps well and can be made several days in advance.

Marcia Adams
Fort Wayne

Maryland Sweet 'n' Sour Sauerkraut

¼ cup butter
1 large onion, chopped
2 Granny Smith apples, peeled and diced
1 32-ounce can sauerkraut, rinsed and drained
1 28-ounce can crushed tomatoes, undrained
¾ cup light brown sugar, packed
½ cup dry white wine
1 tablespoon caraway seed
  freshly ground pepper to taste

Preheat oven to 325°F. Melt butter in large skillet over medium-high heat; sauté onions and apples until softened, 3-5 minutes. Combine with rinsed and drained sauerkraut in a large mixing bowl. Stir in tomatoes, brown sugar and wine. Season with caraway and pepper. Transfer to a 9 x 13-inch dish. Cover tightly with foil and bake 1 hour 15 minutes. Uncover and bake another half-hour. 12 servings.

Pat Staab
Indianapolis

Bean Casserole

½ pound bacon
1 ½ pounds ground beef
½ cup onion, chopped
½ cup green pepper, chopped
½ cup brown sugar
2 tablespoons cider vinegar
1 tablespoon dry mustard
1 cup tomato sauce
2 28-ounce cans pork and beans
1 15-ounce can kidney beans
1 17-ounce can lima beans
½ teaspoon minced garlic
  Worcestershire sauce

Preheat oven to 350°F. Cut bacon into small pieces and fry until done. Brown ground beef in large pot; stir in onion, green pepper, and bacon. Add remaining ingredients and stir well. Pour into large casserole (at least 3 quarts) and bake for 1 hour. Makes about 10 cups. Freezes well.

Jeanne Jerden
Bloomington

Utopia

"I can't think of another place where there were two attempts at a utopian community in the early nineteenth century," says Connie Weinzapfel, public relations director of Historic New Harmony. "We have this incredible legacy of history. Some of the most important things that shaped this country happened here in Indiana."

In 1814, Father George Rapp, a German Lutheran from Pennsylvania, had a vision of the Second Coming of Christ. Rapp feared that the evils of civilization were corrupting his congregation. So he organized a separatist movement to a simpler, purer environment in the wooded lands nestled along the southwestern corner of Indiana territory.

Their first step, Weinzapfel explains, was to clear a lot of land. "The first houses they built here were log cabins, but very quickly they built clapboard houses and then brick houses. In fact, they built the whole town within ten years."

Rapp called the new town Harmonie. The utopian community and its citizens, the Harmonites, dedicated themselves to skilled craftsmanship and quality products, and in turn, they developed a standard of living far better than anything the region's early settlers had ever seen.

By 1824 the tiny community of Harmonie thrived. But late one night, Father Rapp had a second vision that beckoned him and his followers back to Pennsylvania. In a sudden move, Rapp sold the entire town to Robert Owen, an industrialist from Scotland.

Owen had his own vision for a utopian society, rooted not in religion, but in education, science, and the arts. With the help of William Maclure, a philanthropist from Philadelphia, he encouraged some of the country's greatest minds to migrate to this new bastion of scientific and cultural exploration that was renamed New Harmony.

Together, Owen and Maclure established the first free public school system in the United States. Maclure's first free library still stands as a reminder of the philanthropist's ingenuity and vision. And another building, Murphy Auditorium, is a tribute to the country's first civic dramatic club, founded in New Harmony. The auditorium still hosts a summer theater series.

Today, New Harmony has been restored to reflect the skill and craftsmanship of the town's original founders. Much of the restoration effort is due to Jane Owen, wife of a direct descendant of Robert Owen.

"It's the vibrations of the people who came before me," she says to explain her dedication to New Harmony. "They weren't coming here for self-advancement, they were coming here to share. That's what has inspired me from the very beginning—the generosity of mind and heart that made this town what it was."

Dumplings/Noodles

When I was a kid in the fifties, chicken noodle suppers were very popular at churches, schools, clubs and family gatherings. Everyone had their own way of making noodles and they usually did not follow a recipe. Since that time, I received a recipe that, with a slight modification, comes awfully close to the noodles I remember as a child. These are hardy noodles, almost like a dumpling. This noodle is not dried before cooking and can be made in a hurry.

½   teaspoon salt
1 ½ cups flour
3   egg yolks
4   tablespoons milk
¼   cup butter or margarine, melted

Mix salt and flour together. Mix egg yolks and milk together lightly and add to flour and salt mixture. Pour melted butter or margarine over all. Blend well. Mixture will be sticky. Roll approximately ⅛-inch thick on a liberally-floured surface. Cut ¼-inch wide strips for noodles or 2-inch squares for dumplings. Cook in boiling broth until firm and no longer doughy. The best way to test when they are done is to taste! Serves 4.

Cathy A. Trimble
Fishers

Macaroni and Cheese

This is a family favorite at our house. It is a meal in itself when served with a tossed salad or three-bean salad and rolls.

4   cups elbow macaroni, cooked (approximately 3 cups before cooking)
1   pound Colby cheese, shredded
1   small onion, finely chopped
4   cups canned stewed tomatoes or V-8 juice

Preheat oven to 350°F. Combine all ingredients, reserving 1 cup cheese. Pour into casserole dish or 9 x13-inch pan. Spread reserved cheese over top and bake 45–50 minutes or until cheese is browned. Serves 8.

Rita Bulington
Lafayette

Bohemian Dumplings

I would like to say that this recipe reflects a Stoelk family history steeped in the old German tradition. I would like to say that—but I can't . . . My grandmother, Mildred Stoelk, would never think of throwing out a loaf of stale bread. In fact, Grandma never threw anything away! She saved popsicle sticks, toilet paper rolls, the tin foil from Wrigley's Spearmint Gum, and any other item that would otherwise fit easily into a kitchen garbage pail.

10 slices stale bread, white or whole wheat
4 cups flour
2 eggs
2 teaspoons salt
¼ cup milk
¼ teaspoon salt
1 tablespoon vegetable oil
1 tablespoon olive oil

Let bread dry out for 4 to 6 hours, then cut into ½-inch cubes. Mix flour, eggs, and salt in a bowl. Add milk a little at a time until dough has a "sticky" consistency. Fold in bread cubes. (If necessary, add a little more milk to maintain "sticky" texture.)

Roll dough out onto a sheet of waxed paper sprinkled with a little bit of flour. Let stand for 30 minutes.

Form dough into balls about 3–4 inches in diameter. Bring a large pot of water to a boil. Add the salt and vegetable oil and olive oil. Drop dumplings into boiling water and cook for 20 minutes. Drain and cut dumplings in half.

Pour pork juices over steaming dumplings and serve with pork and sauerkraut. Serves 8.

Dave Stoelk
Producer/Director
WFYI

Turkey Dressing

1	10-pound turkey with giblets
¼	pound margarine
3	tablespoons onion, chopped
1	teaspoon salt
¼	teaspoon pepper
¼	teaspoon poultry seasoning
½	pound ground round steak
2	stalks celery, chopped
8	cups dry bread, cut in cubes

Rinse giblets and put in a sauce pan with enough water to cover; lightly salt. Simmer for about 2 hours. (Save juice to baste turkey.) Grind when cool. Melt margarine in large skillet, add onion and cook slowly at low temperature until tender. Add seasonings, ground round steak, and ground giblets. Cook lightly. Add this mixture to celery and bread in large bowl. Toss gently to mix. If not moist enough, add hot water. Stuff turkey and bake according to directions on turkey bag.

Florence Cullen
Indianapolis

Swiss Onion Casserole

Tastes great as a side dish for filet mignon.

½	cup (1 stick) butter or margarine
6–8	large onions
1	can cream of onion soup
	Worcestershire sauce
1	pound grated Swiss cheese
	French bread, sliced and buttered
	Garlic salt

Preheat oven to 350°F. Melt the butter or margarine in a skillet and sauté the sliced onions until translucent. Spread onions in a 9 x13-inch pan. Cover onions with soup and sprinkle lightly with Worcestershire sauce. Top with the grated Swiss cheese. Bake uncovered for 30 minutes. Place bread slices, buttered sides up on the onions to cover. Sprinkle with the garlic salt and bake for another 30 minutes. Serves 12.

Jackie Swats
South Bend

Grilled Asparagus with Morel Vinaigrette

3   pounds fresh asparagus (2–3 bunches)
3   tablespoons olive oil
     Salt and pepper to taste
1   tomato, sliced thinly
½   cup crumbled goat cheese
1   egg, hardboiled and finely chopped
¼   cup fresh chopped chives
     Morel Vinaigrette (recipe follows)

Rinse asparagus in cold water and snap off tough ends of stems. Toss spears with olive oil to coat and sprinkle with salt and pepper. Grill till tender-crisp. Chill. Pour Morel Vinaigrette over asparagus and garnish with tomato slices, goat cheese, egg, and chives.

Morel Vinaigrette

2   cups fresh morel mushrooms
1   tablespoon butter
¼   cup sherry vinegar
⅔   cup vegetable oil
¼   cup chardonnay wine
2   tablespoons truffle oil (optional)
     Salt and pepper to taste

Sauté morels in a little butter. Place morels and vinegar in food processor and puree. Add remaining ingredients slowly. Adjust the seasonings. Pour over grilled asparagus.

Steven J. Oakley, executive chef
Something Different and Snax Restaurant
Indianapolis

Sweets & Treats

As children, our earliest favorite foods are probably sweet treats like ice cream birthday cakes and giant sugar cookies. We take pride in the first batch of brownies we make all by ourselves, and the first pie crust that is actually edible. And we continue to enjoy pleasing our families, friends, and co-workers with both old and new recipes for luscious desserts.

Cakes

White Sheet Cake with Cream Cheese Icing

CAKE

2 ½ cups flour
2 cups sugar
½ cup margarine
½ cup vegetable oil
1 cup water
1 ½ teaspoons baking soda
⅔ cup buttermilk
2 eggs, beaten
2 teaspoons vanilla

ICING

1 8-ounce package cream cheese, softened
½ cup (1 stick) butter or margarine, softened
1 teaspoon vanilla
1 box confectioners sugar, sifted

FOR THE CAKE: Preheat oven to 350°F. Grease and flour a 15 ½ x 10 ½-inch jelly roll pan. Blend flour and sugar together. Bring to a boil the margarine, oil and water. Add it to the flour and sugar mixture. Dissolve the baking soda in the buttermilk and mix with the eggs and vanilla. Combine with the rest of the batter and mix well. Pour in prepared pan and bake for 20 minutes. Cool on a wire rack and then ice with the cream cheese icing.

FOR THE ICING: Combine cream cheese, butter or margarine, and vanilla. Cream the mixture till fluffy and add the confectioners sugar. Beat by hand or with a mixer until it is smooth. Spread icing over cooled cake.

Marge Salisbury
Muncie

Mammy's Spiced Cake

This is a recipe from my husband's grandmother. She was born 146 years ago in June 1852. When I ask my family what cake they want for their birthdays, they always say "Mammy's Spiced Cake!"

3	cups all-purpose flour (do not sift)
1	teaspoon baking soda, scant
1	tablespoon cinnamon
1	teaspoon nutmeg
1 ½	teaspoons ground cloves
½	teaspoon salt
1	cup granulated sugar
1	cup brown sugar
1 ½	cups butter or margarine
1 ½	cups buttermilk
2	eggs, beaten
¾	cup raisins, if desired

Preheat oven to 350°F. Combine flour, soda, cinnamon, nutmeg, cloves, and salt. Using a mixer, cream together granulated and brown sugars with butter or margarine. Combine buttermilk and eggs. Alternately add dry ingredients and buttermilk mixture to the butter and sugar mixture. Add raisins if desired. Prepare three 8-inch pans, greased and lined with wax paper. Equally divide the batter among the pans. Bake for 30 minutes. Cool and ice with your favorite frosting.

Helen D. Vaughn
Indianapolis

One-Bowl Chocolate Cake

2	cups all-purpose flour
2	cups sugar
½	cup baking cocoa
2	teaspoons baking soda
1	teaspoon baking powder
½	teaspoon salt
1	cup vegetable oil
1	cup buttermilk
2	eggs
1	cup hot water
	Frosting of your choice

Preheat oven to 350°F. Grease and flour 9 x 13-inch pan. In a large bowl, combine dry ingredients. Stir in oil, buttermilk and eggs. Add water and stir until combined. Pour into pan and bake for 35 minutes or until a tester inserted near the center comes out clean. Cool completely and frost. Serves 12–16.

Evelyn Harrison
Lafayette

Oatmeal Cake

This was my Grandmother Smith's recipe. When she asked people in for a meal, they would request she bake oatmeal cake for dessert.

CAKE

1	cup quick rolled oats
1 ¼	cups boiling water
½	cup shortening
1	cup granulated sugar
1	cup brown sugar
2	eggs
1 ½	teaspoons cinnamon
½	teaspoon salt
1	teaspoon baking soda
1 ⅓	cups flour

TOPPING

6	tablespoons brown sugar
¼	cup cream or milk
½	teaspoon vanilla
½	cup nuts, chopped
1	cup shredded coconut

FOR THE CAKE: Preheat oven to 350°F. Pour boiling water over oats and let stand for 20 minutes. Cream together shortening and the two sugars. Stir in the eggs, beating well. Add the cinnamon, salt, baking soda and flour. Add the oats mixture and mix all well. Pour into a 9 x 13-inch pan and bake for 45–50 minutes or until it tests done.

FOR THE TOPPING: While cake is baking, combine topping ingredients in a bowl and blend well. Preheat broiler, spread topping over cake and broil about 4 minutes or until lightly browned.

Marsha Grotrian
Flora

Chocolate-Sour Cream Cake

1	chocolate cake mix
1	chocolate instant pudding (small box)
1	6-ounce package chocolate chips
1	cup sour cream
4	eggs
½	cup water
½	cup oil

Preheat oven to 350°F. Grease and flour angel food or bundt cake pan. Mix all ingredients together. Pour into pan and bake 45–55 minutes. Sprinkle with powdered sugar when cool, if desired. Also very good served warm.

Linda Arnot
Indianapolis

Eclair Cake

CAKE
2 3-ounce packages French vanilla instant pudding
3 cups milk
1 9-ounce container whipped topping
1 box graham crackers, left whole

TOPPING
2 10-ounce packages choco-bake
3 tablespoons butter
2 tablespoons white corn syrup
3 tablespoons milk

1 teaspoon vanilla
1 ½ cups powdered sugar

FOR THE CAKE: Butter sides and bottom of 9 x 13-inch pan. Beat pudding and milk. Add whipped topping. Mix well. Line bottom of pan with graham crackers (break to fit). Pour ½ of the pudding over the crackers. Top with another layer of crackers. Spread remaining pudding over crackers. Top with a layer of crackers. Chill 2 hours.

FOR THE TOPPING: Combine all ingredients. Beat until glossy. Gently spread over pudding and crackers. Cover. Refrigerate overnight (better if refrigerated 48 hours).

Mary Foster
Lafayette

Christmas Cake

3 cups flour
1 teaspoon baking powder
1 teaspoon baking soda
1 teaspoon salt
1 teaspoon cinnamon
2 cups sugar
¾ cup vegetable oil or shortening
1 teaspoon vanilla
4 cups chopped apples

2 eggs, beaten
1 cup chopped nuts and dates (optional)

Preheat oven to 350°F. Combine dry ingredients. Add oil, vanilla, and apples. Mix well. Add beaten eggs. Keep blending and add nuts. Put in greased tube pan (batter is very thick). Bake for 1 hour 15 minutes.

In memory of Pearl Britton
Camden

Kate's Apple Cake

CAKE

2	cups diced apples
1	cup sugar
1	egg
1	cup flour
1 ½	teaspoons cinnamon
1	teaspoon baking soda
¼	teaspoon salt
½	cup chopped nuts (optional)

SAUCE

¼	cup brown sugar
¼	cup granulated sugar
1	tablespoon flour
½	cup water
1	tablespoon butter
1	teaspoon vanilla

FOR THE CAKE: Preheat oven to 375°F. Combine the apples and sugar and let stand until sugar dissolves. Add egg and beat well. Sift together the dry ingredients and stir into apple mixture. Add nuts if desired. Bake for 40 minutes. While cake is baking, prepare sauce.

FOR THE SAUCE: Combine first 4 sauce ingredients in a saucepan and cook over low heat until clear. Stir in butter and vanilla. Spread over cake as soon as cake comes from oven.

Barbara Acton
Plainfield

Mom's Apple Cake

2	eggs
2	cups flour
2	teaspoons cinnamon
½	teaspoon salt
1	teaspoon soda
1	cup vegetable oil
1	teaspoon vanilla
2	cups sugar
½	cup nuts, chopped
2	cups sliced apples
½	cup buttermilk
½	teaspoon baking soda
1	cup sugar
⅓	cup butter or margarine
½	teaspoon vanilla
1	tablespoon corn syrup

Preheat oven to 350°F and grease and flour a 9 x 13-inch cake pan. Combine first 8 ingredients and mix well. Add the nuts and apple slices. Pour batter into the prepared pan and bake for 45–60 minutes or until tester comes out clean when inserted near the center.

Combine the remaining ingredients in a saucepan and cook over low heat for about 7 minutes. Poke holes in hot cake and pour this mixture over top of cake.

Mary Wrennick
Indianapolis

Black Walnut Cake

As children, we gathered black walnuts and my mother baked us black walnut cakes. Now I bake black walnut cakes, hulling, rinsing and drying walnuts gathered from the side of the street, then cracking them with a hammer. I have won prizes for my black walnut cakes at the Indiana State Fair.

CAKE

2	eggs, separated
1 ½	cups sugar
⅓	cup shortening
2 ¼	cups cake flour
1	teaspoon baking powder
1	teaspoon salt
1	cup plus 2 tablespoons milk
1	teaspoon black walnut flavoring
¼	cup black walnuts, chopped

BUTTERCREAM FROSTING

1	pound confectioners sugar
½	cup butter
1	teaspoon black walnut flavoring
3	tablespoons milk
⅓	cup black walnuts for decoration

FOR THE CAKE: Preheat oven to 350°F. Beat egg yolks until frothy. Add ½ cup sugar. Beat egg whites until glossy. Set aside.

In another bowl, stir shortening to soften. Sift together flour, 1 cup sugar, baking powder and salt. Add dry ingredients, ¾ cup milk, and flavoring to shortening. Beat 1 minute, scraping bowl. Add remaining milk and egg yolks. Beat 1 minute longer. Fold in beaten egg whites and nuts. Pour batter into two 8-inch greased and floured cake pans. Bake for 25–30 minutes. Frost cooled cake with buttercream frosting.

FOR THE FROSTING: In large bowl, beat together sugar, butter, black walnut flavoring, and milk until smooth. If necessary, add more milk until frosting is of spreading consistency. Frost cake and sprinkle black walnuts on top. Serves 12.

Annie Howard
Indianapolis

Emma Elizabeth's

Black Walnut Buttermilk Cake

This is a cake made for Christmas by my grandmother, Emma Elizabeth Anderson. She prepared it several days ahead, and it was always on a sparkling glass pedestal plate covered with an immaculate white linen napkin.

CAKE

1	cup seeded raisins
2	cups sugar
½	cup shortening
3	cups flour
1	teaspoon nutmeg
1	teaspoon ground cloves
1	teaspoon cinnamon
½	teaspoon salt
2	cups buttermilk
2	teaspoons baking soda
½	cup black walnuts, chopped, or 1 teaspoon black walnut flavoring

ICING

1 ½	cups light brown sugar, packed
1 ½	cups granulated sugar
1	13-ounce can evaporated milk
¾	cup (scant) black walnuts, chopped

FOR THE CAKE: Preheat oven to 350°F. Grease and flour two 9-inch round pans. Steam raisins over boiling water for 15 minutes to plump. Cool and flour the raisins. Cream sugar and shortening. Combine flour, nutmeg, cloves, cinnamon, and salt. Stir baking soda into buttermilk. Add dry ingredients alternately with the buttermilk mixture to the sugar and shortening. Fold in raisins and nuts. Pour batter in pans in equal amounts. Bake for 35–40 minutes, or until done. Allow to stand 10–15 minutes before removing from pans.

FOR THE ICING: Mix sugars and milk; cook, stirring until it boils. Continue cooking to soft ball stage. Let stand about 20 minutes until cool. Beat with mixer until of spreading consistency. If too thick, add a little cold milk. If too thin, add confectioners sugar. Frost cake, then sprinkle on black walnuts or mix them with a little of the frosting and spread on the cake.

Marilyn Anderson
Speedway

Aunt Lillian's Stuffed Angel Food Cake

I grew up in New Albany, Indiana. As a child, I remember many wonderful dinners at my Aunt Lillian's. I continue to remember her fondly today and appreciate the good manners and other lessons learned.

1	tablespoon unflavored gelatin
¼	cup cold water
5	egg yolks, well beaten
2	cups milk, scalded
½	cup sugar
¼	teaspoon salt
1	cup cream, whipped
1	tablespoon vanilla
1	angel food cake
	Maraschino cherries

Dissolve gelatin in water. Beat egg yolks. Add scalded milk, sugar and salt to the eggs. Cook until it coats a spoon (don't overcook). Add dissolved gelatin. Refrigerate until cold. Add whipped cream and vanilla.

Slice top from cake. Create a tunnel by carefully cutting out the center, and pour thickened custard into shell. Replace cake top. Ice the top and sides with remaining custard. Decorate with cherries. Refrigerate until ready to serve. Serves 10–12.

Sandra Schultz Moberly
Shelbyville

Lincoln's Favorite Cake

1	cup butter
2	cups sugar
3	cups cake flour
2	teaspoons baking powder
1	cup milk
1	cup blanched almonds, chopped
1	teaspoon vanilla
6	egg whites, stiffly beaten
¼	teaspoon salt

Preheat oven to 350°F. Grease and flour four 8- or 9-inch pans.

Cream butter and sugar lightly. Stir flour and baking powder together and add alternately with milk to the first mixture. Lightly flour the nuts and and add to the mixture. Add vanilla.

Beat egg whites with salt until stiff peaks form, and fold into the cake batter. Pour batter in the pans and bake for 25 minutes or until done. Ice with boiled icing to which is added ½ cup finely chopped candied pineapple and cherries.

Elaine McVay
Zionsville

Coconut Cake

This recipe came from my paternal grandmother, Mrs. Georgia Pritchett . . . I can remember standing on a chair beating the egg whites and other ingredients for the icing and afterwards being able to lick the beaters and clean up the bowls.

CAKE
2	eggs
⅔	cup oil
1 ½	cups self-rising flour
1 ¼	cups sugar
1	cup sweet milk
1	teaspoon vanilla

ICING
2	egg whites
⅓	cup sugar
½	cup white corn syrup
1	teaspoon vanilla

½	teaspoon salt
	Shredded coconut

FOR THE CAKE: Preheat oven to 400°F. Beat the eggs; add oil, flour, sugar, milk and vanilla. Put in a well-greased 9 x 13-inch pan. Bake for 30–40 minutes. Let cool.

FOR THE ICING: Combine all icing ingredients in a medium mixing bowl. Beat until peaks form. Frost cake and pat shredded coconut over entire cake.

Marilyn Cobb
Sharpesville

Grandma Trout's Banana Cake

This recipe is from my paternal grandmother, probably dating from the late 1800s, long before the days of "healthy" recipes—this one has no salt! I also use black walnuts for a really rich taste.

1	cup buttermilk
1	teaspoon baking soda
⅔	cup shortening
1 ½	cups granulated sugar
2	eggs
2 ½	cups flour
1	cup ripe banana, mashed
½	cup chopped walnuts (optional)

Preheat oven to 350°F. Prepare two 9-inch round pans or one 9 x 13-inch pan. Lightly grease and flour. Stir soda into the buttermilk. Cream shortening with sugar. Add eggs. Add milk mixture alternately with the flour. Stir in banana and nuts. Bake for 35 minutes or until done. Remember, the top will be slightly moist because of the bananas.

Mary Trout Decker
Alexandria

Old-Fashioned Coconut Cake

My mother baked coconut cakes. She shredded coconuts herself. I buy coconut already shredded. I have won prizes for coconut cakes at the Indiana State Fair.

CAKE

⅔ cup butter

1 ¾ cups sugar

2 eggs

1 ½ teaspoons vanilla

¼ teaspoon coconut extract

3 cups sifted cake flour

2 ½ teaspoons baking powder

1 teaspoon salt

1 ¼ cups milk

⅓ cup plus 2 tablespoons coconut

FROSTING

2 egg whites

1 ½ cups sugar

5 tablespoons cold water

1 ½ teaspoons light corn syrup

1 teaspoon coconut extract

1 cup shredded coconut

FOR THE CAKE: Preheat oven to 350°F. Cream butter; add sugar. Cream until light. Add eggs, vanilla and coconut flavoring. Beat until fluffy. Sift together flour, baking powder, and salt. Add dry ingredients to creamed mixture alternately with milk, beating after each addition. Beat 1 minute. Stir coconut into batter. Pour batter into two greased and lightly floured 9-inch round cake pans. Bake for 30-35 minutes. Cool 10 minutes, then remove from pans and continue cooling. Spread frosting on cooled cake, then sprinkle frosted cake with coconut.

FOR THE FROSTING: Combine unbeaten egg whites, sugar, water and corn syrup in upper part of double boiler. Place over rapidly-boiling water, beating constantly with electric egg beater. Cook 7–10 minutes or until frosting will stand in peaks. Remove from heat. Add coconut extract and beat until thick enough to spread. Spread frosting between layers. Frost sides and top of cake with remaining frosting. Sprinkle more coconut over top and sides. Serves 12 to 16.

Annie Howard
Indianapolis

Old Fashioned Chocolate Cake

My grandmother could make this cake, pop it into her old wood stove, and have it on the table while catching up with the latest family news . . .

2	cups flour
2	cups sugar
2	teaspoons baking soda
6	tablespoons cocoa
1	teaspoon salt
2	eggs
2	cups buttermilk (if using sour milk, add 1 more teaspoon baking soda)
2	teaspoons vanilla
5	tablespoons melted butter

Preheat oven to 350°F. Grease and flour a 9 x 13-inch pan. Sift all dry ingredients together. Add eggs, buttermilk, vanilla, and melted butter. Bake for 35–40 minutes. If you halve the recipe, it makes one 9-inch square cake. Serves 6–8.

Sprinkle powdered sugar on top while cake is warm.

Marjorie Riedeman
Indianapolis

Brown Sugar Pound Cake

CAKE

1 ½	cups (3 sticks) butter
1	pound light brown sugar
1	cup white sugar
5	eggs
½	teaspoon salt
3	cups flour
1	teaspoon vanilla
1	cup milk
1	cup walnuts

GLAZE

1	cup confectioners sugar
1	tablespoon butter
1	teaspoon vanilla
1	teaspoon milk
½	cup walnuts, chopped

FOR THE CAKE: Preheat oven to 350°F. Cream together the butter, light brown sugar and white sugar. Add eggs to this mixture one at a time, beating after each one. Mix together the salt and flour. Mix together the vanilla and milk. Add these two mixtures alternately to the creamed mixture. Mix well. Add chopped walnuts. Pour into a 10-inch tube pan that has been sprayed with cooking spray. Bake 1 hour 15 minutes or until tests done. Cool in pan 10 minutes. Remove and cool on rack.

FOR THE GLAZE: Mix all ingredients until thoroughly blended and pour over warm cake. Sprinkle walnuts on top or mix into glaze.

Juanita Smith
Middletown

Peg's Rum Cake

CAKE

1	cup chopped walnuts or pecans
1	yellow cake mix
1	3 ¾-ounce box instant vanilla pudding *
4	eggs
½	cup water
½	cup vegetable oil
½	cup dark rum

GLAZE

¼	pound butter
¼	cup water
1	cup granulated sugar
½	cup dark rum

FOR THE CAKE: Preheat oven to 350°F. Mix all ingredients. Grease and flour bundt pan. Sprinkle nuts over bottom and pour batter over nuts. Bake 1 hour at 350°F. Cool. Invert on plate, prick top and sides with toothpick. Spoon and brush glaze over top and sides, allow cake to absorb. (Do this over a period of several hours.)

* Note: If using a cake mix with pudding already in the mix, omit the pudding and use 3 eggs instead of 4; ⅓ cup oil instead of ½ cup.

FOR THE GLAZE: Melt butter, add water and sugar. Boil 5 minutes, stirring constantly. Remove from heat, stir in rum.

Peg Jones
Indianapolis

Strawberry Shortcake

1 ½	cups sugar
½	cup shortening
1	egg, beaten
1	cup milk
1 ½	cups flour
1	teaspoon baking powder

Preheat oven to 350°F. Grease and flour an 8 x 8-inch pan. Beat the sugar and shortening together. Add all of the other ingredients. Pour into pan and bake for 20–25 minutes. Top with fresh strawberries and whipped cream.

Sandra James
Oxford

Aunt Mamie's Pound Cake

8 medium eggs, separated
2 ⅔ cups sugar
1 pound butter, softened
3 ½ cups sifted all-purpose flour
½ cup whipping cream
1 teaspoon vanilla

Preheat oven to 350°F. Grease and flour a 10-inch tube pan.

Whip egg whites until they hold soft peaks, gradually adding 6 tablespoons of sugar while beating. Beat until stiff peaks form. Refrigerate until needed.

Cream butter thoroughly; add remaining sugar and whip until light and fluffy. With mixer running, add the egg yolks 2 at a time, beating well after each addition. Add flour and cream alternately, beginning and ending with the flour. Add vanilla. Continue beating until mixture is very light, approximately 10 minutes. Fold egg whites into the batter just until well blended.

Pour batter into prepared pan and bake for 30 minutes; reduce heat to 300°F and bake 1 hour more. When done, the top will spring back when touched lightly. Cool in pan for 10 minutes, then turn out onto a wire rack and cool completely. Store in covered container.

Pamela Parker
Indianapolis

Eggnog Cake

CAKE
1 package yellow cake mix
1 cup whipping cream
¼ cup oil
¼ cup rum
3 eggs
½ teaspoon nutmeg

GLAZE
⅓ cup sugar
⅛ teaspoon nutmeg
⅓ cup margarine or butter
2 tablespoons water
2 teaspoons rum

FOR THE CAKE: Preheat oven to 350°F. Grease and flour 12-cup fluted tube pan. In a large bowl, blend cake ingredients until moist. Beat 2 minutes at highest speed. Pour into prepared pan. Bake 30–45 minutes or until toothpick inserted in center comes out clean. Do not remove from pan yet.

FOR THE GLAZE: In a small saucepan, simmer sugar, nutmeg, margarine, and water until sugar dissolves. Remove from heat and add rum. Pour half of glaze around edges of hot cake. Cool upright in pan 5 minutes; turn onto serving plate. Pour remaining glaze over top of cake. Serve warm or cool. Serves 16.

Rosina M. Reese
Morgantown

Hummingbird Cake

3 cups flour
2 cups sugar
½ teaspoon salt
1 teaspoon baking soda
1 teaspoon ground cinnamon
3 eggs, beaten
¾ cup vegetable oil
1 teaspoon vanilla
1 8-ounce can crushed pineapple with juice
1 cup pecans, chopped
3 medium-sized bananas, mashed
½ cup butter, softened
1 8-ounce package cream cheese, softened
1 pound powdered sugar
⅛ teaspoon vanilla
⅛ teaspoon lemon juice
3 tablespoons chopped pecans

Preheat oven to 350°F. Grease and flour three 9-inch cake pans.

Mix together flour, sugar, salt, baking soda, and cinnamon. Fold in eggs, vegetable oil, vanilla, pineapple with juice, pecans and bananas. Blend well and divide into the prepared cake pans. Bake for 25 minutes. Cool cake thoroughly before frosting.

Fold together butter and cream cheese. Gradually add powdered sugar. Add vanilla and lemon juice and stir well. Apply to top of all three cake layers. Stack layers and garnish with pecans.

Randy Wrennick
Indianapolis

Cran-Nut Mini Bundt Cakes

1 ¼ cups flour
¾ teaspoon baking powder
½ teaspoon baking soda
¼ teaspoon salt
6 tablespoons (¾ stick) butter or margarine at room temperature
¾ cup sugar
1 teaspoon vanilla
2 eggs
⅔ cup sour cream
¼ cup chopped pecans
½ cup dried cranberries, chopped

Preheat oven to 350°F. Coat six 1-cup mini bundt cake molds with nonstick cooking spray. Mix flour, baking powder, baking soda, and salt together. Beat butter, sugar, and vanilla in bowl until fluffy. Beat in eggs, one at a time. Stir in flour mixture alternately with sour cream, just to moisten. Fold in pecans and cranberries. Pour into prepared molds. Bake for 20–25 minutes or until wooden pick inserted comes out clean. Unmold onto wire racks to cool. Dust with powdered sugar. Fill center with cooked cranberries if desired.

Mary Wrennick
Indianapolis

Milky Way Bar Cake

8 ounces Milky Way candy bars, chopped
3 sticks margarine
4 ½ cups sugar
4 eggs
1 ¼ cups buttermilk
2 ½ cups flour
½ teaspoon soda
1 cup pecans
1 cup evaporated milk
½ cup (1 stick) margarine
6 ounces chocolate chips
1 cup marshmallow cream

Preheat oven to 325°F. Grease and flour a 9 x 13-inch pan.

In a saucepan, over medium-low heat, melt the candy and 1 stick of margarine together. Remove from heat and set aside.

Cream 1 stick of margarine with 2 cups of sugar. Add eggs and buttermilk; mix in flour and soda. Stir in melted candy mixture and pecans. Bake for 70 minutes. Let cool 5–10 minutes before icing.

Combine the rest of the sugar and evaporated milk; cook to a soft ball stage. Remove from heat and add 1 stick margarine. Add chocolate chips and marshmallow cream. Stir until melted and thick. Spread on cooled cake.

Thelma Crane
Loogootee

Party Cake

Although this is called Party Cake, Mother used this most often as a brunch coffee cake.

½ cup sugar
1 tablespoon Nestle's Chocolate Quik
1 tablespoon cinnamon
1 cup pecan pieces
1 package yellow cake mix
1 package vanilla instant pudding
1 cup canola oil
4 eggs
1 cup sour cream

Preheat oven to 350°F. Grease and flour a bundt pan. Combine sugar, Quik, cinnamon, and pecans; set aside.

Combine remaining ingredients and beat for 7 minutes. Spoon ⅓ of batter into prepared pan and sprinkle with half the sugar mixture. Add another ⅓ of batter and sprinkle with the rest of the sugar mixture. Spoon in the rest of the batter.

Bake 1 hour and 15 minutes or until done. Let cool; remove from pan. and dust with powdered sugar. The cake is better if it "seasons" for a couple of days; it also freezes well.

Gay Burkhart
Zionsville

Mom's Banana Split Cake

2 cups graham cracker crumbs
3 sticks margarine
2 cups powdered sugar
1 egg or pasteurized egg substitute
pinch of salt
3 bananas, sliced
1 large can crushed pineapple, drained
1 large container whipped dairy topping
⅔ cup nut meats, chopped

Melt 1 stick of margarine; blend with crumbs. Press into a 9 x 13-inch pan. Set aside. Melt the other 2 sticks of margarine. Add powdered sugar and egg. Beat for 15 minutes (until thick and creamy). Add salt. Pour over crust. Arrange banana slices and drained pineapple on top. Spread whipped dairy topping over top. Sprinkle with nuts. Chill overnight if possible.

Michael Atwood
Host of Across Indiana
Executive Producer, WFYI

Lindbergh Cake

CAKE

¼ cup butter or margarine, softened

1 cup sugar

2 eggs, separated

1 ½ teaspoon vanilla, divided use

1 cup flour

1 ½ teaspoons baking powder

¼ teaspoon salt

½ cup milk

½ teaspoon rum extract

½ cup pecans, chopped

FILLING

1 cup whipping cream

2 tablespoons powdered sugar

1 teaspoon vanilla

1 8 ¼ ounce can crushed pineapple, drained

FOR THE CAKE: Preheat oven to 350°F. Generously grease and flour two 8-inch round cake pans.

In a small bowl, with an electric mixer, beat together butter and ½ cup of the sugar; add the egg yolks and ½ teaspoon of the vanilla. Beat until light and fluffy. Stir together the flour, baking powder, and salt. Add to the butter mixture alternately with the milk. Pour into prepared cake pans.

Using clean beaters, make a meringue by beating the egg whites with the remaining 1 teaspoon of vanilla and the rum extract until soft peaks form. Gradually add the remaining ½ cup sugar and continue beating on high speed about 5 minutes, or until stiff peaks form.

Drop small spoonsful of the meringue over the unbaked batter in pans, carefully spreading it to cover the batter. Sprinkle the pecans over the meringue and press very lightly into the surface. Bake 25–30 minutes or until a pick inserted in center comes out clean. Remove from oven and cool cakes in pans for 10 minutes.

Carefully remove the cake from the pans. Set the layers meringue-side up on wire racks and cool thoroughly.

FOR THE FILLING: Combine whipping cream, powdered sugar and vanilla. Beat till soft peaks form. Fold in pineapple. Place one layer, meringue side up, on cake plate. Spread filling over top. Place second layer on top with meringue side up and chill 1–2 hours. Store in refrigerator. Serves 10.

Bettylou Schultz
Muncie

German Chocolate Upside Down Surprise Cake

1   cup flaked coconut
1   cup chopped pecans
1   package German chocolate cake mix
1 ¼ cups water
⅓   cup cooking oil
3   eggs
3 ½ cups (about 1 pound) confectioners sugar
1   cup margarine or butter, melted
1   8-ounce package cream cheese, softened

Preheat oven to 350°F. Grease and flour 9 x 13-inch pan. Sprinkle coconut and pecans evenly over bottom of greased pan. In a large bowl, combine cake mix, water, oil and eggs at low speed until moistened; beat 2 minutes at high speed. Spoon batter evenly over coconut and pecans. In another large bowl, combine confectioners sugar, margarine and cream cheese; beat until smooth and creamy. Spoon evenly over batter to within 1 inch of edges. Bake 45–50 minutes, or until tester inserted in center comes out clean; cool completely. Cut into squares; invert each square onto individual plate. Serve warm or cool; store in refrigerator.

Iris J. Kraft
Indianapolis

Lemon-Kiwi Cheesecake

2 ⅔ cups zwieback crumbs
6   tablespoons sifted powdered sugar
1   teaspoon grated lemon peel
6   tablespoons butter
5   8 ounce packages cream cheese
1 ½ teaspoons grated lemon peel
½   teaspoon vanilla
1 ¾ cups sugar
3   tablespoons flour
5   eggs
2   egg yolks
¼   cup whipping cream

Combine first 4 ingredients. Reserve ¾ cup for topping and pat the rest into 9-inch springform pan.

Preheat oven to 250°F. Mix cheese, lemon peel, and vanilla. Gradually beat in sugar and flour, then eggs and egg yolks. Blend in cream. Spread over crust. Sprinkle reserved crust mixture over top. Bake 1 hour. Turn off oven and let stand in oven for 1 hour. Remove from pan and cool at room temperature. Refrigerate overnight. Top with sliced kiwi.

Carol Lumsden
Indianapolis

Irish Cream Cheesecake

CRUST

2	cups finely ground chocolate wafer cookies
¼	cup granulated sugar
6	tablespoons butter or margarine, melted

FILLING

36	ounces (4 ½ 8-ounce packages) cream cheese, softened
1 ⅔	cups granulated sugar
5	eggs
1 ½	cups Irish Cream liqueur
1	tablespoon vanilla extract
1	cup semisweet chocolate chips

TOPPING

1	cup whipping cream
2	tablespoons granulated sugar
½	cup semisweet chocolate chips, melted
2	cups semisweet chocolate chips

FOR THE CRUST: Preheat oven to 325°F. Grease and flour a 9-inch springform pan. For crust, combine crumbs and sugar in a large bowl. Add butter, stirring until mixture resembles coarse meal. Press into bottom and 1 inch up sides of pan. Bake 7–10 minutes.

FOR THE FILLING: Beat cream cheese until smooth. Add sugar and eggs, beating until fluffy. Add liqueur and vanilla, mixing well. Sprinkle chocolate chips over crust. Spoon filling over chocolate chips. Bake 1 hour, 20 minutes to 1 hour, 30 minutes or until center is set. Cool completely in pan. Use a knife to loosen sides of cheesecake from pan and remove sides.

FOR THE TOPPING: Beat cream and sugar in a large bowl until stiff. Continue to beat while slowly adding chocolate. Spread mixture over cooled cake. Melt chocolate in a small saucepan over low heat and pour onto a baking sheet. Let stand at room temperature until set but not firm. To make curls, pull a cheese plane across surface of chocolate (curls will break if chocolate is too firm). Remelt and cool chocolate as necessary to form desired number of curls. Arrange in spoke-like fashion on cake. Refrigerate until ready to serve. Serves 16.

Fran Sercer
Danville

Log Inn Cheese Cake

1   cup margarine, melted
3   cups graham cracker crumbs
1   cup sugar
1   3-ounce package lemon gelatin
½   cup boiling water
½   cup ice cubes
1   8-ounce package cream cheese, softened
¾   cup sugar
1   teaspoon vanilla
1   can condensed milk

Mix crumbs and sugar together and add to melted margarine and mix well. Reserve ½ cup of the crumbs for topping and firmly press remaining crumbs into the bottom and sides of a 9 x 13-inch pan. Set aside.

Pour gelatin in boiling water and stir until dissolved. Add ice cubes, mix well and place in freezer for 3 minutes or until thickened.

Mix cream cheese, sugar, and vanilla together until smooth. Add chilled gelatin and mix well. Return to freezer for 30 minutes.

Meanwhile, beat condensed milk until stiff. Add cream cheese and gelatin mixture and mix until well blended. Pour mixture into the graham cracker crust; sprinkle reserved crumbs on top and freeze for 2 hours or until set. Serves 8 to 10.

The Log Inn
Warrentown

Built in 1825, the Log Inn is one of the oldest original log inn and stage coach stops in the United States. Located on the Old State Road in the village of Warrenton, halfway between Evansville and Princeton, it is officially recognized as the oldest restaurant in Indiana. Visitors can dine in the same log room that Abraham Lincoln visited in 1844. Modern-day dinners are served à la carte or family style.

Cheesecake with Cookie Crust

1 cup flour, sifted
¼ cup sugar
1 teaspoon lemon grated peel
½ teaspoon almond flavoring
1 egg yolk
¼ cup butter, softened
5 8-ounce packages cream cheese, softened
1 ¾ cups sugar
3 tablespoons flour
2 teaspoons grated lemon peel
¼ teaspoon almond flavoring
5 eggs
2 egg yolks

Preheat oven to 400°F. Grease a 9-inch springform pan; remove sides. In medium bowl, combine first 4 ingredients. Make well in center of mixture; blend in egg yolk and butter. Mix with fingertips until mixture is smooth and holds together. Form dough into a ball and place on the bottom of the springform pan. Roll pastry to edge of pan. Bake until light golden brown, approximately 7–8 minutes. Cool. Reattach sides of pan.

Increase oven temperature to 450°F. In large mixing bowl blend cream cheese, sugar, flour, lemon peel, and almond flavoring at high speed. Beat in eggs and egg yolks, one at a time; beat until smooth, scraping bowl often with rubber spatula. Pour into pan. Bake for 10 minutes. Lower oven temperature to 250°F and bake 1 hour longer. Cool on rack for 2 hours. Refrigerate 3 hours.

Loosen from sides of pan with knife and remove sides of pan. Cover entire top of cheesecake with fresh raspberries or fresh fruit of your choice. Serves 16.

Sara Perry
Indianapolis

Mocha Chocolate Chip Cheesecake

3	tablespoons butter
½	cup walnuts, ground
½	cup fine dry bread crumbs
¼	cup sugar
1	teaspoon cinnamon
½	teaspoon nutmeg
4	8-ounce packages cream cheese, softened
¼	cup sour cream
1	tablespoon vanilla
1	tablespoon coffee powder
1 ½	cups sugar
6	eggs
1 ⅓	cups semisweet chocolate chips

Coat the inside of a 10-inch springform pan with the butter; refrigerate until well chilled.

Mix next 5 ingredients and pat evenly into sides and bottom of pan.

Preheat oven to 350°F. Beat cream cheese and sour cream until fluffy. Add coffee powder dissolved in vanilla. Add sugar. Add eggs one at a time, beating well after each. Fold in chocolate chips. Pour into pan and bake 15 minutes. Lower temperature to 250°F and bake 1 ¼ hours longer. Let cool in oven for 1 hour. Remove and cool to room temperature. Refrigerate 12 hours. To serve, remove the sides from the pan; dip a thin knife in hot water and slice the cheesecake. Serves 12–16.

Tippecanoe Place
South Bend

Tippecanoe Place in South Bend was built in 1886 as the home of Clement Studebaker, of the automotive Studebaker family. The 26,000 square-foot mansion was designed by Henry Cobb and built by local craftsmen. It was completed in 1889 at a total cost of $250,000. Then, as today, Tippecanoe Place was known for its hospitality and as a gracious setting for fine dining. Lunch and dinner are offered daily, and brunch is available on Sundays. The restaurant also offers fine banquet facilities.

*P*ies

Butterscotch Pie

This is my mother's recipe; she often made it for us for Sunday dinner as our family of five children was growing up in the 1930s. It is wonderfully full-flavored. Sometimes she would serve it as a pudding, layered with graham crackers and peach halves. Absolutely wonderful!

4	tablespoons (½ stick) butter
1	cup brown sugar
¼	cup milk
1	heaping tablespoon flour
1	cup milk
2	egg yolks, beaten
½	teaspoon vanilla
1	9-inch baked pie shell
2	egg whites
½	teaspoon vanilla
¼	teaspoon cream of tartar
¼	cup sugar

Melt butter in skillet over medium heat. Add brown sugar and ¼ cup milk; cook, stirring occasionally for 5 minutes.

Thoroughly blend flour and 1 cup of milk. Add the beaten egg yolks and vanilla. Add this mixture to the caramel mixture in the skillet and cook until thick and smooth. Pour into pie shell. Let cool.

Preheat oven to 350°F. Beat egg whites, vanilla, and cream of tartar until soft peaks form. Gradually add sugar and continue beating until stiff and glossy. Spread on cooled pie, sealing to pastry. Bake for 12–15 minutes until brown.

Cathie Marvel
Brown County

Chocolate Mousse Pie

"From the Kitchen of Ethelmae M. Russell, February 21, 1962." Ethelmae and I taught at the same school in the early '60s. She was a marvelous cook as well as a super teacher. This is one recipe I have made sure I didn't lose over the years. Just follow the recipe carefully; and you'll have an impressive and scrumptious dessert.

MERINGUE SHELL

2	egg whites
⅛	teaspoon salt
⅛	teaspoon cream of tartar
½	cup granulated sugar
½	teaspoon each vanilla and almond extract
½	cup chopped walnuts or pecans

FILLING

1	6-ounce package semisweet chocolate pieces
1	egg
2	egg yolks
1	teaspoon rum, or vanilla or rum extract
2	egg whites
1 ¼	cup heavy cream, whipped
½	square semisweet chocolate

FOR THE MERINGUE SHELL: Preheat oven to 275°F. Beat egg whites until frothy; sprinkle salt and cream of tartar over them. Continue beating until stiff, but not dry. Gradually beat in sugar, adding vanilla and almond extracts with last of sugar. Continue beating until sugar is dissolved and mixture is smooth and glossy. Line a well-buttered 9-inch pie plate with this mixture. Hollow center out to ¼-inch thickness; do not spread meringue on rim of plate. Sprinkle with nuts. Bake about 1 hour or until delicately browned and crisp to touch. Let cool.

FOR THE FILLING: With a double boiler, melt chocolate pieces over simmering water. Remove from heat. Beat in egg and egg yolks, one at a time. Add rum or extract. Beat egg whites until they peak when beater is raised; fold into chocolate mixture. Whip 1 cup cream; fold into chocolate mixture. Spoon into shell. Chill. Top with ¼ cup cream, whipped. Shave on chocolate. Serves 8.

Marcella J. Taylor
Indianapolis

Chess Pie (1)

This is the original recipe of my mother, Zylpha Adams' family.

1 9-inch unbaked pie shell
3 eggs, separated
1 tablespoon flour
¼ teaspoon salt
1 ½ cups sugar
1 stick butter, melted
⅔ cup cream
¼ teaspoon salt
1 teaspoon vanilla

Preheat oven to 300°F. Beat egg yolks well, then add flour and salt. Add 1 cup sugar and beat well. Stir in butter and cream and mix well. Pour mixture into pie shell and bake for 45 minutes or until set. When done, a knife inserted near the center will come out clean.

Beat egg whites and salt until peaks are formed. Gradually add ½ cup sugar, beating constantly; add vanilla. Pile the meringue on the pie, and bake until light brown, about 15 minutes.

Paul Adams
Anderson

Chess Pie (2)

About thirty years ago this recipe was in the newspaper, and it has been our family favorite all these years. It is a part of all our holiday meals.

1 9-inch unbaked pie shell
½ cup butter
1 ½ cups sugar
3 eggs, separated
2 tablespoons flour
½ cup buttermilk
½ teaspoon vanilla

Preheat oven to 350°F. Cream butter and sugar. Beat egg yolks until light and add to butter and sugar. Add flour and buttermilk. Stir in vanilla. Fold in stiffly beaten egg whites. Pour into pie shell. Bake for 35–40 minutes, or until set.

Deloris Fox
Indianapolis

Dutch Apple Pie

I have won two first-prize ribbons and one second-place ribbon at the Indiana State Fair, Home and Family Arts Building with this recipe.

CRUST

1 ⅓ cups all-purpose flour
½ teaspoon salt
½ cup shortening (I use butter flavor)
3–4 tablespoons water

TOPPING

¾ cup all-purpose flour
¼ cup light brown sugar, firmly packed
¼ cup sugar
⅓ cup butter or margarine, room temperature

FILLING

6 large apples
1 tablespoon lemon juice
½ cup sugar
¼ cup light brown sugar, firmly packed
3 tablespoons all-purpose flour
¼ teaspoon salt
½ teaspoon cinnamon
¼ teaspoon nutmeg

FOR THE CRUST: Spoon flour into measuring cup and level. Mix flour and salt in medium bowl. Cut in shortening using pastry blender or 2 knives until all flour is blended to form pea-size chunks. Sprinkle with water, one tablespoon at a time. Toss lightly until dough will form a ball. Press between hands to form 5- to 6-inch round. Roll dough into circle about ⅛ inch thick. Trim one inch larger than upside-down pie plate. Loosen dough carefully. Fold into quarters. Unfold and press into pie plate. Fold edge under and flute. Makes one 9-inch single crust.

FOR THE TOPPING: Combine all dry ingredients. Cut in butter or margarine with a pastry blender or fork until crumbly.

FOR THE FILLING: Preheat oven to 375°F. Core, peel, and slice apples into small pieces. Stir lightly with lemon juice (omit lemon juice if apples are very tart). Combine next 6 ingredients and toss with apples until apple pieces are all coated. Place in unbaked pie crust and sprinkle with topping mixture.

Set pie on a baking sheet to catch any drips. Bake until topping is golden brown and filling is bubbling, about 50 minutes. Cool on wire rack.

Lori Konermann
Brownsburg

Gooseberry Pie

Gooseberry was the favorite pie of my father, Jim Worland.

He grew up near Shelbyville, Indiana, and told of picking wild gooseberries so his mother could make pies for her large family. Daddy said that those wild gooseberries themselves had very thorny skins. The thorns softened as they cooked in the pies.

Recently we discovered why these sour green berries have such a strange name. We transplanted a gooseberry bush to our lake lot at Shamrock Lakes. Each June the local geese can't wait for the berries to begin to ripen. They strip the bush of every last berry before we can get our share!

	Dough for double-crust pie
3	cups fresh gooseberries
1 ½	cups sugar
3	tablespoons tapioca
⅛	teaspoon salt
2	tablespoons butter

Roll pie dough out for top and bottom of pie, and put bottom crust in 9-inch pie plate.

Preheat oven to 425°F. Remove stems from gooseberries and rinse in water. Crush ¾ cup gooseberries in a saucepan. Add sugar, tapioca, salt, and remaining gooseberries. Cook and stir over medium heat until filling begins to thicken, about 5 minutes.

Pour filling into pastry-lined pie plate. Dot with butter. Apply the top crust and flute edges. Cut vents in top crust. Bake 45 minutes or until crust is golden.

Gooseberry pie is quite tart and needs a sweet topping such as ice cream or whipped topping. Serve warm or at room temperature. Serves 7–8.

Terry McVicker
Hartford City

Grandmother Berg's Mock Mince Meat

1   peck (8 quarts) green
      tomatoes
1   tablespoon salt
8   cups brown sugar
3   1-pound boxes raisins
6   pounds apples, chopped
1   pound suet, chopped
2   tablespoons each cinnamon,
      nutmeg, cloves and allspice
1   cup cider vinegar

Chop tomatoes and put in large pot. Add salt and 2 cups water. Simmer until tender. Add remaining ingredients and cook about 20 minutes. Use immediately for pie filling or can in sterile jars boiling water bath for 45 minutes for later use. Makes 8 quarts.

Alan Cloe
Indianapolis

Grapefruit Pie

This is a good pie to make when grapefruit is in season. It is refreshing, and you will get many requests for the recipe.

3   grapefruits
1   cup sugar
1 ¼ cups water
2   tablespoons cornstarch
⅛   teaspoon salt
1   3-ounce package strawberry
      or raspberry gelatin
½   cup whipped topping
      (optional)
2   9-inch baked pie shells

Peel, seed, and section grapefruits; reserve any juice that results from process.

Combine sugar, water, reserved grapefruit juice, cornstarch, and salt in a saucepan. Simmer until thick and clear. Add gelatin and stir until dissolved. Chill until it begins to set. Add whipped topping, if desired, and mix well. Stir in grapefruit sections and pour into baked pie shells.

Martha Larson
Indianapolis

Ground Cherry Pie

Ground cherries are not a well-known fruit. A ground cherry is a yellow cherry in the tomato family that grows in a pod. When they're ripe and the pods are dry, they'll fall to the ground. Ground cherries have a taste all their own—not too sweet and not too tart- just a pleasant in-between taste. In the Berne area, the Amish often raise and sell ground cherries. The seeds can be purchased in some seed catalogs.

Pastry for one 8-inch double-crust pie
1   cup sugar
1 ⅓ cups water
3   cups ground cherries, hulled and cleaned
3   tablespoons cornstarch or instant tapioca
2   tablespoons vinegar
½   teaspoon salt
1   tablespoon butter
1   tablespoon cream or milk
1   tablespoon sugar

Preheat oven to 425°F. Combine sugar and 1 cup of the water and cook to a syrupy consistency. Boil 1 minute. Add ground cherries and cook till berries are tender.

Combine cornstarch or tapioca, vinegar, salt, and remaining ⅓ cup water. Add to ground cherry mixture and simmer till thickened; add butter; stir and let cool. Pour filling in pastry-lined pie plate, cover with top crust, brush top with cream or milk and sprinkle with sugar. Bake 10 minutes, then lower oven to 375°F and bake until crust is golden and filling is bubbly, about 30 minutes. (Note: If ground cherries are very pale in color, yellow food coloring may be added in the thickening to give a more appetizing appearance. If filling seems too thin before putting in the shell, add a little instant tapioca.)

Berneta Lehman
Berne

Guilt-Free Cream Pie

This is Jane Chapman's recipe. She is an excellent all-around cook, specializing recently in low-fat, low-sugar recipes. I testify this pie is delicious!

2   cups 1 percent milk
3   tablespoons cornstarch
⅓   cup sugar
⅛   teaspoon salt
1   teaspoon vanilla
1   8-inch pastry shell or graham cracker crust

Scald 1 ½ cups of the milk; remove from heat and let cool slightly. Combine cornstarch, sugar, and salt. Blend dry ingredients with remaining ½ cup milk until smooth. Add blended mixture and vanilla to scalded milk. Cover and cook in top of double boiler for 15–20 minutes, until it coats a spoon. Pour into baked pastry shell or graham cracker crust. Top with fresh fruit or whipped cream.

To prepare in microwave: Scald milk in microwave (it does not scorch this way). Cook mixture in microwave-proof large measuring cup or container on high for 2 minutes. Stir. Cook 1 additional minute, until it coats a spoon.

Variations:

1. Top with meringue for less fat. Bake in hot oven until meringue browns.
2. Sprinkle finished pie with coconut for taste and texture.
3. Add 3 tablespoons powdered cocoa to dry mixture for chocolate flavor with no added fat.
4. Serve in dishes without any pastry for pudding dessert.
5. Enrich original recipe with 1 tablespoon butter and 1 egg before blending mixture into scalded milk.

Marcella J. Taylor
Indianapolis

Indiana Sugar Cream Pie

My grandmother, Mary Emma Green Champer, frequently made these pies using the old method, measuring only by sight and feel. Her pies always came out exactly the same and were delicious! This was a good "winter" pie for farmers wives to make when their canned or stored fruit was gone or in short supply and there was extra cream on hand.

1	cup sugar
½	cup flour
¼	teaspoon salt
2	cups whipping cream
1	teaspoon vanilla
½	teaspoon ground cinnamon
1	unbaked 9-inch pastry shell

Preheat oven to 350°F. In a bowl, mix the sugar, flour, salt, cream, and vanilla and let stand for about 20 minutes. Pour mixture into unbaked pie shell; sprinkle with ground cinnamon and bake 50–60 minutes or until filling is set.

Donna Almon
Indianapolis

Mother's Pumpkin Pie

1	15-ounce can pumpkin
¾	cup firmly packed brown sugar
¾	teaspoon cinnamon
½	teaspoon salt
½	teaspoon mace
½	teaspoon ginger
1	tablespoon dark corn syrup
2	eggs, beaten
1	8-inch unbaked pie shell

Preheat oven to 450°F. Mix all ingredients together. Pour filling into pie shell and bake for 30 minutes. Reduce oven heat to 350°F and bake another 30 minutes.

Wayne Johnson
Indianapolis

Oatmeal Pie

½	stick margarine
¾	cup white sugar
¾	cup dark corn syrup
¾	cup quick oats
½	cup coconut
2	eggs well-beaten
¼	teaspoon salt (optional)
1	9-inch unbaked pie shell

Preheat oven to 350°F. Melt margarine; add sugar, syrup, oatmeal, coconut, eggs, and salt, if used. Mix thoroughly. Pour into pie shell. Bake for 45–50 minutes or until brown.

In memory of Mildred Kirkpatrick
Cutler

Orange Cream Pie

1	baked 9-inch pie shell, cooled
½	cup white sugar
4	tablespoons cornstarch
⅛	teaspoon salt
1	cup milk
1	cup orange juice, unstrained
3	eggs, separated
1	tablespoon orange rind, grated
1	teaspoon butter
¼	teaspoon cream of tartar
6	tablespoons sugar

In a saucepan, mix together sugar, cornstarch and salt. Slowly stir in milk and orange juice. Cook until thick, stirring constantly. Slowly beat a little of the mixture in beaten egg yolks. Add to mixture in pan. Stir in orange rind and butter. Pour in pie shell. Cool.

Preheat oven to 400°F. Beat egg whites until frothy. Add cream of tartar and continue beating until they hold stiff peaks. Gradually add sugar and beat till stiff, but glossy. Spread on pie filling, being sure to seal to edge of crust. Bake until lightly browned, about 10–15 minutes.

Bertha Allen
Indianapolis

Shoofly Pie

2　　cups flour
1 ½　cups brown sugar
¼　　teaspoon salt
4　　tablespoons margarine
2　　eggs, beaten
2　　cups molasses
1 ½　cups hot water (not boiling)
2　　teaspoons soda
2　　unbaked pie shells

Mix flour, sugar, salt and margarine together until crumbly. Reserve 2 cups of the mixture for topping.

Preheat oven to 450°F. To the remaining crumb mixture add eggs, molasses, and 1 cup hot water. Mix well. Add soda to ½ cup hot water and add to mixture. Pour the mixture into pie shells and top with reserved crumbs. Bake for 10 minutes. Reduce heat to 375°F and bake an additional 30 minutes or until tops of pies are dry.

(Note: Instead of molasses you can use a combination of 1 ½ cups dark corn syrup, ½ cup light corn syrup, 2 teaspoons vanilla, and ¼ teaspoon maple flavoring.)

Das Dutchman Essenhaus
Amish Country Kitchen
Middlebury

Das Dutchman Essenhaus is in the heart of northern Indiana's Amish country on U.S. 20 in Middlebury. Established in 1971 in a renovated truck stop, it includes a bakery, country inn, shops, and a wholesale food business along with the restaurant.

Staffed by Amish and Mennonite cooks and waitstaff, servings are generous, delicious, and heartwarming. As a testament to satisfied diners, in a busy week, the bakery and restaurant have been known to go through six tons of potatoes, thirty-eight hundred chickens, and fifty-one hundred pounds of roast beef. The record for pies produced is 1,520 in one day.

Peanut-Butterscotch Pie

This is my family and friend's favorite recipe. Sometimes I substitute chocolate pudding in the pie as filling.

2	cups brown sugar
8	tablespoons flour
2	cups milk
4	eggs, separated
1	stick margarine
1	teaspoon vanilla
¼	cup peanut butter
½	cup powdered sugar
1	graham cracker pie crust
½	cup sugar

Make a custard by mixing brown sugar and flour in a medium-size sauce pan and slowly adding milk. Cook over medium heat till thick. Beat egg yolks slightly and slowly stir into mixture. Cook 3 more minutes, stirring constantly.

Remove from heat and add margarine and vanilla. Pour into a bowl and cover with plastic wrap. Let cool to room temperature, then chill.

Preheat oven to 400°F. Mix peanut butter and powdered sugar with a fork. Spread evenly into the pie shell. Pour custard mixture on top.

Beat egg whites and gradually add the ½ cup sugar. Beat until stiff peaks form. Pile on pie, sealing meringue to edge of pastry. Bake until meringue is golden brown, about 15–20 minutes. Let cool to room temperature, then chill.

Virginia Overbay
Straughn

Rhubarb Cream Pie

1 ½	cups sugar
2	eggs, beaten
5	tablespoons water
1	tablespoon flour
1	teaspoon salt
2	cups rhubarb, chopped
2	tablespoons butter
1	teaspoon cinnamon
1	unbaked pie shell

Preheat oven to 350°F. Mix together the sugar, eggs, water, flour, salt, and rhubarb. Pour into unbaked pie shell. Dot with butter and sprinkle with cinnamon. Bake for 1 hour.

Jean Ann McKinnis
Otterbein

Pumpkin Pie

My mother, Clara Mae Getting Rhende, was born in 1890. She used this recipe and I took it with me to bake pies for my classmates when I was in nurses training in the U.S. Cadet Nurse Corps at St. Elizabeth Hospital in Lafayette, Indiana, from 1944–1947. My son, Robert, uses the recipe too.

1	15-ounce can pumpkin
1 ½	cups milk
1	egg, beaten
1 ¼	cups brown sugar
3	tablespoons granulated sugar
2	tablespoons flour
½	teaspoon salt
½	teaspoon baking soda
1	teaspoon cinnamon
¼	teaspoon ground cloves
¼	teaspoon ginger
½	teaspoon nutmeg
¼	teaspoon allspice
1	9-inch unbaked pie shell

Preheat oven to 450°F. Combine pumpkin and milk, mixing well; stir in beaten egg and brown sugar. Sift dry ingredients and spices together and add to pumpkin mixture. Mix well and pour into pie shell. Bake for 15 minutes; reduce heat to 350°F and continue to bake for 35 minutes or until bubbles begin to appear in center. Remove from oven and cool.

Ruth Brown
Marion

Raisin Pie

I have made raisin pie for over fifty-five years.

Pastry for 9-inch double-crust pie
2 ½ cups raisins
1 ½ cups sugar
2 tablespoons corn starch
   rind of 1 lemon, grated
2 tablespoons lemon juice
2 tablespoons butter

Preheat oven to 350°F.

Roll out half the pastry dough and line a 9-inch pie pan. Roll out other half for top crust and set aside.

Put raisins in a small pan with just enough water to cover and simmer until tender. Drain, reserving half of the liquid. Mix reserved liquid, sugar, cornstarch, lemon rind, and lemon juice in a small mixing bowl.

Spoon raisins into the lined pie pan and pour the liquid evenly over the top. Dot with butter and lay top crust over filling. Cut a design in the top crust for venting and crimp or flute the edges. Bake for about 45 minutes or until the crust is a golden brown. Can be served hot or cold. Serves 6–8.

Joy Gore
Stilesville

Lemon Pie

This recipe has been our family and friends favorite since 1934.

1 8-inch baked pastry shell
1 ¼ cups sugar
¼ cup flour or cornstarch
1 cup boiling water
2 eggs, separated
1 tablespoon butter, melted
⅓ cup lemon juice
1 tablespoon lemon rind

Mix 1 cup sugar and flour or cornstarch in a saucepan. Add boiling water slowly and simmer, stirring constantly, until mixture is clear. Beat egg yolks lightly and gradually add butter and yolks to mixture. Cook on low heat (do not boil), stirring constantly, until mixture thickens. Add lemon juice and rind. Let mixture cool and pour in baked pastry shell.

Preheat oven to 300°F. Beat egg whites until stiff; gradually add 4 tablespoons of sugar. Beat until stiff but still glossy. Spread on lemon filling, being sure to seal to edge of crust. Bake for 15 minutes or until a delicate brown.

Anne Carpenter Prosser
Madison

Sugar Cream Pie

In the 1920s my mother, Lizzie Pearl Boswell, rose early two or three times a week to bake pies, and would make these cream pies with the leftover dough. The ingredients were always available, and they also baked better in the cooler oven at the end of the pie-baking period. The pies would be out of the oven just before my brothers and sister and I left for school, so we'd usually have a piece in our lunch boxes. Their fragrance was irresistible, and inevitably someone would ask to exchange their lunch for a piece.

2   cups heavy cream
2   tablespoons butter
1 ½   cups sugar
4   tablespoons flour
1   9-inch unbaked pie shell
     Nutmeg

Preheat oven to 375°F. Combine the cream and butter. Scald this mixture. In a separate bowl mix thoroughly the sugar and flour. Slowly pour the scalded mixture into the sugar and flour and mix carefully. When the sugar is thoroughly dissolved, pour into a pie shell and sprinkle generously with nutmeg. Bake for 40 minutes or until mixture bubbles in the middle. It will thicken as it cools.

Emily Boswell Shambarger
Mexico, Indiana

Rosie's Delicious Ice Cream Pie

A delicious low-fat and low-sugar dessert!

1   quart low-fat butter pecan, caramel, or praline ice cream
8   ounces low-fat cool whipped topping
⅓   cup grape nuts cereal
⅓   cup low-fat peanut butter
1   package sugar-free instant butterscotch pudding, uncooked
1   low-fat graham cracker crust

Let ice cream soften. Mix ice cream with cool whipped topping. Mix in grape nuts, peanut butter, and pudding mix. Pour into the graham cracker crust. Freeze. Before serving, let pie thaw for about 30 minutes.

Rosie Clifton
Indianapolis

Peanut Butter Pie

3 ½ cups Oreo cookie crumbs
10 tablespoons melted butter
2 8-ounce packages of cream cheese
2 cups peanut butter
1 ½ cups sugar
3 ½ cups whipping cream
6 ounces semisweet chocolate chips

Preheat oven to 350°F. Blend crumbs and butter. Press into 2 pie pans. Bake for 10 minutes. Let cool.

Beat cream cheese and peanut butter together until smooth. Add sugar. In a separate bowl, whip 3 cups cream until it forms stiff soft peaks. Add peanut butter mixture gradually. Pour into cooled crusts and refrigerate for 30 minutes.

Combine ½ cup cream and chocolate chips in sauce pan. Heat on medium heat just until mixture boils. Immediately remove from heat and pour over cooled pies in a thin layer. Refrigerate until ready to serve. Makes 2 pies.

Olde Richmond Inn
Richmond

Formerly the home of the Ferdinand Grothaus family, the Olde Richmond Inn was built in 1892. The house was an example of the fine craftsmanship of the "South-end Dutch" carpenters and masons who lived in the neighborhood at the time. The restaurant opened in 1984 and is dedicated to providing customers with fine food in a gracious and professional manner. Chefs at Olde Richmond Inn use classic cooking techniques to provide a unique and elegant dining experience.

Cookies, Puddings & Other Goodies

Amish Whoopie Pies

This is a standard dessert for Amish to take to church dinners, funeral dinners, or any large gathering.

2	cups white sugar
1	cup shortening
3 ½	cups flour
½	cup cocoa
2	teaspoons soda
2	eggs
2	teaspoons vanilla
1	cup buttermilk
1	cup hot water
1	teaspoon salt
2	egg whites
2	teaspoons vanilla
4	tablespoons flour
4	tablespoons milk
1½	cups solid white shortening
2	cups powdered sugar

Preheat oven to 400°F. Cream sugar and shortening until fluffy. Add next 8 ingredients and mix well.

Drop mixture by teaspoonfuls on ungreased cookie sheet. Bake 8 minutes. Let cool completely.

Beat egg whites until stiff peaks form. Combine remaining ingredients and stir until smooth. Fold in egg whites. Spread a bit of the mixture on the bottom of one cookie and place another cookie on that, sandwich-style. Repeat with the rest of the cookies.

Susie Warner
Goshen

Mom's Sour Raisin Jumbles

2 tablespoons sugar
1 teaspoon cinnamon
½ cup butter, softened
1 cup granulated sugar
1 teaspoon vanilla
2 eggs
½ cup sour cream
1 cup seedless raisins
2 cups sifted flour
½ teaspoons baking soda
1 ½ teaspoons salt
¼ teaspoon nutmeg

Preheat oven to 375°F. Combine sugar and cinnamon; set aside. Beat together the butter, sugar, vanilla, and eggs. Stir in the sour cream and raisins. Sift the flour, baking soda, salt, and nutmeg together and add to batter.

Drop the dough onto ungreased baking sheets by spoonfuls and sprinkle with the sugar and cinnamon mixture. Bake for 10–15 minutes or until the edges are lightly browned and the top of the cookie springs back when touched lightly. Makes 2 ½ dozen cookies.

Geneva Parker
Indianapolis

Candied Fruit Bars

These are better than fruitcake.

2 eggs
1 cup brown sugar
2 teaspoons vanilla
1 cup flour
1 teaspoon baking powder
½ teaspoon salt
⅔ cup nuts
½ cup raisins or dates, chopped
1 cup candied fruit of your choice
Powdered sugar

Preheat oven to 350°F. Beat eggs and brown sugar, add vanilla. Sift flour, baking powder and salt together and add to egg mixture. Stir in nuts, raisins or dates, and candied fruit. Pour into greased 9 x 13-inch pan and bake for 30 minutes. Remove from oven and sprinkle with powdered sugar. Let cool and cut into 1 x 3-inch bars. Makes two dozen.

Bettylou Schultz
Muncie

Breezy Brownies

BROWNIES

1	cup sugar
½	cup margarine or butter, softened
4	eggs
⅛	teaspoon salt
1	16-ounce can chocolate syrup
1	cup plus 1 tablespoon flour

ICING

1 ½	cups sugar
6	tablespoons margarine or butter
6	tablespoons milk
½	cup semisweet chocolate chips
1	cup pecan pieces

FOR THE BROWNIES: Preheat oven to 350°F. Cream together sugar and margarine or butter. Add eggs one at a time and then add salt. Beat well. Blend in chocolate syrup and flour. Pour into greased and floured 10 ½ x 15 ½-inch baking pan. Bake 22 minutes, or until done when toothpick comes out clean.

FOR THE ICING: Boil together the sugar, margarine or butter, and milk. When mixture comes to a boil, cook and stir for one minute. Add chocolate chips and beat well until melted. Add nuts and beat to spreading consistency. Spread over warm brownies in pan. Allow to cool; then cut into bars.

Sally Ouweneel
Indianapolis

Caramel Nut Cookies

A favorite at Christmas, these are so rich—like eating candy.

15	graham crackers
2	sticks butter or margarine
1	cup brown sugar, firmly packed.
1	cup cashews or pecans, chopped

Preheat oven to 325°F. Line a 10 x 14-inch jellyroll pan with graham crackers. In medium size pan melt butter. Add brown sugar and bring to a rolling boil for only one minute. Add nuts to melted mixture and spoon evenly over graham crackers. Bake for 10 minutes. Remove and let cool for 10 minutes. When cooled, cut into squares.

Beverly Reynolds
Brownsburg

Chewy Coconut Squares

CRUST
½   cup butter
½   cup brown sugar
1   cup flour

FILLING
1   cup brown sugar
¼   cup flour
¼   teaspoon salt
1   teaspoon vanilla
2   eggs
1   cup coconut
1   cup nuts, chopped

FOR THE CRUST: Preheat oven to 375°F. Cream butter and brown sugar for 5 minutes. Stir in flour and pat into greased 8 x 8-inch pan. Bake for 10 minutes. Remove.

FOR THE FILLING: Combine brown sugar, flour and salt; add vanilla and eggs; mix well. Stir in coconut and nuts. Spread over crust and bake for 20 minutes.

Betty Schultz
Muncie

Chrissy's Special Cookies

2   cups butter
2   cups sugar
2   cups brown sugar
4   eggs
2   teaspoons vanilla
5   cups oatmeal
4   cups flour
1   teaspoon salt
2   teaspoons baking powder
2   teaspoons soda
24   ounces chocolate chips
1   8-ounce chocolate bar, grated
3   cups chopped nuts

Preheat oven to 375°F. Cream butter and both sugars. Add eggs and vanilla. Put oatmeal in container of food processor and process until it is flour-like. Combine oatmeal, flour, salt, baking powder, and soda. Add chocolate chips, chocolate bar and nuts. Roll into balls and place two inches apart on an ungreased cookie sheet. Bake for 10 minutes. Makes about 9 dozen cookies.

In memory of Warren M. Schnaiter
Martinsville

Coconut Macaroons

My late aunt, Mabel Ann Oldham, of Evansville, wrote to our family newsletter in 1983 describing a trip to Kashmir that she had once made and included in her account this recipe for coconut macaroons. She prefaced the recipe with these comments: ". . . Our host unpacked the hamper, brewed our tea, and served the most delicious Coconut Macaroons I've ever eaten . . . we sat on the Oriental rugs, munching macaroons and sipping tea, while feasting our eyes on the ever-present white fleecy clouds floating by the snow-capped mountain peaks etched against the bluest of skies . . ."

2	egg whites
3	tablespoons sugar
2	tablespoons flour
6	tablespoons coconut, grated
1	ounce butter, softened

Preheat oven to 300°F. Whip egg whites with a wire whisk until soft peaks form; gradually add sugar and flour and continue beating until stiff. Stir in coconut and butter. Dab onto an ungreased cookie sheet. Bake in center of oven for 25 minutes. Makes 1 dozen.

Cathie Marvel
Brown County

German Brown Sugar Cookies *(Braun Zucker Plätchen)*

1 ½	cups brown sugar, firmly packed
⅔	cup shortening
2	large eggs
2	tablespoons milk
1	tablespoon grated orange rind
1	teaspoon baking soda
1	teaspoon cinnamon
2	cups flour
1	cup raisins
½	cup slivered almonds

Preheat oven to 350°F. Cream sugar and shortening until light and fluffy. Beat in eggs, milk, and grated orange rind. Sift together baking soda, cinnamon, and flour. Mix flour mixture into sugar mixture. Stir in raisins and nuts. Drop dough by large teaspoonfuls onto greased cookie sheets. Bake for 9 minutes until done. Remove from oven; cool one minute on cookie sheet before removing cookies to a rack to further cool. Store in tight tins.

Elaine McVay
Zionsville

Dream Bars

These are wonderful cookie treats my mom had waiting for me when I came home from school. Now my three-year-old daughter helps me bake "Grandma's cookies," so we add another generation of little ones to the list of fans.

CRUST

½   cup butter
1   cup flour
2   tablespoons sugar

FILLING

2   eggs, well beaten
½   cup brown sugar
¼   teaspoon salt
⅛   teaspoon baking powder
½   teaspoon vanilla
¾   cup coconut
½   cup finely chopped nuts

FROSTING

1   cup confectioners sugar
2   tablespoons milk
2   tablespoons butter, softened
1   square dark chocolate, melted
1   teaspoon vanilla

FOR THE CRUST: Preheat oven to 350°F. Combine butter, flour, and 2 tablespoons sugar and mix with fingers until well-blended. Press in small cake or pie pan. Bake for 20 minutes.

FOR THE FILLING: Mix eggs and brown sugar together and add salt, baking powder, and vanilla. Stir in coconut and nuts. Pour over crust and bake at 350°F for 30 minutes. Let cool.

FOR THE FROSTING: Mix remaining ingredients together, adding a bit more milk if needed. Spread over baked and cooled cookie; cut into bars.

Hilary Bruce
Indianapolis

Famous Sugar Cookies

1 cup shortening
1 cup sugar
2 large eggs
1 teaspoon vanilla extract
2 ½ cups all-purpose flour
½ teaspoon baking powder
¾ teaspoon salt
½ teaspoon baking soda
1 16-ounce can vanilla
frosting

Preheat oven to 350°F. Cream shortening and sugar. Beat in eggs and vanilla. Gradually blend in dry ingredients. Wrap in plastic wrap and chill at least 3 hours or overnight. (Dough keeps up to 2 days.)

On a lightly floured surface roll dough to ⅛-inch to ¼-inch thickness. Cut with cookie cutters. Bake for about 8 minutes. Do not let the cookies get brown. When cookies cool, frost and decorate as desired. Makes 20 cookies.

Kathy Patterson
Carmel

Icebox Cookies

My grandmother, Blanche Reed, never drove up from southern Indiana to visit us without bringing baked goods. This is one of her recipes. She loved her family and always fed us well. When she died, I inherited her chicken-frying pan. It is one of my most cherished possessions.

1 cup butter or lard
1 cup white sugar
1 cup brown sugar
3 eggs, beaten
1 teaspoon vanilla
1 cup nuts, chopped
4 cups flour
1 heaping teaspoon soda
1 tablespoon cinnamon
½ teaspoon salt

Lightly grease cookie sheet. Cream butter, then add brown and white sugars, beaten egg, vanilla and nuts. Sift flour, soda, cinnamon and salt together and add to sugar mixture. Mix and form into a firm roll. Refrigerate until well chilled.

Preheat oven to 375°F. Slice roll of dough into thin rounds and bake for 8–10 minutes.

Julie Reed
Indianapolis

Girl Scout Ice Box Cookies

These are great for dunking. They keep well when put in airtight containers. We took these when we went camping in the early fifties.

1	cup butter or margarine
1	teaspoon salt
1	teaspoon vanilla
1	cup brown sugar
1	cup white sugar
2	eggs
1 ½	cups flour, sifted
1	teaspoon soda
3	cups rolled oats
½	cup nuts, chopped

Preheat oven to 350°F. Blend butter, salt, and vanilla; cream in sugars gradually. Add eggs, one at a time; beat well. Sift flour and soda together. Add flour, rolled oats, and nuts. Shape into 2 rolls; wrap in waxed paper and chill. Slice ¼ inch thick; place on ungreased cookie sheet. Bake for 10 minutes.

Mary Anne Weiss
West Lafayette

Crunch & Raisin Cookies

These are excellent! A good chewy cookie!

1 ¾	cups unsifted all-purpose flour
1	teaspoon baking soda
¼	teaspoon salt
½	cup butter or margarine at room temperature
½	cup creamy or chunky peanut butter
1	cup granulated sugar
1	cup light brown sugar, firmly packed
1	teaspoon vanilla
2	eggs
¼	cup milk
2 ½	cups granola
1	cup raisins or dried cranberries

Preheat the oven to 350°F. Lightly grease cookie sheets. Combine flour, baking soda and salt; stir to mix well. Beat together butter, peanut butter, granulated and brown sugars and vanilla in large bowl until light and fluffy. Beat in eggs and milk until smooth. Stir in flour mixture until well blended. Gently mix in granola and raisins or dried cranberries. Drop batter by rounded teaspoonfuls 2 inches apart on prepared cookie sheets. Bake for 12–15 minutes or until lightly browned. Remove to wire racks or paper to cool. Makes 7 dozen.

Rosina M. Reese
Morgantown

Raisin Oatmeal Cookies

This recipe became a family favorite sometime between 1948 and 1956. During that time, I was a member of IPS School 70 Brownie and Girl Scout troops. We took orders for homemade oatmeal cookies, and then made the cookies and delivered them.

1	cup raisins, simmered with 5 tablespoons water
¾	cup shortening
1	cup sugar
2	eggs
1	teaspoon salt
1	teaspoon soda
1	teaspoon cinnamon
2	cups flour
2	cups oatmeal
½	cup pecans, chopped (optional)

Preheat oven to 375°F. Simmer raisins with water in covered pan for 5 minutes. Set aside to cool. Cream shortening and sugar. Add eggs, then dry ingredients, except for oatmeal. Add oatmeal and raisins and liquid from raisins. Stir in pecans. Drop by teaspoonfuls onto lightly greased cookie sheet. Bake for 7 minutes or until lightly browned.

Claudia Clark
Whitestown

Toll House Oatmeal Cookies

¾	cup granulated sugar
¾	cup brown sugar
1	cup solid white shortening
2	eggs
1	teaspoon vanilla
1 ½	cup flour
1	teaspoon baking soda
1	teaspoon salt
2	cups quick oatmeal
1	cup finely chopped nut meats
1	12-ounce package chocolate chips

Preheat oven to 375°F. Grease baking sheets. In a large mixing bowl, cream sugars and shortening; add the eggs and mix well. Add vanilla.

Sift together the flour, baking soda, and salt. Add to creamed mixture and mix well. Stir in the oatmeal, nuts, and chocolate chips. Drop by teaspoonfuls on the prepared baking sheets.

Bake for 10–12 minutes (do not overbake). Makes about 100 cookies.

J. Robert Cook
Producer/Director
WFYI

Mint Stick Brownies

BROWNIES

2 squares semisweet baking chocolate

½ cup butter

2 eggs, well beaten

1 cup sugar

¼ teaspoon peppermint flavoring

½ cup flour, sifted

⅛ teaspoon salt

½ cup pecans, chopped

MINT FROSTING

2 tablespoons soft butter

1 cup powdered sugar, sifted

1 tablespoon heavy cream

½ teaspoon peppermint flavoring
Green food coloring (optional)

GLAZE

1 square semisweet baking chocolate

1 tablespoon butter

FOR THE BROWNIES: Preheat oven to 350°F. Melt chocolate and butter together over hot water. Cool. Add remaining ingredients. Blend. Pour batter into a well-greased 9-inch square pan. Bake for 20–25 minutes. Cool. Top with the mint frosting and glaze.

FOR THE FROSTING: Mix frosting ingredients together until creamy and spread on cooled brownies. Add a few drops of green food coloring if desired. Refrigerate while making glaze.

FOR THE GLAZE: Combine chocolate and butter and melt over hot water. Blend well. Dribble glaze over mint frosting. Carefully tilt pan back and forth to cover surface. Refrigerate to set chocolate glaze. Cut into fingerlike sticks. Yields 4 dozen brownies.

Kathy Patterson
Carmel

Peanut Butter Cookies

This recipe is good using smooth or chunky peanut butter. It was my first year 4-H project in Foods. What a treat for a ten-year-old to see these make it all the way to the State Fair! They still take first place with my husband today!

½	cup shortening
½	cup butter
1	cup granulated sugar
1	cup brown sugar
3	eggs, beaten
1	cup peanut butter
3	cups flour
1	teaspoon soda
⅓	teaspoon salt
1	teaspoon vanilla

Preheat oven to 350°F. Cream together shortening and butter. Add sugars and beat until light and fluffy. Blend in eggs. Add peanut butter and mix well. Sift together dry ingredients and gradually mix in with peanut butter mixture. Mix in vanilla extract. Drop by teaspoonfuls two inches apart onto ungreased baking sheet. Flatten slightly with a fork, making tine marks both vertically and horizontally. Bake for 12–15 minutes. Makes approximately 2 dozen cookies.

Rita Bulington
Lafayette

Ginger Snaps

This is a recipe I've used for over forty years.

¾	cup shortening
1 ½	cups sugar
1	egg
¼	cup molasses
2	cups flour
1	tablespoon ginger
2	teaspoons soda
1	teaspoon cinnamon
½	teaspoon salt

Preheat oven to 350°F. Cream shortening and 1 cup sugar; add egg and molasses and mix well. Combine dry ingredients and add to creamed mixture. Form into 1-inch balls and roll in remaining granulated sugar. Place 1 inch apart on cookie sheet and bake 12–15 minutes. Makes about 3 dozen cookies.

Edith Tucker
Terre Haute

Peanut Butter Sticks

2 loaves very thin bread
1 12-ounce jar peanut butter
1 teaspoon sugar
¾ cup vegetable oil

Preheat oven to 250°F. Remove crusts from bread and cut each slice of bread into thirds. Put bread and crusts on a cookie sheet in a single layer; toast in the oven for 45 minutes. Remove from oven. When cool, roll crusts to make crumbs.

Combine peanut butter, oil, and sugar in top of double boiler and mix well. When mixture is hot and well blended, dip each bread stick in peanut butter mixture until completely covered. Roll lightly in crumbs. Place on waxed paper to cool. Store in the freezer in an airtight container. Serve directly from freezer.

Jane Bengsten
Monticello

Rice Krispie Scotcheroos

This recipe was originally on the cereal boxes about 50 years ago.

1 cup sugar
1 cup white corn syrup
1 cup peanut butter
5 cups Rice Krispies
1 cup chocolate chips
1 cup butterscotch chips

Combine sugar and corn syrup in a large kettle and bring to a boil. Remove from heat as soon as it comes to a rolling boil. Add the peanut butter and mix well, then add the Rice Krispies and stir it until well blended. Spoon into a greased 9 x 13-inch pan and smooth out evenly.

Pour the chocolate and butterscotch chips into a microwave safe bowl and microwave on high for about 1 ½ minutes or until melted. Blend well and spread over Krispie mixture as "icing." Do not refrigerate!

Ruth Lewman
Indianapolis

Capers in Copper

Unfortunately, I don't make anything that anybody really needs—I'm making a living by just making it up as I go along and convincing people they should go along with me.

I tell folks that if you need something to keep food in, you can get Tupperware. If you need something to serve food with, you can use a paper plate. But I guess people do still appreciate the human touch.

My name is Michael Bonne, and I'm a coppersmith in Knightstown.

I love copper. It's soft, so you can move it around and shape it any way you want to. It's my favorite metal because it's so warm. When you see a copper pan, you instantly think of hearth and home, and it gives you a warm, fuzzy feeling. You don't get that with aluminum or stainless steel. When I think of aluminum, I think of a beer can in a ditch by the side of the road.

My wife and I love antiques, and we started our copper business based on old things and old ways. We bought some antique machinery that was used to make copper goods a hundred and fifty years ago. We bought antique cups and plates and cookie cutters and dissected them and tried to discern how they were made in the old days. There was no school at that time where you could go to learn traditional metal smithing.

We sell copper cups that are just like the old coffee cups that granddad drank out of years ago. We do baking pans in various sizes and shapes; they're made just like they were a hundred years ago. People then had decorative pans—not just square or round ones. But probably our most popular items are cookie cutters. During one month, we produced about a ton of cookie cutters a week, which just blows my mind. I can't even picture a ton of cookie cutters. I can't picture how many cookies you could make with a ton of cutters.

We don't have giant machines that press out a thousand cutters an hour. We have specialists. After they've worked here for a few weeks, our craftspeople generally gravitate into a particular job classification they like. I'm still the master craftsman. I make all the designs and do the design work and prototypes. I get to do the fun stuff! Then we all work as a team. There's no way I could do this without my teammates helping me.

We've been fortunate to have some really neat contracts with some neat companies that love cookie cutters. And we love to make them, so it's quite a match. For Martha Stewart, we made a series of oversized cookie cutters of various shapes and sizes. And the whole process took place in a Knightstown shop that has a crew of sixteen.

The really neat thing about copper is that it lasts. They've dug up burial mounds and ancient cities, and the copper is virtually unchanged. Copper is something that doesn't go away very easily. Who knows? My copper creations might be around for ten generations.

Pumpkin Cookies

1	cup sugar
1	cup shortening
1	cup pumpkin
1	teaspoon vanilla
1	egg
2	cups flour
1	teaspoon baking soda
1	teaspoon baking powder
1	teaspoon cinnamon
½	teaspoon ginger
3	tablespoons butter
¾	tablespoon vanilla
4	tablespoons milk
½	cup brown sugar
1	cup powdered sugar, sifted

Preheat oven to 350°F. Cream sugar and shortening; add pumpkin, vanilla, and egg. Add flour, baking soda, baking powder, cinnamon, and ginger, and stir well. Drop by teaspoonfuls onto ungreased cookie sheets. Bake for 10-12 minutes.

Combine butter, vanilla, milk and brown sugar in a saucepan. Stirring constantly, bring just to a rolling boil. Remove from heat. Let cool and stir in powdered sugar. Frost cookies while still warm. Return icing mixture to heat if mixture becomes too thick. Yield 3-4 dozen cookies.

Charlie and June Williams
Fashion Farm Restaurant
Ligonier

Chocolate Tower

1	9 x 13-inch pan of brownies, baked and broken into pieces
2	packages instant chocolate mousse, prepared
6	large chocolate-covered toffee bars, crushed
1	16-ounce container whipped topping
3	tablespoons shaved chocolate

In a trifle bowl, layer ½ of each ingredient: the brownies, chocolate mousse, toffee bars, and whipped topping. Repeat layering. End with whipped topping. Garnish with shaved chocolate.

Carol and Michael Lumsden
Indianapolis

Swedish Spritz Cookies

A traditional cookie I make every Christmas, served at the Christmas Eve dinner with the Swedish Fruit Soup, or Fruktsoppa (see page 234).

1	cup butter
¾	cup sugar
1	egg
1	teaspoon almond extract
2 ½	cups sifted all purpose flour
½	teaspoon double-action baking powder
⅛	teaspoon salt

Preheat oven to 400°F. Cream butter; add sugar and cream well. Beat in egg and extract. Sift together flour, baking powder and salt. Add to first mixture and mix well by hand. Force dough through cookie press onto ungreased cookie sheets, in an "O" shape, using disk with small star opening. Bake 10-12 minutes, until brown on the bottom, but not too brown on top. Makes about 2 dozen large cookies.

Martha Larson
Indianapolis

Whiskey Balls

My Aunt Lucy allowed Uncle George to have whiskey in the house only for "medicinal purposes"—and for her whiskey ball cookies!

3	cups vanilla wafers, rolled fine
1	cup chopped nuts
3	tablespoons dark corn syrup
1 ½	tablespoons cocoa
½	cup whiskey
1	cup confectioners sugar

Mix first 5 ingredients thoroughly, and roll into balls, about 1 inch in diameter. Roll in confectioners sugar.

Barbara Keene
Indianapolis

Chocolate Ice Cream Roll

Variation at Christmastime: I omit the chocolate; add ¼ cup more of flour and enough red or green cake coloring to make the dough the color you want. Spread with peppermint or other seasonal ice cream of choice.

4	eggs
1 ⅓	cups sugar
1	teaspoon vanilla
½	cup cold water
1	cup sifted flour
⅓	cup cocoa
1 ¼	teaspoon baking powder
¼	teaspoon salt
1	cup powdered sugar
1	pint ice cream, softened

Preheat oven to 375°F. Have eggs at room temperature. Beat eggs about 5 minutes at medium speed with electric mixer. Gradually add sugar, beating constantly. Stir in vanilla and water. Sift flour, cocoa, baking powder and salt. Add sifted ingredients all at once to egg mixture, blending only until batter is smooth. Spread evenly in lightly greased, waxed-paper lined 10 ½ x15 ½ x 1-inch pan. Bake about 25 minutes or until center of cake springs back when lightly touched with finger. Loosen edges and immediately turn out on towel sprinkled with powdered sugar. Sprinkle more powdered sugar on top of cake roll. Roll up, beginning at narrow end. Wrap in towel until cool (1 hour). Unroll, spread softened ice cream on top, then reroll. Wrap tightly in foil and put in freezer. Slice to serve.

Sandra James
Oxford

Forgotten Meringues

6	egg whites
½	teaspoon cream of tartar
2	cups sugar

Preheat oven to 400°F. Beat egg whites with cream of tartar until frothy. Gradually beat in sugar until stiff and glossy. Heap into high mounds on brown paper on baking sheet and hollow out with back of spoon. Put into oven, close door, then turn off oven. (Don't peek!) Let stand overnight in oven. Store in airtight container. Makes 18–20 meringues.

Carol "Kayo" Walker
Fishers

Meringue Shells

¼ teaspoon salt
1 teaspoon vinegar
1 teaspoon vanilla
6 egg whites
2 cups sugar

Preheat oven to 300°F. Place egg whites in a glass or metal mixing bowl. Add salt, vinegar, and vanilla and beat until mixture forms stiff peaks. Add sugar gradually and continue beating until very stiff.

Cover a cookie sheet with ungreased brown paper which has been cut into squares. Spoon mixture onto the squares in mounds and indent each mound with the back of a spoon. Bake for 45 minutes. Remove from oven and let cool. Store meringues in a covered container until ready to use. Fill with your favorite ice cream and top with fruit or sauce. Makes 12–14 shells.

Sally Lugar
Indianapolis

Strawberry Stürm

Strawberry stürm is a dessert that has been a tradition in the Swiss, Amish, and Mennonite communities. During strawberry season, we always served stürm when we had company. Having large families, we often made it in a dishpan.

1 quart strawberries (frozen can be used)
¾ cup sugar
5–6 slices dry bread
1 ½ cups light cream or ice cream and milk

Crush strawberries in a bowl. Add the sugar (use less sugar if ice cream is used). Break bread into small pieces into the strawberries and mix until all juice is absorbed. Stir in cream or ice cream and milk until a soup-like consistency is reached. (If ice cream is used, add slivers over strawberry mixture and let it melt. Add more cream or milk to desired consistency.) Mix lightly and serve. Serves 6–8.

Berneta Lehman
Berne

Chrusciki *(Angel Wings)*

3 cups flour
½ stick butter, melted
1 whole egg
5 egg yolks
1 teaspoon lemon flavoring or brandy
2 tablespoons sugar
¼ teaspoon salt
1 cup sour cream
1 cup powdered sugar

Mix flour and melted butter together. Beat egg, egg yolks, and lemon flavoring or brandy with sugar and salt. Add sour cream to the egg mixture and mix well again. Add all this to butter and flour mixture; stir until mixture forms a ball. Cover and let stand for 30 minutes.

Cut dough into four pieces. Roll out each piece very thin. Cut in strips 1 ½ inches by 3 inches long. Cut slit lengthwise in each strip. Pull through an end of it so it looks like a bow tie. Fry in deep fat. Drain well on paper towel and when cool sprinkle with powdered sugar. Makes 7–8 dozen.

Helen Lopinski
South Bend

Brandy Peaches

This is a wonderful finale to a holiday dinner. It can be prepared in advance and baked while dinner is being enjoyed.

16 canned peach halves
1 cup maple syrup
1 cup brown sugar, firmly packed
⅓ cup butter or margarine, melted
 ground cinnamon
⅓ cup brandy
 Vanilla ice cream

Preheat oven to 325°F. Place peach halves cavity side up in a lightly greased 9 x 13-inch baking dish; spoon about 1 tablespoon syrup, 1 tablespoon brown sugar and 1 tablespoon butter into each cavity. Sprinkle lightly with cinnamon; bake uncovered for 20 minutes. Remove from oven; pour brandy over peaches. Place each peach half in an individual serving dish; top with ice cream. Spoon sauce from baking dish over ice cream. Serves 16.

Mary Rinck
Indianapolis

Chocolate Delight

½ cup butter
1 cup flour
½ cup ground pecans
1 8-ounce package cream cheese
1 cup powdered sugar
1 cup whipped topping
3 cups milk
2 3-ounce packages instant chocolate pudding
1 large container whipped topping
  Chocolate shavings

Preheat oven to 375°F. Mix butter, flour, and pecans. Bake for 15 minutes. Mix cream cheese and powdered sugar until creamy. Add whipped topping. Spread mixture on cooled crust. Beat milk and instant pudding together until thick. Spread on creamy layer. Cover the top with contents of a large container of whipped topping. Garnish with shavings of chocolate.

Leslie F. Knox
Indianapolis

Chocolate Mousse

6 ounces semisweet chocolate chips
½ cup (1 stick) unsalted butter
3 eggs, separated
2 tablespoons sugar
¾ cup heavy cream
½ teaspoon vanilla

Melt chocolate and butter in top of double boiler over simmering water. Transfer to a mixing bowl and set aside to cool.

When the chocolate mixture has reached room temperature, add egg yolks and stir well. Beat egg whites to soft peaks, then beating continuously, add the sugar. Whisk a small portion of egg white into chocolate mixture to lighten it; gently fold in remaining egg whites.

Whip cream with the vanilla until stiff, then fold into chocolate mixture carefully but thoroughly. Spoon the mixture into individual serving dishes and chill until serving time. Serves 4.

Mary Ann Smith Kendall
Columbus

Chocolate Espresso Mousse

BAKED MOUSSE BASE

4	ounce bittersweet chocolate
½	cup unsalted butter
4	eggs
½	cup sugar
2	tablespoons espresso liqueur
1	teaspoon instant espresso

MOUSSE

4	ounces bittersweet chocolate
½	cup butter
4	eggs
½	cup sugar
2	tablespoons espresso liqueur
1	teaspoon instant espresso
2	tablespoons instant gelatin
2	tablespoons espresso, warmed

FOR THE MOUSSE BASE: Preheat oven to 350°F. Line a 9-inch spring-form pan with parchment paper. Melt chocolate and butter in a *bain-marie**, taking great care to not let any water get into the ingredients. Stir until smooth. Pour mixture into large bowl and set aside. Clean the top of double boiler.

Whisk eggs and sugar in bain-marie until sugar dissolves. Continue whisking until triple in volume. Cool.

Add espresso liqueur and espresso to chocolate and butter mixture. Carefully fold in egg mixture. Pour into spring-form pan and bake 30–40 minutes or until knife comes out clean. Cool.

FOR THE MOUSSE: Melt chocolate and butter in a bain-marie. Stir until smooth. Whisk eggs and sugar in a bain-marie until sugar dissolves. Whisk until triple in volume. Pour into large bowl and let cool.

Add espresso liqueur and espresso to chocolate and butter mixture. Dissolve gelatin in warmed espresso. Add to chocolate mixture. Fold in egg mixture. Pour on top of baked mousse. Freeze until mousse is set.

* A *bain-marie* is much like a double-boiler, used for foods that would burn easily. For this type of recipe, a large bowl, preferably metal, positioned over simmering (not boiling) water would work well. It is extremely important to be sure that no water or moisture gets into the mixtures, and to not have the bottom of the bowl touching the hot water. For maximum volume, a balloon whisk should be used for the beating.

Steven J. Oakley, Executive Chef
Something Different and Snax Restaurant
Indianapolis

Pear and Almond Tart

Sweet pear halves atop almond-flavored cream in a buttery tart shell make an elegant springtime dessert. Resembling the more complicated French poires Bourdaloue (poached pears and almond cream), this make ahead tart is assembled in a series of easy steps.

1 ⅓ cups flour

¼ cup sugar

1 ½ teaspoon grated lemon peel

½ cup cold butter or margarine, cut into pieces

1 egg yolk

1 3-ounce cream cheese, at room temperature

1 cup whipping cream

¼ cup powdered sugar

½ teaspoon lemon peel

1 teaspoon lemon juice

¼ teaspoon almond extract

¼ teaspoon vanilla

2 tablespoons kirsch (optional)

4 medium size fresh pears, poached (recipe next page)

⅔ cup apricot jam

¼ cup sliced almonds

Preheat oven to 300°F. In a small bowl, blend together flour, sugar, and 1 teaspoon lemon peel. Add butter or margarine. Crumble with your fingers until mixture is mealy and has no large particles. With a fork, stir in one egg yolk until blended. Then work dough with your hands until it holds together in a smooth ball. Press dough evenly over bottom and sides of an 11-inch tart pan with a removable bottom, or use a 10-inch springform pan, pressing dough 1 ¼ inches up the sides. Bake for 30 minutes or until golden brown.

In small bowl of an electric mixer, beat the cream cheese; then slowly blend in the whipping cream. Add powdered sugar, lemon peel, lemon juice, almond extract, vanilla and kirsch. Beat until mixture is thick as stiffly beaten cream. Spoon filling into the pastry shell, spreading evenly.

Poach pears; cool. Cut the end off one pear half to shape into a round; place in center of tart. Arrange remaining pear halves, cavity side down, around the center; gently push pears into filling. Cover and chill until firm, about 1 hour.

Rub the apricot jam through a wire strainer into a small saucepan to obtain a smooth puree. Heat just until melted. With a spoon, lightly drizzle jam over pears and filling, forming a thin glaze over all. Cover with a tent of foil and refrigerate until serving time. Before serving, arrange almonds around the edges and the center pear. Serves 7–14.

Poached Pears

1 ½ cups water
¾ cup sugar
1 teaspoon grated lemon peel
1 teaspoon vanilla
4 medium-size fresh pears

Combine water, sugar, lemon peel and vanilla in a 4-quart pan. Bring to a boil, stirring until sugar dissolves. Peel the pears; cut in half lengthwise and remove cores. Place halves in syrup, cover, and simmer about 10 minutes or until fork tender. Drain well; save syrup to sweeten other fruits. (Note: A large can of pear halves, drained, may be substituted for poached pears.)

Peggy Rapp
Indianapolis

Apricot Dessert Supreme

1 large box apricot gelatin
2 ½ cups boiling water
¾ cup apricot nectar or cold water
1 20-ounce can crushed pineapple, well drained (reserve juice)
3 medium size bananas, quartered
1 cup miniature marshmallows
2 tablespoons butter
2 tablespoons flour
½ cup sugar
1 egg, beaten
½ cup pineapple juice
1 8-ounce package cream cheese, softened
1 package Dream Whip
¾ cup pecans, chopped

Mix gelatin with boiling water. Add cold apricot nectar. Pour gelatin into a 9 x 13-inch glass baking dish. Chill until mixture starts to firm. Add drained pineapple, bananas and marshmallows. Refrigerate again until firm. Combine butter, flour, sugar, egg and pineapple juice in a saucepan. Cook until thick and smooth. Remove from heat. Add cream cheese; mix well. Let mixture cool. Whip dream whip according to package directions. Add Dream Whip to cooled mixture; blend. Spread over cooled gelatin. Sprinkle with pecans. Refrigerate until time to serve. Serves 24

Yolanda Heritier
Indianapolis

Coconut Crunch

1   cup sifted flour
¼   cup light brown sugar
½   cup soft butter or margarine
1   cup flaked coconut
1   8-ounce package slivered
    almonds
1 ½ cup very cold milk
1   3-ounce package vanilla
    instant pudding
1   cup whipped topping,
    thawed

Preheat oven to 350°F. Mix flour, sugar, butter, coconut, and almonds until crumbly. Spread out very thinly on an ungreased jelly roll pan. Brown for 15 minutes. Stir often (every 2 or 3 minutes). Set aside to cool. Crumble it up more after it is cool. In a small deep bowl combine milk and instant pudding according to directions on pudding package but using only the amount of milk specified above. Fold whipped topping into pudding mixture until just blended. Into the bottom of an 8 x 8 x 2-inch glass dish place half the crumb mixture. Spoon all the pudding mixture over the crumbs and spread evenly. Top with remaining crumbs. Place in refrigerator until ready to serve.

Pam Parker
Indianapolis

Russian Cream

I like to finish a meal with in-season fruits, a perfect accompaniment to this fluffy-white dessert.

1 ½ pints heavy cream
1 ½ cups sugar
½   cup water
1   tablespoon unflavored
    gelatin
1 ⅓ cups sour cream
1   tablespoon vanilla extract

In a medium saucepan, heat heavy cream and sugar to 180°F. In a separate pan, heat water and gelatin to a boil. Combine cream and gelatin blends. Set pot containing mixture in an ice bath and fold in sour cream and vanilla extract. Chill. Serve with fresh berries or fruit. Serves four.

Fletcher Boyd
Fletcher's Restaurant
Atlanta

Pumpkin Squares

1 package yellow cake mix
½ cup melted butter or margarine
3 eggs
3 cups pumpkin pie mix
⅔ cup milk
¼ tablespoon sugar
1 tablespoon cinnamon
¼ cup butter, softened

Preheat oven to 325°F. Grease bottom only of 9 x 13-inch glass pan. Reserve 1 cup cake mix for topping. Combine rest of cake mix, ½ cup melted butter, and 1 egg. Stir well. Press into pan.

Blend pumpkin pie mix, 2 eggs, and milk. Pour over crust.

Combine the reserved cake mix, sugar, cinnamon, and ¼ cup butter and sprinkle over top. Bake for 45–50 minutes.

Nancy Lugar Fogle
Indianapolis

Mae Rose's Custard

This recipe came from Kentucky some sixty years ago. Don't hurry. It needs to cook slowly. Unlike eggnog, do not add any flavoring, such as nutmeg.

½ gallon whole milk *
1 cup sugar
pinch of salt
6 eggs, beaten
1 tablespoon vanilla

Mix milk, sugar and salt in a large pan. Heat slightly. Beat eggs and add to warm milk. Cook on medium to low until liquid coats a metal spoon. It will thicken as it cools. Set in pan of cold water or on cold wet cloth to stop the cooking. When cool, add vanilla. Put in glass pitcher or jars to store. Serve with ice cream.

* You can use 1 percent or 2 percent milk, but the richer the milk, the richer the custard.

Mae Rose Poynter
Franklin

Baked Custard

Nourishing for a sick child.

2	eggs
¼	cup sugar
¼	teaspoon salt
½	teaspoon vanilla
2	cups milk, scalded
	cinnamon

Preheat oven to 400°F. Beat eggs; add sugar, salt, and vanilla. Add hot milk. Pour into buttered baking dish and set baking dish in pan of warm water. Sprinkle with cinnamon. Bake for 35 minutes.

Freeda Murphy
Indianapolis

Baked Indian Pudding

My grandmother, Carrie, was a strong-willed lady from the little town of Bicknell in Knox County. At a time when women were discouraged from becoming involved in things beyond home and family, she became a powerful force in both local and state politics. She even served as the local justice of the peace for a time. What I remember most about her is her warm smile, gentle voice and her kitchen that always seemed to smell like the holidays. As a young girl, she learned traditional southern Indiana recipes from her mother. This recipe for Indian pudding was one of her favorites.

2	tablespoons butter
2	quarts milk, scalded
½	teaspoon salt
1 ½	cups yellow corn meal
1	tablespoon ginger
2	eggs, beaten
1	cup molasses

Preheat oven to 300°F. Grease a large casserole with the butter. Mix milk, salt, cornmeal and ginger. Let stand a couple of minutes. Add eggs and molasses and mix well. Bake 2 hours.

J. Robert Cook
Producer/Director
WFYI

Tapioca with Pineapple Pudding

9 tablespoons tapioca
6 cups milk
3 egg yolks
9 tablespoons sugar
3 egg whites
6 tablespoons sugar
1 ½ teaspoons vanilla
1 15-ounce can crushed pineapple, including juice

Put the tapioca, milk, egg yolks, and 9 tablespoons sugar into a large 3-quart cooking pan. Set 5 minutes; then bring to a full boil. In a large bowl, beat egg whites until frothy. Add 6 tablespoons sugar. Beat to soft peaks. Set aside. Add vanilla. Slowly add hot cooked tapioca ingredients to egg white mixture and mix together. Add pineapple and juice. Makes 12 half-cup servings.

Myrna Sommers
Indianapolis

Old-Fashioned Apple Pudding

This recipe was given to me by a lovely German lady over fifty years ago. She said it was a favorite in her family for over fifty years, which makes it over a hundred years old.

1 egg
¾ cup sugar
1 cup flour
1 teaspoon baking powder
1 teaspoon baking soda
1 teaspoon cinnamon
2 cups chopped apples
1 lump butter (size of an egg), melted
½ cup chopped nuts

Preheat oven to 350°F. Beat egg, add sugar, beat again. Mix dry ingredients and add to egg mixture. Stir in apples, butter and nuts. Bake in 8 x8-inch square pan for 45 minutes. When still warm, cut in 4 generous squares. Serve with a dollop of vanilla ice cream.

Helen Turner
Terre Haute

Raisin Bread Pudding

This has been enjoyed by our family and friends for the last sixty years.

3	eggs, beaten
1	cup sugar
3	cups milk
1 ½	teaspoons cinnamon
½	cup raisins
3	slices bread
4	tablespoons butter
2	tablespoons flour
1	cup brown sugar
½	cup hot water

Preheat oven to 350°F. Combine eggs, sugar, and milk. Add cinnamon and raisins. Mix well and pour into 8 x 8-inch baking dish. Lay bread on top of mixture, pressing into mixture until bread is coated. Bake for about 45 minutes. Cool.

Blend butter, flour, brown sugar, and hot water and cook over medium-low heat until thick. It will scorch easily, so watch closely. Cool and pour on top of baked mixture.

Sarah Fields
Ridgeville

Chocolate Pudding Dessert

2	cups sugar
4	tablespoons cocoa
4	tablespoons flour
2	teaspoons vanilla
5	cups hot water
2	cups flour
4	tablespoons cocoa
1 ½	cups sugar
4	teaspoons baking powder
1	teaspoon salt
1	cup milk
4	tablespoons melted margarine

Combine first 5 ingredients in a saucepan. Cook over low heat until smooth and sugar is dissolved. Set aside and let cool.

Preheat oven to 350°F. Combine next 5 ingredients in a mixing bowl. Add milk and margarine. Pour in ungreased 9 x 13-inch pan. Ladle sauce over batter. Bake for 35 minutes. Serves 12.

In memory of Opal Fetterhoff
Cutler

Upside-Down Date Pudding

This recipe was given to me forty-five years ago by my sister and has become a special favorite with our family at Christmas. It is a very good dessert to take to family gatherings or "carry-in" dinners.

PUDDING

1	cup chopped pitted dates
1	cup boiling water
2	tablespoons butter or margarine
½	cup dark brown sugar
½	cup granulated sugar
1	egg
1 ½	cups flour
½	teaspoon baking powder
1	teaspoon soda
½	teaspoon salt
1	cup walnuts, chopped

SAUCE

1 ½	cups boiling water
1 ½	cups dark brown sugar
1	tablespoons butter or margarine

FOR PUDDING: Preheat oven to 375°F. Combine dates with boiling water. Set aside to cool. Melt butter or margarine. Using electric mixer, combine brown sugar, granulated sugar, egg, and melted butter or margarine. Mix well. Sift together dry ingredients; gradually add to sugar mixture. Stir in walnuts and cooled date mixture. Pour into ungreased 2-quart rectangular baking dish.

FOR SAUCE: Combine boiling water, brown sugar, and butter or margarine. Stir well until sugar is dissolved. Carefully spoon over cake mixture. Bake for 40 minutes. As it bakes, the cake rises to the top and the dates and sauce thicken and settle to the bottom. Cool on rack. To serve, cut into squares and use a pancake turner to invert onto plates so the sauce runs down from the top. Top with whipped topping or whipped cream. Serves 15–18.

Mary Hood
Terre Haute

Rhubarb Crunch

1	cup flour
¾	cup rolled oats
1	cup brown sugar, packed
1	teaspoon cinnamon
½	cup melted butter
4	cups diced rhubarb
1	cup sugar
2	tablespoons cornstarch
1	cup water
1	teaspoon vanilla

Preheat oven to 350°F. Mix flour, oats, brown sugar, cinnamon, and melted butter until crumbly. Press half of crumbs in a greased 9 x 13-inch baking pan. Add diced rhubarb. Combine sugar, cornstarch, water and vanilla and cook until thick and clear. Pour over rhubarb. Top with remaining crumbs. Bake for 1 hour.

Annabelle May
Noblesville

Apple Dumplings

We make these in the fall when the apples ripen and freeze batches for use all year long.

12	apples
	Dough for 3 single-crust pies
1	stick butter or margarine
1 ½	cups sugar
2	cups water
1	teaspoon salt
1	teaspoon vanilla or almond extract
1	teaspoon cinnamon
	Red food coloring

Peel and dice apples into ½-inch pieces. Dip in salt water to keep from turning dark. Drain in colander.

On floured surface roll pie dough out into 8-inch circles about ⅛ inch thick. Place ½–¾ cup apples in center of each circle. Fold dough around filling and pinch closed. Wrap in cellophane wrap and freeze.

Preheat oven to 375°F. Spray a 9 x 13-inch pan with cooking spray and place frozen dumplings in pan.

Combine sugar, water, salt, extract, cinnamon, and food coloring in a saucepan and bring to a boil. Reduce heat and simmer until sugar is dissolved. Pour over frozen dumplings, making sure each is coated. Sprinkle tops with cinnamon and sugar to taste and bake 30 minutes. Reduce heat to 350°F and bake another 30 minutes. (Time may need to be extended for larger dumplings.) Makes 12 dumplings.

Mary Beth Wiggins
Evansville

Mom's Persimmon Pudding

2 cups brown sugar
2 cups flour
1 teaspoon baking soda
1 cup persimmon pulp
1 teaspoon butter, melted
3 eggs, beaten
1 quart milk

FOLLOWING ARE OPTIONAL:
½ cup chopped walnuts
½ cup raisins
¼ teaspoon nutmeg
¼ teaspoon cinnamon

Preheat oven to 350°F. Grease and lightly flour 9 x13-inch cake pan.

Combine brown sugar and flour in large mixing bowl. Dissolve baking soda in 2 tablespoons water; add persimmon pulp, butter, eggs, and milk. Mix well. Add brown sugar and flour mixture and stir until blended. Add optional ingredients as desired. Pour into prepared cake pan. Bake for 1 hour, stirring occasionally.

John W. Snyder
New Augusta

Prize-Winning Persimmon Pudding

Mrs. O. E. VanCleave of Mitchell won first prize in a persimmon pudding contest at the 1959 annual persimmon festival in Mitchell with this recipe. In her hurry to bake the pudding for the contest, she left out the cinnamon and vanilla. She believed that because of the omission, her pudding had more of the persimmon taste and was judged the best.

2 cups persimmon pulp
2 cups sugar
3 large eggs
1 teaspoon soda
1 ½ cups buttermilk
1 ½ cups flour
⅛ teaspoon salt
1 teaspoon baking powder
¼ cup cream
⅛ pound butter, melted
½ teaspoon cinnamon
1 teaspoon vanilla

Preheat oven to 325°F. Mix pulp and sugar; add eggs and beat well. Add soda to buttermilk, stirring until mixture stops foaming. Add to mix and stir. Sift flour, salt, and baking powder together into persimmon mixture and beat well. Add cream. Melt butter in a 9 x 13-inch pan and add to batter, leaving enough to grease the pan for baking. Stir in cinnamon and vanilla. Bake for 45 minutes or until done or thumbprint tested. Serve with ice cream or whipped cream. Serves 12.

Helen T. Ernestes
Indianapolis

Peanut Brittle

2 cups granulated sugar
1 cup white corn syrup
½ cup water
2 cups salted peanuts
2 teaspoons baking soda

Butter pan or cookie sheet. Bring sugar, corn syrup and water to a boil and cook to hard crack stage on candy thermometer until it starts to brown. Stir in the salted peanuts. Add baking soda and remove from heat. Spread quickly on pan or cookie sheet. Let cool. Break into pieces and store in airtight container.

Sandra James
Oxford

Crispy Caramel Popcorn

½ cup sugar
¼ cup butter or margarine
¼ cup dark corn syrup
¼ teaspoon vanilla extract
¼ teaspoon salt
2 quarts freshly popped corn, unsalted

Combine all ingredients except popcorn in a saucepan; bring to a boil. Reduce heat and simmer 5 minutes. Remove from heat. Pour over popcorn and mix well

Preheat oven to 250°F. Spread mixture in a 10 x 15 x 1-inch jellyroll pan. Bake for 1 hour, stirring every 15 minutes. Remove from oven and stir immediately. Stir occasionally while mixture cools. Store in airtight container.

Mary Lou Hurst
Indianapolis

Peanut Butter Fudge

1 18-ounce jar peanut butter, crunchy or smooth
1 can vanilla frosting

Empty contents into a large bowl and mix thoroughly with a large spoon. When well mixed, put into two 4 x 7-inch pans or one 9 x 13-inch pan. Cover with foil or waxed paper, and refrigerate for 3 hours or overnight. Cut into squares.

Mary E. Wagner
Indianapolis

Praline Pecan Crunch

This is a great snack!

1	16-ounce package oat squares cereal
2	cups pecan pieces
½	cup light corn syrup
½	cup brown sugar, firmly packed
¼	cup margarine
1	teaspoon vanilla
½	teaspoon baking soda

Preheat oven to 250°F. Combine cereal and pecans in 9 x 13-inch pan. Set aside. Combine corn syrup, brown sugar and margarine in 2-cup microwaveable bowl. Microwave at high for 1 ½ minutes; stir. Microwave on high for ½ to 1 ½ minutes more or until boiling. Stir in vanilla and baking soda and pour over cereal mixture. Stir to coat evenly. Bake for 1 hour, stirring every 20 minutes. Spread on baking sheet to cool; break into pieces. Makes 10 cups.

Rosina M. Reese
Morgantown

Microwave Peanut Brittle

This recipe has been adapted for use in the microwave oven. My grandfather Papenmeier raised the peanuts to be used in peanut brittle. I'm the third generation to use this recipe.

1	cup raw peanuts
1	cup sugar
½	cup light corn syrup
⅛	teaspoon salt
1	tablespoon butter or margarine
1	teaspoon vanilla
1	teaspoon baking soda

Grease cookie sheet with butter or margarine. Combine peanuts, sugar, syrup, and salt in an 8-cup glass measure or 2 quart glass casserole. Microwave for 4 minutes on high. Stir down. Microwave for 4 more minutes. Add butter and vanilla and microwave on high for 1 minute more. Add baking soda. Stir mixture down and then pour onto prepared baking sheet. Let cool. Break into pieces and store in airtight container. (Note: Cashews, pecans, almonds, or walnuts may be substituted.)

JoBerta Hein Campbell
Wadesville

Puppy Chow

1	box Golden Grahams cereal
1	large jar peanuts
1	box raisins
12	ounces chocolate chips
18	ounces peanut butter
6	tablespoons margarine
4	cups powdered sugar

Combine first three ingredients and set aside. Melt chocolate chips, peanut butter, and margarine in microwave. Pour over cereal mixture and mix well. Place mixture in a large plastic bag in which the powdered sugar has been placed. Tie bag and mix well to coat cereal. Let stand in bag several hours or overnight. Store in refrigerator in an airtight container.

Debra Johnson
New Harmony

Cranberry Sherbet

Over fifty years ago this recipe was given to me by my mother-in-law. Through the years I cannot recall a Thanksgiving or Christmas family dinner when a sherbet glass did not appear at each place and its contents eaten with the turkey and rest of the main course.

4	cups cranberries (1 pound)
2 ½	cups water
2	cups sugar
1	teaspoon unflavored gelatin
½	cup cold water
	Juice of 1 lemon

Cook cranberries with water until the berries start popping, about 5–10 minutes. Put a strainer over a pan or bowl. Place some of the berries and water in the strainer and work with a wooden spoon, forcing the berry pulp through the strainer. Continue until all berries and water have been put through strainer. Add sugar and cook just a few minutes until dissolved. Dissolve gelatin in cold water; add to cooked mixture. Cool and stir in lemon juice. Pour into a square plastic container with a lid. Place in freezer and stir occasionally, about 3 times, before it freezes solid. Allow 2–3 hours to freeze before serving. Serves 10–12.

Betty Parkhurst, Jr.
Indianapolis

Chocolate Fudge

Mother loved this fudge and she always made a batch for Christmas.

4 ½ cups sugar
4 tablespoons (½ stick) butter
1 large can evaporated milk
2 teaspoons vanilla
1 large chocolate bar
2 cups nuts, pecans or walnuts, chopped
12 ounces chocolate chips
1 can marshmallow cream

Combine sugar, butter, and evaporated milk in a saucepan. Bring to a boil; reduce heat and simmer for 6 minutes, stirring constantly.

Remove from heat and combine with the remaining ingredients in a large bowl. Beat until creamy and pour into well-buttered 9 x 13-inch pan. Makes 5 pounds.

Gay Burkhart
Zionsville

Creamy Caramels

My family raves about this candy. It really is delicious! When I made them for Christmas last year, Caitlyn, my four-year-old, helped by wrapping the pieces in waxed paper.

1 cup sugar
2 sticks butter
1 cup light or dark corn syrup
1 14-ounce can sweetened condensed milk
1 teaspoon vanilla

Line an 8-inch square pan with foil and butter the foil. Combine sugar, butter and corn syrup in a 3-quart saucepan. Bring to a boil over medium heat, stirring constantly. Boil slowly for 4 minutes without stirring. Remove from heat, add milk and stir. Reduce heat to medium-low and cook until candy thermometer reads 238°F (soft-ball stage), stirring constantly. This part takes quite a while. Remove from heat and stir in vanilla. Pour into prepared pan. Cool completely. Remove from pan and cut into 1 inch squares. Wrap individual pieces in waxed paper. Twist ends closed. Yields 64 pieces.

Kim Carmony
Nineveh

Swedish Fruit Soup *(Fruktsoppa)*

This is a traditional Swedish dish served as a dessert, which I do at our Christmas Eve dinner with Swedish Spritz Cookies (page 214).

1	pound assorted dried fruits (such as raisins, prunes, peaches, or apricots)
½	cup sugar
½	stick of cinnamon
2	fresh apples, unpeeled and cut into bite sizes
2	tablespoons tapioca
⅓	cup lemon juice
1	4 ¾-ounce packet of Junket raspberry Danish dessert
1	can red sour cherries (if desired)

Cut dried fruit as needed into bite sizes. Place in a pan with enough water to cover fruit. Let soak until fruit is puffed. Add sugar and cinnamon and cook until fruit is tender, about 20 minutes. Add apples, tapioca, and lemon juice; cook until apples are tender.

Meanwhile, prepare Danish pudding according to package directions. If using cherries, use the juice to make the pudding; otherwise use either orange juice or water. Add pudding to the fruit mixture. Serve chilled. Serves 8–10.

Martha Larson
Indianapolis

Good Morning!

BREAKFAST AND

BRUNCH SELECTIONS

Early settlers to Indiana recorded in letters and diaries their reactions to unfamiliar landscapes, plants, and animals. In a letter to a friend on the eastern side of the Appalachians, one pioneer woman wrote of her delight at seeing flocks of jewel-colored parakeets when she rose each morning to prepare her family's breakfast. Today, early-rising Hoosiers can enjoy the sight and songs of brilliant red cardinals, sunny goldfinches, and perky chickadees when they sit down to their morning meal.

Apple Fritters

Watch them disappear!

1 cup sweet milk
2 eggs, separated
1 tablespoon sugar
2 cups flour
1 teaspoon baking powder
¼ teaspoon salt
2 sour apples, thinly sliced
  lard or shortening for frying

Heat milk and add slowly to egg yolks and sugar. Combine flour, baking powder, and salt. Beat egg whites until frothy. Add four mixture and egg whites to milk mixture.

Add apple slices and stir well. Drop by spoonfuls into hot oil or shortening. Fry to a light brown. The same recipe may be used substituting bananas for the apples.

Friend of WFYI
Vincennes

Wild Rice Quiche

1 10-inch unbaked pie shell
1 egg, slightly beaten
1 tablespoon water
2 cloves garlic, chopped
2 tablespoons oil
1 14 ½-ounce can Italian tomatoes, chopped
1 6-ounce package long grain wild rice, cooked
1 8-ounce package cream cheese, softened and cubed
1 teaspoon salt
⅛ teaspoon pepper
4 eggs, slightly beaten

Preheat oven to 425°F. Prick crust with a fork and line with foil. Bake for 15 minutes or until edges are lightly browned. Remove foil and brush with egg and water mixture. Return to oven for 2 minutes to set. Reduce temperature to 375°F.

In a skillet, brown the garlic in the oil; add tomatoes with liquid. Simmer 10–15 minutes. Stir in cooked rice and cream cheese; stir until cheese is melted. Add seasonings and eggs. Pour into crust. Bake 25–30 minutes at 375°F. Let stand for 10 minutes before serving. Serves 6–8.

Kathy Mulvaney
Carmel

French Onion Pie

This makes a good brunch dish or complement to Beef Fondue.

Pastry for a 9-inch pie crust

1 3 ½-ounce can (2 cups) french fried onions

4 eggs

2 cups milk

2 ½ cups shredded sharp cheddar cheese

½ teaspoon salt

⅛ teaspoon cayenne pepper

Preheat oven to 450°F. Bake pie shell for 7–8 minutes. Remove from oven and reduce oven temperature to 325°F. While pastry is warm, fill with french fried onions, reserving ½ cup.

Beat eggs slightly. Blend in milk, 1 ½ cups cheese, salt, and cayenne pepper. Pour over onions in pie shell. Sprinkle 1 cup cheese over pie. Bake at 325°F for 45 minutes. Sprinkle reserve onions around edge. Bake 5–10 minutes longer or until knife inserted comes out clean. Let stand for 10 minutes before cutting.

Mary Lou Curtis
West Lafayette

Sausage Quiche

This is so easy and really good, it's almost sinful!

1 8-ounce package refrigerated crescent dinner rolls

¾ pound pork sausage

3 eggs, use 4 if small

8 ounces Monterey jack cheese, grated or cubed

⅔ cup milk

Preheat oven to 325°F. Line 10-inch quiche or pie pan with rolls. Brown and drain sausage. Sprinkle over crust in pan. Mix eggs, cheese, and milk together and pour over sausage. Bake at 325°F for 40–45 minutes. Let set 10 minutes before serving.

Jacqueline Leonard
Indianapolis

Egg and Chilies Casserole

Great for a brunch served with ham slices or sausage links!

12	eggs
½	cup flour, sifted
1	teaspoon baking powder
1	teaspoon salt
16	ounces creamed small curd cottage cheese
1	pound Monterey jack cheese, shredded
½	cup butter, melted
1	4-ounce can diced green chilies

Preheat oven to 350°F. Beat eggs until light and lemon-colored. Add flour, baking powder, salt, cottage cheese, Monterey jack cheese and melted butter, blending smoothly. Stir in chilies. Pour into buttered 9 x 13-inch casserole dish. Bake for 35 minutes or until top is browned and center is firm. Serve immediately.

Joan Waits
Oakland

Breakfast Pizza

1	package crescent dinner rolls
1	pound sausage
1	cup frozen hash browns, thawed
1	cup cheese, shredded
5	eggs, beaten
½	cup milk
½	teaspoon salt
½	teaspoon pepper
2	tablespoons Parmesan cheese

Preheat oven to 375°F. Spread crescent roll dough on a pizza pan like a pizza crust.

Brown and drain sausage. Layer sausage and hash browns over dough and sprinkle cheese on top.

Thoroughly blend eggs, milk, salt, and pepper and pour over the pizza. Sprinkle Parmesan cheese over all and bake for 15–20 minutes.

Mary Ann Sturges
Zionsville

Grandma Deel's Cornmeal Pancakes

This recipe was found in a letter written by my grandma in 1954 stating that she had just located her grandmother's recipe for pancakes. They are delicious and my family's favorite.

1	cup yellow cornmeal
2	tablespoons sugar
1	teaspoon salt
1	cup boiling water
½	cup flour
2	teaspoons baking powder
1	egg
2	tablespoons butter, melted

Blend first three ingredients together and stir in boiling water. Cover and let stand for 10 minutes. Add remaining ingredients, stirring briskly. Fry on well-oiled griddle.

Molly Been Cline
Lafayette

Virgie's Virginia Cream Waffles

This recipe is from the state of Virginia, the Old Dominion, as my grandmother Virgie called it.

4	eggs, separated
4	cups milk
5	cups flour
4	teaspoons sugar
4	teaspoons baking powder
1	cup butter, melted

Beat egg yolks and add milk. Sift together flour, sugar, and baking powder and add to beaten yolks. Add melted butter and mix well.

Beat egg whites until very stiff and fold into batter. Bake on a hot waffle iron until golden. Serves 6.

Barbara Fausett
Frankfort

Sunday Morning Pancakes

I grew up on these simple but wonderful pancakes. Once you make these, you may never make "boxed" pancakes again! You can also freeze these. Just microwave frozen pancakes on high for 1 minute.

3	eggs, separated
1	cup milk
1	cup flour
	pinch salt
1	tablespoon sugar
2	heaping teaspoons baking powder
2	tablespoons butter, melted

Beat yolks and milk together. Sift dry ingredients together and add to milk and yolks. Add melted butter. Beat egg whites until stiff and fold into batter. Cook pancakes on hot, ungreased griddle. Makes about a dozen 4-inch pancakes.

Laura Padfield
Columbus

Aunt Peg's Grits Casserole

1 ½	cups cooked grits
½	pound processed cheese, cubed
½	pound sharp cheddar or longhorn cheese, cubed
1	heaping teaspoon seasoning salt
¼	pound margarine, melted
3	eggs, well-beaten

Preheat oven to 350°F. In a mixing bowl, combine all ingredients and blend well. Pour the mixture into a well-greased 8 x 8-inch casserole dish and bake uncovered for 45 minutes.

Peg Guard
Evansville

Eggs à la Goldenrod

Another breakfast favorite in our house.

14   hard-boiled eggs
1   stick butter or margarine
½   cup flour
½   teaspoon each salt and pepper
1   quart milk (can use skim milk)

Peel eggs; slice in half and remove yolks. Chop the whites coarsely. Push the yolks through a coarse sieve with the back of a spoon or run them through a ricer. Set aside.

Melt butter or margarine over low heat. Add flour and salt and pepper. Cook, stirring, until mixture is smooth and bubbly. Slowly stir in milk and heat to boiling, stirring constantly.

Add chopped hard-boiled egg whites to sauce. Spoon sauce over toast and sprinkle a liberal amount of the yolk on each serving. Serves 12.

Gay Burkhart
Zionsville

Cheese Soufflé

This is a stand-by recipe which many of you already have but was one of Mother's favorites. Our standard Christmas morning fare was baked ham, cheese soufflé, fresh fruit and orange juice and Party Cake. It is also wonderful for a light luncheon with salad and French bread. If you choose, you can add things to it such as cooked sausage or green pepper, but they should all be pre-cooked.

11   slices soft white bread, crusts removed
¼   pound jar Old English cheese
1   stick butter
4   eggs, beaten
2   cups milk

Grease a 2-quart soufflé dish. Cream together the cheese and butter and spread mixture on bread rather liberally, so all the mixture is used.

Cut each slice in quarters. Layer in soufflé dish. Blend milk and eggs thoroughly and pour over cheese and bread. Cover dish and refrigerate overnight.

Preheat oven to 350°F and bake soufflé for 1 hour. Serve at once. Serves 8.

Gay Burkhart
Zionsville

French Crêpes

On Shrove Tuesday, the beginning of Lent, the French cooked thin pancakes, or crêpes. The crêpes were often folded and drenched in liqueurs.

1 ½ cups flour, sifted
⅛ teaspoon salt
1 tablespoon sugar
2 whole eggs
1 egg yolk
1 ¼ cups milk
3 tablespoons butter, melted
    Butter for frying

Make a well in the flour and add salt, sugar, eggs and egg yolk. Start whisking the flour from the side, gradually adding the milk to make a batter the consistency of light cream (add a bit more milk if needed). Add cooled melted butter. Whisk again. Let stand for 30 minutes.

Place a large spoonful of butter in a 5-inch heated frying pan. Add a rounded tablespoon of batter; cook for 30 seconds, turn, and cook for another 30 seconds. Stack and reserve. Makes about 18 crêpes.

Crêpes are quite versatile. They may be served plain, with syrup or filled with any type jam desired. Wrap around fresh fruit for a light taste or for a fancy dessert, fill with whipped cream and chocolate.

Friend of WFYI
Vincennes

Cheese, Egg, and Ham Bake

¾ cup Swiss cheese, shredded
1 ¾ cups shredded sharp
    cheddar cheese
12 slices of bread
1 cup chopped ham or
    cooked sausage, crumbled
4 eggs
2 cups milk
¼ teaspoon nutmeg
⅛ teaspoon dry mustard

Combine cheeses. Trim crusts from bread and butter slices well on one side. Line a 9 x 13-inch pan with 6 slices of bread, buttered side down. Top with ½ of the cheese and all of the ham or sausage. Top with remaining bread, buttered side down. Sprinkle remaining cheese over top. Beat eggs, milk, and spices; pour over all. Refrigerate overnight.

Preheat oven to 350°F and bake until set and golden brown, about 1 hour 15 minutes. Serves 6–8.

Edith J. Wampole
Centerville

Pineapple Escalloped

Great as a side dish for a brunch.

2	20-ounce cans pineapple chunks, drained and liquid reserved
2	tablespoons flour
1	cup sugar
2	cups shredded cheddar cheese
1	cup crushed Ritz crackers
¼	cup butter or margarine, melted

Preheat oven to 350°F. Combine pineapple, flour, sugar and cheese. Place in greased glass baking dish. Pour ⅓ cup of reserved liquid over this. Mix cracker crumbs and margarine together and sprinkle on top. Bake for 25 minutes or until bubbly.

Friend of WFYI
Indianapolis

Tomato Pie

A good accompaniment to any of your egg casseroles, as well as barbecue, hamburgers, or chicken.

1	cup biscuit mix
¼	cup water
1	tablespoon soft butter
4–5	medium tomatoes
	Salt and pepper to taste
1	cup shredded cheddar cheese
½	cup mayonnaise
½	cup minced green onions
2	tablespoons minced fresh parsley

Preheat oven to 350°F. Mix biscuit mix, water and butter together and press into 9-inch pie pan. Peel and slice tomatoes ½ inch thick and sprinkle with salt and pepper. Layer tomato slices on crust. Sprinkle cheddar cheese on top. Mix mayonnaise, green onions, and parsley and spread over cheese. Bake for 3 minutes in lower half of oven. Serve immediately. Serves 6.

Sa
In

Pineapple Cheese Salad

This is delicious and was served to many church circles of West Washington Street Methodist Church.

1	envelope unflavored gelatin
	water
1	8-ounce can crushed
	pineapple
1	teaspoon lemon juice
¾	cup sugar
1	8-ounce package cream
	cheese, cubed
1	cup whipped topping

Dissolve gelatin in 2 tablespoons cold water. Then add ½ cup boiling water. Add pineapple, lemon juice and sugar to gelatin mixture. Mix well, pour in mold and place in refrigerator until almost set. Mix cream cheese with the mixer, leaving some small chunks. Fold in whipped topping. Pour over gelatin in mold. Refrigerate until set. Serves 6–8.

Ruth M. Wolfe
Indianapolis

en Fruit Salad

gar

package cream

nce tub

ng

chopped

zen

Cream sugar and cream cheese. Fold in whipped topping and remaining ingredients one at a time. Spread in 9 x 13-inch glass dish and freeze. Serve in squares on lettuce leaf.

Mary Lou Curtis
West Lafayette

ly Lugar
lianapolis

Pineapple Escalloped

Great as a side dish for a brunch.

2   20-ounce cans pineapple
    chunks, drained and liquid
    reserved
2   tablespoons flour
1   cup sugar
2   cups shredded cheddar
    cheese
1   cup crushed Ritz crackers
¼   cup butter or margarine,
    melted

Preheat oven to 350°F. Combine pineapple, flour, sugar and cheese. Place in greased glass baking dish. Pour ⅓ cup of reserved liquid over this. Mix cracker crumbs and margarine together and sprinkle on top. Bake for 25 minutes or until bubbly.

Friend of WFYI
Indianapolis

Tomato Pie

A good accompaniment to any of your egg casseroles, as well as barbecue, hamburgers, or chicken.

1   cup biscuit mix
¼   cup water
1   tablespoon soft butter
4–5   medium tomatoes
      Salt and pepper to taste
1   cup shredded cheddar
      cheese
½   cup mayonnaise
½   cup minced green onions
2   tablespoons minced fresh
      parsley

Preheat oven to 350°F. Mix biscuit mix, water and butter together and press into 9-inch pie pan. Peel and slice tomatoes ½ inch thick and sprinkle with salt and pepper. Layer tomato slices on crust. Sprinkle cheddar cheese on top. Mix mayonnaise, green onions, and parsley and spread over cheese. Bake for 30 minutes in lower half of oven. Serve immediately. Serves 6.

Sally Lugar
Indianapolis

Pineapple Cheese Salad

This is delicious and was served to many church circles of West Washington Street Methodist Church.

1	envelope unflavored gelatin
	water
1	8-ounce can crushed
	pineapple
1	teaspoon lemon juice
¾	cup sugar
1	8-ounce package cream
	cheese, cubed
1	cup whipped topping

Dissolve gelatin in 2 tablespoons cold water. Then add ½ cup boiling water. Add pineapple, lemon juice and sugar to gelatin mixture. Mix well, pour in mold and place in refrigerator until almost set. Mix cream cheese with the mixer, leaving some small chunks. Fold in whipped topping. Pour over gelatin in mold. Refrigerate until set. Serves 6–8.

Ruth M. Wolfe
Indianapolis

Frozen Fruit Salad

¾	cup sugar
1	8-ounce package cream
	cheese
1	10- or 12-ounce tub
	whipped topping
2	bananas, mashed
½	cup pecans, finely chopped
1	10-ounce package frozen
	strawberries
1	can crushed pineapple

Cream sugar and cream cheese. Fold in whipped topping and remaining ingredients one at a time. Spread in 9 x 13-inch glass dish and freeze. Serve in squares on lettuce leaf.

Mary Lou Curtis
West Lafayette

Company Brunch

An informal time for a family gathering or neighborly get-together is a breakfast or brunch served in the often most-popular room in the house—the kitchen! Piping hot mugs of coffee served with warm muffins and scones are only the beginning to a warm and relaxing time of sharing your favorite recipes in a casual atmosphere.

A delicious brunch can really make a weekend special. Treat late-morning guests to Grilled Salmon Napoleon (page 126), Poached Eggs Chesapeake (page 251), Grilled Tuscan Shrimp Salad (page 36), Asparagus and Prosciutto Appetizer (page 14), and assorted muffins and scones. Thanks to Joseph Heidenreich, executive chef at California Café in Circle Centre, Indianapolis, for these wonderful eye-openers. (Photo by Matthew Musgrave)

Backyard Picnic

A picnic in Indiana is one of summer's greatest enjoyments for the young and old alike. Your basket can be filled with delectable finger foods, fresh fruit or garden vegetables, and, of course, your favorite cookies or desserts. The place can be your own backyard or perhaps a state or community park. And when autumn arrives, it's a Hoosier tradition to "tailgate" a picnic at many of the universities and colleges in our state. Everyone loves a picnic!

There's nothing like fresh air to enhance a meal. Enjoy the outdoors while dining on Pork Loin on Pepper Biscuits (page 65), Marinated Beef Tenderloin on Peasant Rolls, Garden Sundried Medley on Seven-grain Buns, Stuffed New Potatoes with Sour Cream and Chives, Fresh Fruit Kabobs with Sweet Orange Dip (page 257), Antipasto Tray, Pasta Salad with Dill Marinade, and an assortment of cookies. Sue Kobets, owner of the Illinois Street Food Emporium, Indianapolis, is the clever designer of this moveable feast. (Photo by Matthew Musgrave)

Sherried Egg Casserole

3   dozen eggs
1 ⅓   cups milk
2   cans cream of mushroom
       soup
1   large can mushrooms,
       drained
¼   cup sherry
2   cups grated cheddar cheese

Beat the eggs and milk together. Heat a large skillet over medium heat, and, working in batches if necessary, scramble the egg mixture just until soft. Place in a large casserole.

Combine the soup, mushrooms, and sherry, and fold the mixture into the eggs. Top with cheese. (The dish can be prepared ahead of time to this stage; cover and refreigerate.)

Place the casserole in a cold oven and set the heat for 250°F. Bake for 1 ½ hours.
Serves 12–18.

The Frederick-Talbott Inn
Fishers

For those who want accommodations close to Indianapolis but who prefer a more rural setting, the two deep-green structures that comprise the Frederick-Talbott Inn make a delightful choice.

The inn includes an 1870s Gothic-style farmhouse and a 1906 cottage. Guestrooms are furnished in antiques and reproductions. Also available is the Talbott Hall, a fully appointed conference room for business meetings.

Marinated Asparagus

Serve with an egg casserole, ham slices, fresh fruit and hot biscuits for a great brunch on Easter morning.

24	fresh asparagus spears
	Vinaigrette dressing
2	hard-boiled eggs
	fresh parsley, minced
	chives, minced
1	red pimento, cut into long strips
	Fresh parsley and chives

Wash asparagus spears and snap off ends. Using steamer pan with small amount of water, steam asparagus for 2 minutes until it can be pierced with a knife. Drain and rinse with cold water. Toss lightly with vinaigrette and marinate in refrigerator for 1–2 hours.

Put the eggs through a sieve or ricer.

To serve, place lettuce leaves on a platter or individual salad plates. Drain asparagus spears and arrange on lettuce. Sprinkle with sieved egg. Garnish with pimento strips, parsley, and chives.

Friend of WFYI
Merrillville

Mrs. Underwood's Coffee Cake

This recipe has been in our family for four generations. It came to my mother upon her marriage in 1920. Mrs. Underwood lived in the Elnora area of Daviess County.

4	cups flour, sifted
2	cups sugar
1	teaspoon baking powder
½	teaspoon salt
½	cup solid white shortening
2	cups buttermilk
1	teaspoon baking soda
	cinnamon
2	tablespoons butter

Preheat oven to 350°F. Mix the flour, sugar, baking powder and salt in a bowl. Add in shortening with a pastry blender until it is crumbly. Reserve ¾ cup for topping. Beat baking soda into the buttermilk and add to the flour mixture. Grease two 8-inch pans. Pour batter into prepared pans and cover the tops with the reserved crumb mixture. Sprinkle with cinnamon and dot with butter. Bake for 30 minutes or until center springs back when lightly touched.

Sarah Jane Waitt
Sheridan

French Breakfast Puffs

These won't last long if eaten warm right out of the oven. A real treat for Sunday morning!

5	tablespoons shortening
½	cup sugar
1	large egg, separated
1 ½	cups flour
2 ¼	teaspoons baking powder
¼	teaspoon salt
¼	teaspoon nutmeg
½	cup milk
1	tablespoon sugar
1	teaspoon cinnamon
½	stick butter, melted

Preheat oven to 350°F. Cream shortening and sugar. Blend in egg yolk and mix well. Sift dry ingredients together and add to creamed mixture alternately with milk. Fold in stiffly beaten egg white. Pour into greased muffin tins. Bake 25 minutes. Combine cinnamon and sugar. Remove muffins from tins and while still warm, roll tops in melted butter and then in cinnamon-sugar.

Laura Villanyi
Fishers

Grandmother Adele's Crullers

This recipe is from the late 1800s or early 1900s. The original "oil" was lard.

2	eggs
1	cup sugar
1	cup milk
¼	teaspoon salt
⅛	cup butter, melted
2	teaspoons baking powder
1	teaspoon lemon flavoring (or 1 tablespoon fresh lemon juice)
2 ½	cups flour

Combine first 7 ingredients and blend well. Add flour, adding more as needed to make dough easy to handle. Knead lightly and shape into a ball.

Roll dough out on lightly floured surface to about ¼-inch thickness. Cut dough in diamond shapes and deep fry in oil until golden color. Drain on absorbent paper. Sprinkle with confectioners sugar and serve with currant jelly or lemon sauce. Makes about 3 dozen.

Virginia Simmons
Indianapolis

Sticky Buns

1	package active dry yeast
2	cups warm water
6	cups flour
½	cup sugar
2	teaspoons salt
½	cup shortening
1	egg
1	package pecan pieces, chopped
1	cup softened butter or margarine
1	box light brown sugar
2	tablespoons orange blossom honey

Dissolve yeast in ½ cup warm water and set aside. In a large mixing bowl, combine flour, sugar, salt, and shortening. Add egg, yeast, and the rest of the water and mix well. Turn dough out on a floured surface and knead until smooth. Place dough in a large, greased bowl; cover and let rise in a warm place until double in size.

Grease a 9 x 13-inch baking pan and spread pecans on bottom. Combine butter or margarine, brown sugar, and honey.

Roll a section of dough out into a very thin rectangle. Spread a thin layer of brown sugar mixture over dough and roll dough up, starting at wide end, like a jelly roll. Cut rolls to desired size and spread cut sides with some brown sugar. Place coated-side down on pecans in prepared pan. Lightly cover buns and let them rise again for an hour or so. Preheat oven to 400°F and bake until light golden brown, about 25 minutes.

Remove from oven and turn pan upside down on aluminum foil. Pick rolls apart lightly with a fork, let them cool for a few minutes and serve.

Kate Esterline
Indianapolis

Orange Knots

I won a blue ribbon at the 1997 Johnson County Fair with these in the Sweet Breakfast Roll category. They are a nice, light roll, perfect for Easter breakfast.

1	package active dry yeast
¼	cup warm water (110–115°F)
1	cup warm milk (110–115°F)
⅓	cup sugar
½	cup butter or margarine, softened
1	teaspoon salt
2	eggs
¼	cup orange juice
2	tablespoons grated orange peel
5 ½	cups flour
1	cup powdered sugar
2	tablespoons orange juice
1	teaspoon grated orange peel

In a mixing bowl, dissolve yeast in water. Add the next seven ingredients and 3 cups flour; beat until smooth. Add enough remaining flour to form a soft dough. Turn onto a floured board; knead until smooth and elastic (about 6-8 minutes). Place in a greased bowl, turning once to grease top. Cover and let rise in a warm place until doubled, or about 2 hours. Punch dough down; roll into a 10 x 16-inch rectangle about ½-inch thick.

Cut into ¾ x 10-inch strips; roll lightly and tie each strip into a knot. Place on greased baking sheets; tuck the ends under. Cover and let rise until doubled, or about 30 minutes.

Preheat oven to 400°F and bake rolls for 10 to 12 minutes or until golden brown. Cool on wire racks. Makes about 2 dozen rolls.

While rolls are baking, combine powdered sugar, orange juice, and grated orange peel. Mix well and drizzle over cooled rolls.

Kim Carmony
Nineveh

Topsy-Turvy Coffee Ring

1	cake yeast
¼	cup lukewarm water
3	tablespoons shortening, melted
½	cup warm buttermilk
1	teaspoon salt
½	cup sugar
2	large eggs, well beaten
3	cups flour
¼	cup soft butter
⅓	cup brown sugar
1	teaspoon cinnamon
¾	cup raisins
⅓	cup finely chopped nuts
½	cup confectioners sugar
1	tablespoon milk
½	teaspoon vanilla

Dissolve yeast in water. Combine shortening, buttermilk, sugar and salt. Blend eggs into the yeast mixture. Add flour and mix well until mixture forms a soft mass. Place in greased bowl and cover. Let dough rise until double in bulk, about 1 ½–2 hours.

Roll dough out on floured board into a 10- to 12-inch rectangle. Spread with butter. Combine brown sugar, cinnamon, raisins, and nuts. Sprinkle over dough. Roll as for jelly roll. Cut into 2-inch slices and arrange cut-side-down in a circle in a well greased 9-inch tube pan. Let rise until double, about 30–45 minutes. Preheat oven to 350°F and bake for 35–40 minutes. Let cool a bit and turn out onto a large plate.

Blend confectioners sugar, milk, and vanilla until spreading consistency. Spread over warm ring.

Mary Alice Norris
New Whiteland

Maryland Style Crab Cakes
with Poached Eggs Chesapeake

Serve with fruit and home fried potatoes.

Maryland Style Crab Cakes

½	cup mayonnaise
¼	cup red bell pepper, minced
¼	cup scallion, minced
¼	cup celery, minced
4	teaspoons parsley, minced and squeezed to reduce liquid
¼	teaspoon salt
2	teaspoons dry mustard
⅛	teaspoon cayenne pepper
⅛	teaspoon white pepper
½	teaspoon Tabasco
1	3 ⅜ ounce crab meat, well picked-over
⅔	cup bread crumbs (Japanese preferred)
6	eggs
	Cajun Hollandaise Sauce (recipe follows)

Cajun Hollandaise Sauce

6	egg yolks
1	teaspoon lemon juice
	Salt and pepper to taste
	Water, as needed to thin the sauce
1 ½	pounds clarified butter
2	tablespoons Cajun spice (or to taste)

FOR THE CRABCAKES: Combine first 11 ingredients and mix gently by hand. Add ¾ of the bread crumbs and mix. Refrigerate about 30 minutes to absorb liquids. After mixture has rested, additional crumbs may be added to obtain proper consistency. Form into individual portions with a 2-ounce scoop. Flatten cakes, dredge in seasoned flour, dip in beaten whole egg, and coat with reserved bread crumbs. Deep fry in vegetable oil until golden.

Poach the eggs. Place a crab cake on each individual plate, top with a poached egg and Cajun Hollandaise Sauce. Serves 6.

FOR THE HOLLANDAISE: Combine egg yolks, lemon juice, salt and pepper, and 1 tablespoon of water in a stainless steel bowl or top of double boiler. Cook over a just simmering pan of water until it begins to thicken, whisking constantly. Remove from heat and add butter a drop at a time, whisking constantly until all the butter is added. If necessary, add more water a few drops at a time to keep the desired consistency. Add the cajun spice.

Joseph Heidenreich, Executive Chef
California Café
Indianapolis

Polish Bismarcks

1   cup milk
¼   pound butter
½   cup sugar
¾   teaspoon salt
¾   teaspoon vanilla
1   cake or 1 package yeast
4 ½ cups sifted all-purpose flour,
     divided use
3   eggs, well beaten
¼   cup rum
     Jelly (your favorite)
     Powdered sugar

Scald milk. Remove from heat and add butter, sugar, and salt. Stir until butter melts and sugar and salt are dissolved. Cool to lukewarm. Add vanilla and yeast and stir until yeast dissolves. Add half of flour and beat. Mix in eggs and rum. Add remainder of flour to make heavy dough. When too stiff to mix, turn on floured board and knead. Place in greased bowl and let rise until double in bulk. Punch down and let double again.

Punch dough down and turn out on floured surface. Pat out dough to ½-inch thickness and cut out 2-inch circles. Place ½ teaspoon jelly in center of each. Dampen edge of each circle and fold in half, enclosing jelly. Once sealed, shape into ball. Let rise 1 hour.

Heat oil in deep fryer or deep pan to 370°F. Carefully lift each bismarck with pancake turner and drop into hot oil. Cook until brown. Cool on cooling rack, sprinkle with powdered sugar before serving. Makes about 3 dozen.

Helen Cybulski
South Bend

Sausage Apple Balls

1   pound bulk pork sausage
2   cups biscuit mix
1   cup raisins, chopped
1   cup apple, unpeeled and
     grated
½   cup walnuts, chopped
½   teaspoon apple pie spice

Preheat oven to 350°F. Mix all ingredients together and shape into 1-inch balls. Place on an ungreased baking sheet, and bake for 20 minutes or until lightly browned. These can be frozen on a sheet, then bagged and baked at a later date. Great for brunch buffet delight. Makes about 4 ½ dozen.

Marilyn Sherbrooke
Evansville

Polish Coffee Cake

COFFEE CAKE

3	3-ounce cakes yeast
½	cup warm water
2 ½	cups sugar, divided use
3	cups milk, warmed
12	cups flour, divided use
1	cup raisins
4	egg yolks
4	whole eggs
2	teaspoons salt
1	orange
1	teaspoon vanilla
1 ½	cups butter, melted

TOPPING

3	cups flour
1 ½	cups sugar
1	stick butter or margarine
1	teaspoon lemon flavor
1	teaspoon almond flavor

FOR THE CAKE: Dissolve the yeast in lukewarm water with 2 tablespoons of sugar. Let stand 5 minutes. Take half of the remaining sugar and dissolve in warm milk. Add 5 cups of flour. Beat well and add yeast mixture and mix well together. Let the sponge dough stand in warm place 30–40 minutes. Place the raisins in water to soak.

Meanwhile, beat egg yolks and whole eggs with the rest of the sugar and salt until light. Squeeze the juice from the orange and grate the rind (orange part only). Add this to sponge dough with vanilla. Beat well. Add some flour and add melted butter a little at a time. Work it out for about 20 minutes. Squeeze water out of the raisins, coat them with some flour and mix into the dough. Cover and let rise for 1 ½ hours or until doubled. Push the dough down and let rise again.

Preheat oven to 350°F. Grease five 9-inch coffee cake pans. Fill with dough to ¾ full. Sprinkle with topping and let rise 45 minutes. Bake for 45 minutes.

FOR THE TOPPING: Combine flour and sugar; work in butter or margarine into a crumbly mixture adding flavorings as you work. Crumbs should not be too sticky and should be the size of peas or smaller. Makes 5 cakes.

Helen Lopinski
South Bend

Kuchen

Being an area of the state with a German heritage, there are many recipes for kuchen but this is one of my favorites. It is used like coffee cake for breakfast or dessert. It can be topped with heated apple or cherry pie filling if you like.

1 ¼ cups sugar
3 tablespoons chopped pecans
1 tablespoon cinnamon
½ cup (1 stick) butter or margarine
1 egg
1 8-ounce container sour cream
1½ cups flour
1 teaspoon baking soda
1½ teaspoons baking powder
1 teaspoon vanilla

Preheat oven to 350°F. Grease and flour an 8 x 8-inch pan or spring-form pan.

Combine 3 tablespoons sugar, chopped pecans, and cinnamon. Set aside.

Cream margarine and remaining sugar. Add remaining ingredients and mix well. Pour half of batter in prepared pan. Sprinkle half of nut mixture over batter; add remaining batter, then topping. Bake for about 1 hour, or until tester inserted in the middle comes out clean. Don't overbake.

Margaret Rapp
Poseyville

Odds & Ends

SAUCES, JAMS AND PICKLES

Sometimes a stray jar in the pantry or an errant plastic container in the freezer inspires a marvelous meal. Far from being extraneous, sauces, condiments, and relishes can help make for a memorable dining experience.

Roasted Pumpkin Seeds

Preheat oven to 350°F. Clean and wash pumpkin seeds and dry on paper toweling. Butter cookie sheet and roast seeds until they turn golden. Stir often with a fork. Salt to taste.

Sally Lugar
Indianapolis

Rhubarb Jam

So easy and delicious.

3   cups rhubarb, cut in 1-inch
    pieces
1 ½ cups sugar
½   cup water
1   small package red raspberry
    gelatin

Combine rhubarb, sugar and water. Cook until rhubarb is soft (approximately 5 minutes). Remove from heat and add dry gelatin; stir until gelatin is dissolved. Place in covered container and refrigerate.

Freeda Murphy
Indianapolis

Dip for Fresh Fruit

2   eggs, beaten
½   cup sugar
4   teaspoons cornstarch
1   6-ounce can limeade
    concentrate
    Green food coloring
1   cup whipped cream or
    whipped topping
    Fresh fruit for dipping

Mix first four ingredients together. Cook till thickened, then remove from heat and add 2–3 drops green food coloring. When cool, add whipped cream or whipped topping. Serve with fresh fruit pieces.

Ginny Mulkey
Poseyville

Sweet Orange Dip

This is a great dip for fresh fruit!

½	cup sugar
⅓	cup flour
¼	teaspoon salt
2	cups milk
2	eggs, slightly beaten
1	teaspoon vanilla
2	cups sour cream
½	cup orange juice

In a saucepan combine sugar, flour and salt. Slowly stir in the milk and cook until boiling; simmer about 2 minutes more, stirring constantly. Stir a little hot mixture into the beaten eggs, then add that back to the saucepan and stir all together over low heat until smooth. Remove from heat and add vanilla. Let cool, then refrigerate. When completely chilled, fold in the sour cream and orange juice. Keep refrigerated. Makes 4 ½ cups.

Sue Kobets, owner
Illinois Street Food Emporuim

Uncooked Relish

This recipe comes from the Dubois County Extension Homemaker Club cookbook originally published in 1962. My grandmother, Iretha Ahrens of Huntingburg, was a farm wife who raised six children. She always knew how to cook for a crowd.

1	peck (8 quarts) ripe tomatoes
2	cups celery, chopped
2	cups onions, chopped
3	hot red peppers, chopped
2	green peppers, chopped
1	cup horseradish
½	cup mustard seed
2	cups sugar
½	cup salt
6	tablespoons mixed spices
6	cups vinegar

Peel tomatoes; chop fine and drain. Combine tomatoes and vegetables with all the other ingredients and blend well. This keeps well in jars all winter in refrigerator without cooking.

Julie Reed
Indianapolis

Red Sweet Pepper Relish

Any sweet red peppers will do. This relish is wonderful to have on hand for tuna salad, chicken salad, potato salad, cheese spreads, etc.

8	sweet red peppers
1	tablespoon salt
1	pint vinegar
3	cups sugar

Remove seeds from peppers and put through a food grinder or coarsely chop with a food processor (makes about 3 ½ cups). Sprinkle with salt. Let stand 3–4 hours.

Drain peppers in a sieve and put in a pan. Add sugar and vinegar and simmer until thick. Pour, while hot, into hot jars and seal with paraffin.

Sandra James
Oxford

Strawberry Preserves

My great-grandparents, the Hetricks, with their five-year-old daughter, who became my grandmother, came to Indiana from Pennsylvania in 1846 in a covered wagon. With them came this unique recipe which is never stirred; the pan is shaken so the berries remain plump and whole.

1	quart strawberries
3	cups sugar

Boil strawberries and 2 cups of the sugar gently for 10 minutes. Then add the additional cup of sugar and boil for 3 minutes. Shake at intervals while cooking. Do not stir! Spoon carefully into jars so the berries will remain whole and not be crushed.

(Note: Originally these preserves were canned hot, but I now cool and freeze them. When frozen, they taste as fresh as though they just came from the garden. Let them thaw at room temperature so they will come out of the jars whole.)

LeVaughn Harper Stong
Rossville

Freezer Pickles

4–5 cups unpeeled cucumbers,
       thinly sliced
1   medium onion, sliced thin
1 ½   teaspoons salt
½   teaspoon celery seed
1   cup sugar
½   cup white vinegar

Mix the cucumber slices, onion, and salt. Refrigerate for 2 hours. Drain thoroughly in a colander and place in jars or freezer containers.

Combine the celery seed, sugar, and vinegar. Pour the mixture evenly over the cucumber and onion slices. Cover and refrigerate. (These will keep in refrigerator for a week or more, or can be frozen in small packages.)

Sue Brames
Indianapolis

Homemade Mayonnaise (Spitikia Mayoneza)

1   tablespoon powdered
       mustard
¼   teaspoon sugar
       Dash of white pepper
1   teaspoon salt
2   teaspoons white vinegar
       Yolks of 2 eggs
1 ⅔   cups olive oil
3   tablespoons fresh lemon
       juice

Combine mustard, sugar, pepper and salt. Add vinegar and egg yolks and beat together with a whisk until well combined. Add oil one drop at a time beating constantly. When mayonnaise starts to thicken, thin with lemon juice and continue beating, alternately adding lemon juice and oil. Makes 2 cups.

Doris Bowman
Indianapolis

Watermelon Pickles

½ gallon watermelon rind
1 cup kosher salt
1 lump alum, size of a whole pecan
3 cups sugar
1 cup vinegar
6 whole cloves
1 stick cinnamon
¼ teaspoon nutmeg
½ lemon cut into very thin slices
Small amount of preserved ginger

Trim all green and red from watermelon rind. Cut the white rind into small pieces and let stand overnight in a brine made of the salt and 1 gallon of water. Drain and rinse well and place in a large pot. Add enough water to cover the rind and add the alum. Bring to a boil; reduce heat and simmer until the rind is tender and translucent. Remove from heat and let cool. Drain and squeeze as much liquid as possible by hand.

Combine the remaining ingredients in a saucepan. Bring to a low boil and cook until sugar is dissolved. Pour the boiling mixture over the drained watermelon rind and let stand overnight.

Drain the syrup from the rind into a saucepan, bring to a boil, and again pour over the rind; let stand overnight again. Repeat process 2 more days.

On day 4, place the hot rind and syrup in sterile canning jars. Follow canning procedure for sealing and store.

Jane Scott
Evansville

Index

"Ardath's Favorite" recipes are indicated by an asterisk *
"Landmark Restaurant" recipes are indicated by a cross mark †
Across Indiana features and "Landmark Restaurant" names are listed in bold print

Recipes from Across Indiana
THE BEST OF HEARTLAND COOKING

WFYI TELEPLEX

Please send _____ copies of **Recipes from Across Indiana** at $24⁹⁵ each _____

Please write name and address for mailing below. (Please note if book is to be sent to a different name and/or address.)

Indiana residents, add 5% sales tax _____

Postage & Handling at $4⁰⁰ per book _____

_____

GRAND TOTAL _____

_____

☐ My check is enclosed (payable to WFYI)

_____

☐ Please charge my Visa, MasterCard, American Express, or Discover

Send orders to

WFYI – COOKBOOK

_____
Card Number

1401 N. Meridian Street, Indianapolis, IN 46202

Tel. 317-636-2020 • Fax 317-633-7418

_____
Exp. Date

Recipes from Across Indiana
THE BEST OF HEARTLAND COOKING

WFYI TELEPLEX

Please send _____ copies of **Recipes from Across Indiana** at $24⁹⁵ each _____

Please write name and address for mailing below. (Please note if book is to be sent to a different name and/or address.)

Indiana residents, add 5% sales tax _____

Postage & Handling at $4⁰⁰ per book _____

_____

GRAND TOTAL _____

_____

☐ My check is enclosed (payable to WFYI)

_____

☐ Please charge my Visa, MasterCard, American Express, or Discover

Send orders to

WFYI – COOKBOOK

_____
Card Number

1401 N. Meridian Street, Indianapolis, IN 46202

Tel. 317-636-2020 • Fax 317-633-7418

_____
Exp. Date

Recipes from Across Indiana
THE BEST OF HEARTLAND COOKING

WFYI TELEPLEX

Please send _____ copies of **Recipes from Across Indiana** at $24⁹⁵ each _____

Please write name and address for mailing below. (Please note if book is to be sent to a different name and/or address.)

Indiana residents, add 5% sales tax _____

Postage & Handling at $4⁰⁰ per book _____

_____

GRAND TOTAL _____

_____

☐ My check is enclosed (payable to WFYI)

_____

☐ Please charge my Visa, MasterCard, American Express, or Discover

Send orders to

WFYI – COOKBOOK

_____
Card Number

1401 N. Meridian Street, Indianapolis, IN 46202

Tel. 317-636-2020 • Fax 317-633-7418

_____
Exp. Date